Sylvia Plath and the Language of Affective States

Advances in Stylistics

Series Editor: Dan McIntyre, University of Huddersfield, UK

Other Titles in the Series:

Corpus Stylistics in Principles and Practice, Yufang Ho

Chick Lit: The Stylistics of Cappuccino Fiction, Rocío Montoro

D. H. Lawrence and Narrative Viewpoint, Violeta Sotirova

Discourse of Italian Cinema and Beyond, Roberta Piazza

I. A. Richards and the Rise of Cognitive Stylistics, David West

Oppositions and Ideology in News Discourse, Matt Davies

Opposition in Discourse, Lesley Jeffries

Pedagogical Stylistics,
Michael Burke, Szilvia Csábi, Lara Week and Judit Zerkowitz

Style in the Renaissance, Patricia Canning

Stylistics and Shakespeare's Language, Mireille Ravassat

Text World Theory and Keats' Poetry, Marcello Giovanelli

The Stylistics of Poetry, Peter Verdonk

Sylvia Plath and the Language of Affective States

Written Discourse and the Experience of Depression

Zsófia Demjén

Bloomsbury Academic
An imprint of Bloomsbury Publishing Plc

B L O O M S B U R Y
LONDON • OXFORD • NEW YORK • NEW DELHI • SYDNEY

Bloomsbury Academic
An imprint of Bloomsbury Publishing Plc

50 Bedford Square
London
WC1B 3DP
UK

1385 Broadway
New York
NY 10018
USA

www.bloomsbury.com

First published 2015
Paperback edition first published 2017

British Library Cataloguing-in-Publication Data
A catalogue record for this book is available from the British Library.

ISBN: HB: 978-1-4742-1266-3
PB: 978-1-3500-2425-0
ePDF: 978-1-4742-1268-7
ePub: 978-1-4742-1267-0

Library of Congress Cataloging-in-Publication Data
Demjen, Zsofia.
Sylvia Plath and the language of affective states: written discourse and the experience of depression/Zsofia Demjen.
pages cm. – (Advances in stylistics) Includes bibliographical references and index.
ISBN 978-1-4742-1266-3 (hardback) – ISBN 978-1-4742-1267-0 (epub) – ISBN 978-1-4742-1268-7 (epdf) 1. Emotive (Linguistics) 2. Affect (Psychology) 3. Plath, Sylvia–Psychology. 4. Corpora (Linguistics) 5. Narration (Rhetoric) 6. Psycholinguistics. 7. Stylistics. I. Title.
P325.5.E56D46 2015
818'.5403–dc23
2014046975

Series: Advances in Stylistics

Typeset by Deanta Global Publishing Services, Chennai, India

Anyunak és apunak: ezt tették lehetővé.

Contents

List of Abbreviations

CLAWS	Constituent Likelihood Automatic Word-tagging System
CMT	Cognitive metaphor theory
FPN	First-person narration
FPN + Shifts	First-person narration and shifting narration
LL	Log-likelihood
MIP	Metaphor identification procedure (Pragglejaz, 2007)
POS	Parts-of-speech
SEM	Semantic
SFL	Systemic functional linguistics
Smith Journal	The first journal (pp. 3–187) in *The Unabridged Journals of Sylvia Plath* (Kukil 2000) written between July 1950 and July 1953. It covers her summers at home in Wellesley, as well as her school years at Smith College, in Massachusetts
SPN	Second-person narration
SWTPAuto	The autobiography section of the Speech Writing and Thought Presentation corpus (Semino and Short, 2004)
USAS	UCREL Semantic Analysis System

List of Concordances

List of Figures and Tables

Acknowledgements

This book and its previous incarnations never would have seen the light of day without one exceptional teacher, supervisor, mentor, colleague and friend: Elena Semino. For the past eight years, she has gone far beyond the call of duty to encourage, challenge and support me. She (still) never lets me get away with less than I am capable of, and I do not think I could be more fortunate than having her to call on.

I want to thank everyone at the Department of Linguistics and English Language, Lancaster University, who supported me in various ways over the past years. In particular, Mick Short, my upgrader and internal examiner, who taught me about the importance of operationalizable methodology; Paul Rayson for his dedicated support with Wmatrix; Marjorie Wood for always having an open door; the PASTY and CRG research groups for listening to half-baked ideas; and Helen Hargreaves and Sharon McCulloch for summers of wit and banter. I must also thank Dan McIntyre, for taking an interest in my work and encouraging me to take it further. I thank the editors at Bloomsbury Academic and an anonymous reviewer for kind words of guidance.

Finally, I have to thank Pavle. I am not sure if it is possible to capture his contribution to all this in a few words, but he has been there for me and us throughout this roller coaster of a process, listening, questioning, reading, supporting or letting me be, instinctively knowing what was required. He helped keep things in perspective with his patience and affection and challenged and clarified my thinking on this and many other things.

Two chapters in this book draw on previous publications:

- Chapter 6 draws on Demjén, Z. (2011), 'Motion and Conflicted Self Metaphors in the Sylvia Plath's Smith Journal', *Metaphor and the Social World*, 1(1): 7–25.
- Chapter 7 draws on Demjén, Z. (2011), 'The Role of Second-person Narration in Representing Affective States in Sylvia Plath's Smith Journal', *Journal of Literary Semantics* 40(1): 1–21.
- Figure 3.2 is reproduced from Eggins, S. (2004), An Introduction Systemic Functional Linguistics. London: Continuum with the permission of Bloomsbury Publishing Plc.

1

Introduction

What is this book about?

In this book, I explore what the language of Sylvia Plath's 'Smith Journal' tells us about the writer's mental and emotional life. In light of her diagnosed depression and documented suicidal tendencies, I am interested in Plath's *affective states* – aspects of her cognition and inner world, such as emotions, feelings and moods that can be placed on a cline of positive to negative – as embedded in the style, grammar and lexis of her private journal. Specifically, I discuss what linguistic features of Sylvia Plath's journal are most important for conveying these affective states; what these states feel like based on Plath's language; whether she perceives them as within her control and whether her language indicates changes in such things as valence and intensity. The Smith Journal, the first in *The Unabridged Journals of Sylvia Plath* (Kukil 2000), is particularly appropriate for this purpose: throughout much of the text, Plath explicitly focuses on her inner turmoil, reflecting eloquently and creatively on her own experience of her affective states.

Throughout the chapters, I draw connections between Plath's linguistic patterns and those commonly associated with various mental disorders. As a diagnosed depressive with suicidal tendencies, Plath's experience of her affective states is, to some extent, also her experience of these disorders, so what her language reveals about her experience may be relevant for the experience of depression more broadly. Of course, I hesitate to generalize too far: Plath, as an accomplished and talented writer, is exceptional, and her language primarily tells us something about her. At the same time, precisely because of her facility with language, she may have been able to express what others also feel but cannot articulate. Poets and writers, like Plath, who suffer from mental disorders often write about their experiences, putting into words experiences and sensations that are close to inexpressible (Jamison 2006). Such individuals are able to create an authentic and vivid feel for the phenomenology of their disorders, thereby providing valuable insights to others experiencing or interested in these more broadly (Jamison 2006). In addition, because of their status as prominent and respected writers, the way Sylvia Plath and others like her express their experiences of such affective states may also influence how others perceive and describe their own – just as Plath's writing reflects the influences of Freudian psychoanalysis (Bundtzen 2006). In this way, although the Smith Journal is the voice of just one person, it has bearings on many others.

Using language as a way of accessing what goes on in the mind is a relatively well-established technique. It has to do with the unique human ability of self-reflection (Ramachandran and Blakeslee 2005), coupled with language's communicative function. The linguistic choices people make – *how* they say what they say – provide clues about the nature of their perceptions, experiences, attitudes and sense of self (Schiffrin 1996) beyond what could be gleaned from simply engaging with the content of their propositions. Linguistic analysis can therefore reveal meaning beyond content 'to fill in for what is left unsaid' (Gumperz 1999: 458). In stylistics, for example, the concept of mind style (Fowler 1977) rests on the assumption that a character's 'mental self' can be accessed through language. Particularly revealing aspects of language include metaphor and patterns of lexico-grammatical choices (cf. Halliday and Matthiessen 2004). In fact, looking to linguistic patterns for inferences about the mind is a practice common not only in linguistics. A more empirical basis for it can be found in clinical and narrative psychology, where Pennebaker and colleagues, for instance, have done extensive research on the link between mental health and changes in language use (e.g. Pennebaker and King 1999). At the same time, in narrative psychology (e.g. Lászlo et al. 2007) the focus has been on the correlation between the way stories are told/written and mental health.

Situated at this interface of applied linguistics, narrative studies and psychology, this book presents a mixed-methods corpus stylistics approach to the analysis and interpretation of language in relation to affective states. It combines qualitative and quantitative analytical techniques from linguistics and narratology (e.g. metaphor analysis and corpus-based comparisons), refers to facts and events in Sylvia Plath's life where relevant and draws on studies in social, clinical and narrative psychology in the interpretation of findings. The combination of qualitative and quantitative techniques makes it possible to exploit the strengths, while also offsetting the weaknesses, of both. Qualitative linguistic analysis in the tradition of stylistics, for example, can provide rich insights but may be difficult to generalize. Corpus-based comparisons, on the other hand, provide robust results but require substantial interpretation and may miss some of the subtleties of language use. The methodology presented here is therefore characterized by a constant interplay between different frameworks, techniques and approaches in a data-driven manner.

I draw on studies and literature beyond the field of linguistics, because this brings with it the advantages of interdisciplinarity, facilitating the cross-fertilization of ideas and methods between different disciplines (Banich and Mack 2003). For example, while clinical psychologists have mapped correlations between language use and various mental and affective states using specially developed, automated methods, these tools do not provide the same kind of detail and precision as currently available corpus analysis software (e.g. WordSmith Tools or Wmatrix). Frameworks developed broadly in the area of linguistics also have their shortcomings. A case in point is cognitive metaphor theory (CMT), which, until recently, not only was unsupported empirically but also relied on artificially produced examples to substantiate its claims. The importance of authentic data has been widely recognized and propagated, including within CMT, but it is in the field of psychology that the theory has found some empirical support (e.g. Casasanto 2008a and 2008b).

Throughout this book, I refer to two terms that are neither uncontroversial nor simple to define: affective state and depression. I have already indicated that by *affective state* I mean aspects of Sylvia Plath's inner world, such as emotions, feelings and moods, that can be placed on a cline of positive to negative, that is, are intrinsically valenced. I choose this particular term and definition as they are sufficiently narrow and, at the same time, sufficiently broad to include all relevant aspects of Sylvia Plath's inner world. An *affective state* is narrower than the more common *mental state,* which could include anything from emotions, cognition, perception, dispositions, goals, attitudes and even background knowledge (Palmer 2004). At the same time, an *affective state* is also broader than *emotion* and can include curiosity, uncertainty, enthusiasm and anxiety. These 'experiences' would not necessarily be called emotions, but they do share the aspect of valence.

The concept of *valence* stems from the tradition of mood research, which has tended to focus on the relatively broad dimensions of negative and positive affect. These refer, respectively, to 'the extent to which a person is non-specifically experiencing aversive states such as fear, sadness, anger and guilt' and 'the extent to which someone is experiencing pleasant states such as cheerfulness, enthusiasm, confidence, and alertness' (Gray and Watson 2001: 36). *Mood* and its research are also significant, because *mood* includes a temporal element: the affective state can persist over a period of time (Thayer 1996). In this way, there is also an, albeit indirect, connection with depression. While depression itself cannot be called a mood, it is sometimes referred to as a *mood disorder* (cf. *DSM-IV*). It is 'a profound and persistent feeling of sadness or despair and/or a loss of interest in things that were once pleasurable' (Fundukian and Wilson 2008: 339) that can take on more or less severe forms lasting for extended periods of time. In light of Sylvia Plath's diagnosed depression (Kirk 2004), attempted suicide in 1953 and suicide in 1963, this connection is highly relevant to the subject at hand.

The link between affective states and language, like the term affective state itself, is also not straightforward. Generally speaking, almost any example of language can lead to inferences about affective states (Palmer 2004). Descriptions of physical appearance or behaviour are as valid objects of study as creative metaphors. In this book, however, what I am particularly interested in are references that are more explicitly related to these states. These include language that directly or indirectly describes feelings and other valenced states (e.g. *I am depressed; I am scared; I am trembling*) as well as their effects on the writer (e.g. *it was exhilarating*). They can take the form of, or be signalled by, some types of mental process verbs (e.g. *I felt …*) as well as relational process types (Halliday 1994). Also relevant for conveying Plath's experience of affective states is the statistical composition of her language use. Specifically, the relative frequencies of grammatical categories, including personal pronouns, negation and polarized language (e.g. all, always, never, everyone, nobody etc.), have been shown to correlate with affective states (cf. Pennebaker and King 1999, Fekete 2002).

Through this analysis of different linguistic features, and using different methodologies, I show that Plath's affective states and experience of depression are conveyed through the metaphors she uses; the changes in the personal pronouns she uses to refer to herself and the frequency with which she does so; and the correlation of such changes with temporal orientation and negation, among others. I also discuss the ways in which she describes herself and how she seems to construct her world in categorical terms using dichotomous structures. Overall, in the Smith Journal, Sylvia Plath frequently describes herself in a negative light and appears to experience negative affective states more frequently and more intensely than positive ones. She also seems to introspect and focus on herself more than would be expected even in a personal journal. Notably, these tendencies are particularly pronounced in entries where she writes about herself using the second-person pronoun *you*. This kind of self-focus has repeatedly been associated with depression and can be a particularly worrying sign in combination with certain types of metaphors and grammatical structures. In the final two entries in the Smith Journal, written one month before Plath attempts suicide, precisely this dangerous combination is apparent. At other points in the journal, her language suggests inner conflict and turmoil, a sense of two conflicted selves and an inability to control or overcome her predicament. All together, these findings present a troubled mind in the broadest sense.

1.1 The structure of this book

This book is in two parts. In Part I, I set the theoretical and methodological context and establish the key linguistic characteristics of Sylvia Plath's Smith Journal using corpus linguistic tools. After an introduction to Sylvia Plath and the Smith Journal, Chapter 3 outlines the theoretical background for this book. It begins with an overview of linguistic approaches relevant for the study of affective states through language, such as stylistics, mind style and functional grammar, especially transitivity. These sections are followed by relevant research in social, clinical and narrative psychology, outlining literature important for assessing what linguistic features need to be considered in relation to the experience of affective states.

Then, in Chapter 4, I discuss the results of a corpus comparison of the Smith Journal with a reference corpus of autobiographies. After a brief introduction to corpus linguistics and the specific methodologies used in this study, I discuss the key grammatical and semantic features of the data with a view to establishing how Plath's language differs from a norm. This preliminary quantitative analysis informs the second half of the study in Part II of the book. Of course, not all of these differences are relevant to affective states, and not all relevant language is statistically significantly overused. However, focusing the study primarily on language that is both relevant and different from a norm helps to ensure that the most important ways that language can convey affective states and aspects of the self receive most attention. From Chapter 4 onwards, excerpts from the Smith Journal will include parts-of-speech (POS) or semantic (SEM) tags, as appropriate.

In Part II of the book, I explore qualitatively, and in greater depth, aspects of Sylvia Plath's language that are statistically significant or have implications for her experience of affective states, or both. In this way, the principles of a mixed-methods approach are embodied by the structure of this book. An initial quantitative, corpus-based comparison with a relevant norm informs more qualitative, manual intensive investigations of particular aspects of Plath's language, before the qualitative findings are once again subjected to further scrutiny using corpus-based tools. Although Part II is mainly qualitative in nature, the chapters do draw on further corpus analyses to substantiate the discussions and longer excerpts will continue to show POS or SEM tagging for further information. Combining manual, qualitative analyses with quantitative corpus results in this way increases comprehensiveness and improves reliability, while still providing the necessary amount of detail.

The first chapter in Part II, Chapter 5, looks at self-descriptions and direct references to affective states, and Chapter 6 then discusses metaphorical expressions relevant to affective states and the self in the Smith Journal. Metaphors have an important role to play in the communication of abstract, sensitive and subjective experiences, such as that of affective states: 'the study of metaphor is central to the study of mind' (Barnden 1997: 312). In Chapter 7, I discuss the role of personal pronouns in conveying affective states, focusing on the role of *you* in the Smith Journal. As outlined in Chapter 4, personal pronouns are significantly overused in the Smith Journal, but their role in conveying affective states is also well documented in the psychology literature. Finally, in Chapter 8, I conduct intra-textual (Adolphs 2006) corpus comparisons to characterize differences between journal entries written in the expected first-person *I* and those written using *you*.

In the final chapter of the book, Chapter 9, I zoom out from the data to explore the implications of linguistic patterns in the Smith Journal for Plath's experience of her affective states and for affective states more broadly. I discuss Sylvia Plath's language in the context of theories of depression and tentatively suggest possible practical applications for research of this kind.

Part One

Background to the Study

2

Sylvia Plath and her Journals

Introduction to the data

Sylvia Plath was a novelist and poet born in 1932 in the United States. She later lived in the United Kingdom after her marriage to the British poet Ted Hughes. Plath published a novel, *The Bell Jar* (1963); two major collections of poetry, *The Colossus* (1960) and *Ariel* (1965); and a collection of short stories, *Johnny Panic and the Bible of Dreams* (1977). Plath suffered from documented mental health problems from her late teenage years onwards and was reportedly diagnosed with depression (Kirk 2004) and borderline personality disorder (Cooper 2003). She died by suicide in 1963, but also attempted suicide at least once before then, in the summer of 1953. These are just some of the most well-known facts about Plath, and it is striking how her work, for better or for worse, seems forever interlinked with her life and death.

While attempts to interpret all her creative output through the lens of her personal tragedy are frustrating and inevitably favour certain interpretations over others, her personal journals can undoubtedly be seen as enlightening with regard to what it was like to be her (or what might be called the 'lived experience'; van Manen 1997). Among other facets, this experience included being a person with depressive and suicidal tendencies. Her talent as a writer and her turbulent mental life make her private journals an ideal ground for exploring what her language reveals about how she experienced her affective states.

Karen Kukil's 2000 edition of Plath's *Journals* appears under two different titles – *The Unabridged Journals of Sylvia Plath* in the United States and *The Journals of Sylvia Plath 1950–1959* in the United Kingdom – but neither edition is complete. The final two journals, written immediately prior to Plath's death, were never released and may possibly have been lost. The data and examples in this book come from Kukil's US edition of the *Journals*. *The Unabridged Journals of Sylvia Plath* consists of eight journals and fifteen fragments. Kukil remained as true as possible to the original formats (Brain 2006), reserving any notes for the end of the edition and retaining every physical nuance of Plath's originals:

> The transcription of the manuscripts at Smith College is as faithful to the author's originals as possible. Plath's final revisions are preserved and her substantive deletions and corrections are discussed in the notes. Plath's spelling, capitalization, punctuation, and grammar, as well as her errors, have been carefully transcribed and are presented without editorial comment. Every nuance of the physical journals has been preserved, including Plath's practice of underlining certain words and passages in her journals. (Kukil 2000: ix–x)

At various points in this book, I refer to events in Plath's life; the brief chronology of Plath's life juxtaposed with the dates and numbers of the journals with which they coincide in Table 2.1 below helps to contextualize this. Dates and events in grey indicate the absence of published journal entries from those times.

The journal entries sometimes deal with the life events outlined above, but they also include excerpts from letters, rough drafts of future poems, ideas for short stories, descriptions and narrations of Plath's feelings and preoccupations. Example 1 is a fairly typical journal entry written in the summer of 1951, while she was working for the Mayo family.

Example 1

> Tonight, after playing ping pong down in the Blodgett basement playroom I walked back into the house with a perceptible sense of proprietorship. If nothing else, in one month I have come to regard this place with an air of home. Upstairs, especially, I am complete sovereign. I still remember the day I drove up with Dick and stood in awestruck fear outside the gate, gazing at the great lawn, the long white house, the clump of huge copper beech trees spaced carefully on the grass. Never, I thought, could I walk with carefree equanimity on that carefully clipped lawn. But I do now. (Entry 95)

Some event is described, together with the concurrent perceptions and internal reactions. On the apropos of arriving back to the Mayo house after a party, she describes how at home she feels in the rather lavish environment. Sometimes, as in this case, the immediate topic is also related to something in the past.

To a certain extent, *The Unabridged Journals of Sylvia Plath* can be considered an example of a private journal (see Section 2.1 for more details), but it has to be acknowledged that a self-aware artist such as Plath may have intended her journals to be published at some point. This potentially means that all entries were written with an audience in mind. At the same time, the journals cannot

Table 2.1 Chronology

Journal number	Approximate date	Important events in Plath's life
	27 October 1932	Birth
	5 November 1940	Otto Plath dies
Journal 1	1950	Wins a scholarship to Smith College
1950–53	September 1950	Begins freshman year
	July 1951	Mother's helper at Mayo household
	September 1951	Begins second year at Smith College
	July–August 1952	Mother's helper at Cantor household Story 'Sunday' is published in *Mlle*, other stories in *Seventeen* and *Christian Science Monitor*
	January 1953	Fractures a fibula while skiing
	April 1953	Poems published in *Harper's Bazaar*. Editor of *Smith Review*
	June 1953	Guest editor of *Mlle* for a month
	24 August 1953	First suicide attempt
	September 1953	Stays at McLean Hospital, treated by Dr Ruth Beuscher
	February 1954	Returns to Smith
	summer 1954	Attends Harvard summer school
	June 1955	Graduates 'Summa cum laude' from Smith. Wins Fulbright scholarship
	October 1955	Begins studies at Cambridge
Journal 2–4	February 1956	Meets Ted Hughes at a party
November 1955–August 1956	16 June 1956	Marries Ted Hughes
	June–August 1956	Summer in Benidorm, Spain
Journal 5–6	June 1957	Finishes Bachelor of Arts studies
January 1957–August 1957		

Table 2.1 (Continued)

Journal number	Approximate date	Important events in Plath's life
Journal 7	September 1957	Starts teaching at Smith
August 1957–October 1958	May 1958	Finishes teaching
	summer 1958	Quarrels with Ted over seeing him with a girl
		Settles in Boston with Ted. Takes on secretarial work at a psychiatric ward
	October 1958	Resumes therapy with Beuscher
Journal 8	December 1958	
December 1958–November 1959	June 1959	First pregnancy begins
	summer 1959	Stays at artists' colony in Yaddo
Appendix: 1961	December 1959	Returns to England with Ted
Descriptions of people	January 1960	They settle in London
	April 1960	Frieda is born
	October 1960	*Colossus* published
	February 1961	Second pregnancy ends in miscarriage
	August 1961	Move to Devon
	November 1961	Receives Saxton grant to work on a novel
	January 1962	Nicholas born
	July 1962	Learns of Ted's affair with Assia Wevill
	September 1962	Separates from Ted
	December 1962	Moves to London with children and prepares *Ariel*
	January 1963	*The Bell Jar* is published pseudonymously
	11 February 1963	Commits suicide

easily be considered one homogeneous genre. Plath used her journals partly as a writer's notebook (Brain 2001) testing out versions of future poems (a good example of this is Entry 65, Example 2, which includes a poem now known as 'April 18') and also included letters (as in Example 3).

Example 2

And so I will write to you a few lines that came during class on Monday after your visit, after I said things to you that I should not have said, and so, here it is:

The slime of all my yesterdays [...]
(from Entry 65)

Example 3

March 8 – letter excerpt:

'Firstly of all I was horrified to hear that the dear bearshooting imaginative adorable very lovable bright southernaccented sandy' I knew for such a little nice while is gone away. it is unjust, unnecessary, and difficult to comprehend. (Entry 183)

While a reasonable argument can be made that entries such as Example 1 can be considered 'private writing', these types of entries were obviously written with an audience in mind. For this reason, I exclude entries consisting of letters and work in progress from my data set.

In fact, the actual data set discussed in this book is much smaller than the complete published journals. Only the first journal in *The Unabridged Journals of Sylvia Plath*, written between 1950 and 1953 (Kukil 2000: 3–187), constitutes my data. It spans the years that Plath spent at Smith College and is henceforth referred to as the Smith Journal or the Journal. This particular journal was selected for several reasons. First, the rich imagery so characteristic of the Smith Journal almost disappears from Plath's second, third and fourth journals, although it does reappear in the final ones. Secondly, the later journals are influenced by important people in Plath's life: Ted Hughes, for example, not only becomes the topic of her preoccupations but also influences the way she thinks as she tries to emulate a husband she much respects. Her later writing is also affected by her therapist, Dr Beuscher, and books on Freudian therapy that she reads. Finally, and perhaps most importantly, the first journal is not necessarily comparable with the rest of the journals, but it does have good internal comparability and encompasses a relatively contained period of Plath's life.

The Smith Journal begins just before Plath goes to university and ends just before her first suicide attempt. Although the entries are not always dated, it seems that they were written with reasonable frequency and without too many lengthy interruptions. Due to this regularity, the entries reflect both positive and negative experiences, emotions and states, providing a relatively comprehensive picture of Plath's affective states. After Plath's first suicide attempt, there is an interruption of over two years before the journals resume again. In this period, Plath goes through a substantial amount of therapy, resumes university, finishes it and moves to England to study at Cambridge. When she begins writing her journals again, they are written in the form of letters to a former boyfriend. It is not until almost four years after the Smith Journal leaves off that Plath returns to her initial style of writing – and by this point she is a married woman. Her preoccupations as a woman and a wife are markedly different to those of a young adult going to university.

2.1 Personal journals

Diaries have been written for centuries and are traditionally seen as something therapeutic, spiritual and, above all, private. The genre is relatively difficult to define, as diaries or journals are 'artless, without rule, fragmentary, and personal' (McNeill 2005: 2). In addition, the genre may or may not remain stable, as journals are generally not circulated, and people have to rely on 'cultural osmosis' to acquire journal writing skills/norms.

Although diaries are traditionally not included in the genre of autobiographies, it can be argued that they may be similar in 'the inner compulsion to write of the self' (Marcus 1994: 3). According to Marcus (1994), diaries and autobiographies are similar also in the sense that they are a means of self-discovery. The main difference between autobiographies and journals is that the former, by definition, are written for an audience. While this may also be true for some diaries (Bloom 1996), it is not necessarily true for all of them. Autobiographies also retrospectively interpret/narrate events, emotions and thoughts (Schiwy 1994) and have to rely on a less than perfect memory (Stanley 1992). A journal, on the other hand, is a record of the life as it is happening: 'the journal writer writes in the midst of living her [sic] life' (Schiwy 1994: 236). This means that journals, by virtue of being written at the time (or temporality close to) when things happen, are less likely to be refined or revised. In Sylvia Plath's case, there are indications that she used her journals as a writer's notebook with the (perhaps subconscious) intentions of publication (Brain 2001 and 2006): as Bloom says, 'a professional writer is never off-duty' (Bloom 1996: 25). But there are also suggestions that they were primarily of a personal nature (Rose 1992), and, at the time of writing the Smith Journal (1950–53), Plath could not yet be described as a 'professional' writer.

Morson (1981) attempts to make concrete distinctions between literary diaries (those written to be read) and non-literary ones (those written for the self only). He believes that a literary diary will contain a lot of information that is unnecessary for the person writing it, as the writer is part of their own context. These details need to be included in literary diaries, because the intended audience does not share the writer's context. In addition, a literary diary will have a sense of being complete, whereas a personal journal has a tendency to seem more fragmentary: truly private diaries are often elliptical and do not identify people or places (Bloom 1996). 'Such diaries march along chronologically, their day-by-day progress dictated by the format and textually insulated from the rest of the work. They exhibit no foreshadowing and scarcely a retrospective glance except to keep score' (Bloom 1996: 26).

Based on Morson's (1981) and Bloom's (1996) distinctions, Plath's journals cannot be seen as entirely literary, except in entries that are explicit works in progress or letters to people. Arguably, Plath introspects a lot more than what would be expected from a private diary as described by Bloom (1996), but she does not seem to provide excessive detail for the benefit of a potential external reader. In fact, it is often difficult to follow her narrative due to a lack of context. It is sometimes difficult to chronologically place her entries (especially in the first journal), and it is often challenging to keep the various people she writes about separate. She often writes about the men she dates, and yet it is difficult to distinguish between them – some are not named at all. Plath also did not write in a logical and orderly fashion – she wrote on loose-leaf paper and notebooks, typed and handwritten (Kukil 2000). There is also no sense of beginning or end to any of the journals. The journals do not seem complete – and not only because some parts are actually missing. All this seems to suggest that the journals were private, at least to some extent.

An interesting issue arising from this is the notion of an authentic 'self'. As discussed, journals are more likely to be written close to the events they report and are less likely to be edited substantially to cater to an audience. However, this does not necessarily mean that diarists like Plath write their authentic 'self' in their journals. In one of her lectures, Anaïs Nin, another prominent diarist, describes the struggle she experiences between the often conflicting demands that society and she herself put on her own person (Plath experienced similar difficulties, according to Brain (2006)). She states that it is, of course, possible to be more than one person/more than one self in a diary:

> You can see the story in the *Diary.* You can see how first of all I tried to be the ideal woman and that didn't work. Then I tried to be the mirror for others and the muse, the one that helped to get their books done. (Nin 1975: 52)

However, all the personalities she chose for her diary were representative of who she was, wanted to be, would be, sometimes was etc. Nin is very clear about this: 'my genuine self was in the diary' (Nin 1975: 52). In discussing Dorothy Wordsworth's journals, McGavran (1988) similarly describes how, even though she tried, Dorothy could not avoid putting her 'self' down.

Obviously, all this does not mean that everything that is narrated in the journals is factually true. After all, '"fiction" cannot actually be separated from fact, both in autobiography, and in lives as they are lived' (Stanley 1992: 65). It does, however, give credibility to the idea that an analysis of Plath's language will lead to some insight into the way she really experienced her affective states – especially considering that even the conscious 'performance' of one's self can give some insights into the person's 'true' self.

2.1.1 A note on discourse types

Texts have always been classified according to their function, topic, style, social context, etc. The discussion of the 'genre' of journals above mainly made reference to function, for example. According to Faigely and Meyer, there are two main traditions of text classification: 'one tradition classifies texts according to purpose, the other by mode or type' (Faigely and Meyer 1983: 305). Such classifications have led to different categories, such as genres, text types, discourse types and discourse modes. These terms are largely interchangeable and can be associated with certain scholars or traditions. What Werlich (1976) calls *text types* are what Faigely and Meyer (1983) and Fludernik (1996) would call *discourse types* and what Smith (2003) calls *discourse modes*. In general, the differences in terminology allude to various levels of precision in defining the terms and the characteristics of the texts that they are meant to denote.

Broadly speaking, text types can be considered 'an idealized norm of distinctive text structuring which serves as a matrix of rules and elements for the encoder when responding linguistically to specific aspects of his experience' (Werlich 1976: 39). Various text types have been recognized by linguists over time: for example, description, narration, exposition, argumentation and instruction (Werlich

1976). However, although the vast majority of work on text types uses this term to refer to texts at supra sentence and paragraph level (Fludernik 2000), the exact unit of analysis is rarely specified, and it is generally acknowledged that a single text can be made up of smaller units of various text types (Fludernik 2000, Smith 2003, Herman 2008). Therefore, as Smith (2003) points out, researchers always need to find a fruitful level or unit of analysis.

Considering the Smith Journal as a whole in terms of form would not constitute a fruitful level of analysis since, as noted earlier, personal diaries are less bound by convention than other genres (McNeill 2005) and can therefore take a variety of forms. And precisely this heterogeneity necessitates a way of distinguishing various text types or discourse modes. In this book, *discourse type* refers to passages or segments of the overall text of the Smith Journal. The exact length of the passages that constitute a discourse type is not clear-cut: their delimitation is largely context- and content-dependent (Werlich 1976, Herman 2008).

2.1.1.1 The descriptive and narrative discourse types

I have already alluded to different kinds of 'description' that Plath included in her journals, and, in subsequent discussions, the presence of such description will help to explain various linguistic characteristics of the data. It makes sense, therefore, to consider what the descriptive discourse type is like and to contrast it with anther common form, the narrative discourse type.

Description seems to be characterized by its static nature, involving progression only in space (Merlini Barbaresi 2004), while narration is more dynamic and involves progression in time. 'In Narrative, situations are related to each other and dynamic Events advance narrative time' (Smith 2003: 13). In contrast, a descriptive text is one where the 'focus is on factual phenomena (i.e. persons, objects, relations) in the spatial context' (Werlich 1976: 19), rather than the temporal. Although it is useful to distinguish between description and narration, Herman offers a word of caution. He states that the two overlap significantly 'since representations and discourses falling under both rubrics have the net effect of coupling properties with situations, events or objects' (Herman 2008: 451). Herman (2008) suggests that context determines whether a particular statement functions as a description or narration.

Meyer understands the function of description to be an expression of a relationship between ideas that 'gives more information about a topic by presenting attributes, specifics, manners, or settings' (Meyer 1985: 17). In conjunction with the all-important spatial locators, descriptions therefore often refer to other visual characteristics, such as shape, dimensions, colour and light (Merlini Barbaresi 2004). This leads in to the linguistic features of the discourse types. The narrative mode's focus on temporal progressions results in frequent use of temporal references (e.g. adverbials), complex tenses and sequencing conjunctions (Merlini Barbaresi 2004). This mode is also often composed of a sequence of events, which are also understood as involving/signalling temporal progression (Smith 2003). By contrast, Werlich notes that, in impressionistic description, phenomena are presented as

> subjective impressions of relations, qualities, positions and directions in space. [The encoder] accordingly makes linguistic choices which, apart from describing something, also give expression to the associations, attitudes, feelings and moods which the phenomena release in the perceiver. (Werlich, 1976: 47)

This often involves the use of hyperbole, metaphor, comparisons and evocative language (although metaphor and comparisons are common in the narrative text type as well), designed to help the addressee infer the scene being outlined in all its significance (Merlini Barbaresi 2004).

The subjectivity outlined above appears in all discourse modes. However, there is an inherent subjectivity in descriptions as they are presented from the point of view of the speaker (often in first person; Werlich 1976). According to Merlini Barbaresi (2004), subjectivity may be increased by making objective reference points obscure and less accessible, using abstractions and resorting to idiosyncratic preferences as opposed to conventionalized forms (linguistically speaking). These subjective forms represent an access to the mind of the narrator (Smith 2003) and are also evident in the frequent use of modals, adverbials and parentheticals.

In the following analyses, *description* should be understood as outlined here. It consists of the part of a text that provides a subjective, 'vivid, often emotionally suggestive mental picture of factual phenomena, such as [specific] objects, people, and places in space' (Werlich 1976: 50). Its main linguistic features are hyperbole, metaphors, comparisons and evocative language, atelic verbs, first-person pronouns, lexis of vision (but also references to other senses), modals, adverbials and parentheticals.

3

Language and Affective States – Setting the Theoretical Scene

Continuing to set the scene, in this chapter I introduce some concepts, frameworks and areas of research that underpin the approach of this study. I start broadly, from a background of applied linguistics and stylistics, and zoom in on specific notions such as transitivity and mind style. I then consider the interface between language and psychology and focus on research into the language of affective disorders.

3.1 Stylistics and applied linguistics

Stylistics has always assumed 'that the different ways in which people express their thoughts indicate, consciously or unconsciously, their personalities and attitudes' (Fowler 1996: 168), making it an appropriate backdrop for a study of language and affective states. Traditionally the study of language use and style in literature (Leech 1969), stylistics is essentially a collection of frameworks and methods drawn from a number of linguistic subdisciplines to investigate texts and language in terms of 'context, purpose, author and period' (Semino and Culpeper 1995: 513), among others. Authorial style, the style of genres, reader response, character construction, text world construction, point of view, metaphor, speech presentation etc. have all been investigated under the umbrella of stylistics. The strength of the stylistics approach, in contrast with traditional literary theory, for example, lies in its rigour. It aims to be explicit, systematic and verifiable (Short 1996).

While stylistics has traditionally applied the theories and methods developed in theoretical linguistics and discourse analysis, more recently it has benefited from advances in pragmatics, psychology and the cognitive sciences in particular, making it a potentially interdisciplinary approach to language analysis (Semino and Culpeper 1995). It has also broadened out to include the study of non-fictional and/or non-literary texts (see, for example, Jeffries 2009). For this study, the most pertinent notion to emerge from stylistics has been *mind style* (Fowler 1977, Leech and Short 1981).

3.1.1 Mind style

The term *mind style* was first coined by Roger Fowler in *Linguistics and the Novel* 'to refer to any distinctive linguistic representation of an individual mental self' (Fowler 1977: 103). It was a way of analysing and understanding the world views of characters in novels. A few years later, Leech and Short defined mind style as 'a realization of narrative point of view' (Leech and Short 1981: 188) and applied it not only to the analysis of characters but also to the analysis of implied authors, since 'it is a commonplace that a writer's style reveals his habitual way of experiencing and interpreting things' (Leech and Short 1981: 188). Since the publication of these seminal works, the meaning of the term and its applications have evolved, but the principle of systematic linguistic choices being seen as sources of inferences about minds has remained.

More recently, and not surprisingly, the concept of mind style has benefited from developments and ideas in psychology and the cognitive sciences. Bockting, for example, draws on psychology and psychiatry in her interpretations of characters' linguistic patterns in Faulkner's *The Sound and the Fury*, making the notion of mind style more specific to the individual character, as opposed to a broader world view (cf. Leech and Short 1981):

> Mind style is concerned with the construction and *expression in language of the conceptualizations of reality in a particular mind*. This individual structuring is *unique in all its details*, even though it is built up of elements that are also found in the realities of others. (Bockting 1994: 159, my emphasis)

Semino (2002) makes the distinction between mind style and world view even clearer. She suggests that world view represents aspects of ideology that are determined by external circumstances such as culture; while mind style is 'most apt at capturing those aspects of world views that are primarily personal and cognitive in origin' (Semino 2002: 97). In this definition, the focus on cognitive aspects is already quite clear, but it is Boase-Beier who explicitly equates mind style with (a broad notion of) mental state: 'I define mind style as the linguistic style that reflects a cognitive state. In particular, it is a linguistic style characterized by distinctive and striking textual patterns' (Boase-Beier 2003: 254). Not only is it distinctive and striking textual patterns that are of interest to an investigation of mind style; it is, in particular, those that are persistent:

> If style is the result of choice, and choice is the result of cognitive state, then it could be argued that all style is in a sense mind style. However, what is peculiar to the notion of mind style is *a consistent stylistic pattern* in the text as evidence of a particular cognitive state. (Boase-Beier, 2003: 263; my emphasis)

In principle, almost any persistent pattern of language can be indicative of mind style, but establishing the link requires two interconnected steps: identifying distinctive and systematic linguistic patterns; and linking these patterns to representations of characteristics of an individual mind (Semino 2005). The first of these steps can be done, to some extent, through corpus analysis. But the second step does not arise directly as a result of the first: distinctive or statistically significant patterns may or may not be related to mind style (Semino 2005). In addition, statistically insignificant patterns may also be significant for mind style. The following linguistic features have established links to mind style: sentence structure (e.g. Bockting 1995), over/under use of particular semantic fields (e.g. Bockting 1995), figurative language (e.g. Semino and Swindlehurst 1996), transitivity (Halliday 1971), use of (formal) logic (McIntyre 2005), conversational style (Semino 2005), the use of negation and the use of deictic expressions (e.g. Fowler 1986). These features overlap, to some extent, with those identified by psychologists as indicators of individuality and pathology (see Section 3.2). It is important to remember, however, that none of these features in isolation is enough to establish a particular mind style. The interplay between a number of features is what is particularly interesting and fruitful for analysis (Semino 2005).

Although the concept of mind style is now well established, there is ambiguity over whether the term refers to linguistic features or people's attribution of those as characteristics of particular minds (Semino 2007) and over whether it is an expression of an unconscious state or a manipulation of language to create the impression of a state (Boase-Beier 2003). In both cases, the two options do not seem to be mutually exclusive. Linguistic patterns and people's interpretations of those are part of the same analytical process, though in the current context I understand mind style as characteristics attributed to a mind by a reader. This is, of course, related to my understanding of affective states, which are also based on concrete linguistic indicators but are deduced from those indicators by myself as the analyst. Similarly, on unconscious expression versus intentional manipulation, Boase-Beier suggests that 'both mind style in a text and the cognitive state of which it is a manifestation will contain both conscious and unconscious elements' (Boase-Beier 2003: 254).

In the same way that mind style within stylistics links language and affective states, systemic functional grammar in applied linguistics more broadly can be useful for exploring character (Toolan 1998) and minds (Fine 2008).

3.1.2 Systemic functional grammar

Essentially, functional grammar (or systemic functional linguistics/grammar – SFL – as it is sometimes referred to), as originally put forward by Halliday in 1985, is a way of describing and understanding language based on meaning (semantics) in context, rather than form (syntax). This is based on the idea that language is a social semiotic system (Halliday 2006), and its interpretation is therefore dependent on social function: the internal organization of language 'embodies the functions that language has evolved to serve in the life of social man' (Halliday [1973] 2003: 317). A further assumption of SFL is that language is made up of sets of viable options of meaning – something that Halliday ([1972] 2003) describes as *meaning potential*. Simply put, this means that, in communicating information in the broad sense, the actual language one uses is a matter of choice. Each choice 'acquires its meanings against the background of other choices which could have been made' (Eggins 2004: 3), so the linguistic choices people actually make are meaningful in themselves – this, of course, echoes the underpinnings of mind style.

According to SFL, the uses/meanings of language can be grouped into three *metafunctions* that encode various aspects of reality (Halliday 2006). The *ideational* metafunction encodes meanings about the world (i.e. understanding and expressing perceptions of the internal and external world) and includes experiential and logical modes (Bloor and Bloor 2004). The former is captured by the notion of transitivity with the aim of describing *who does what to whom*, while the logical mode is captured by the logical relationships between ideas (Bloor and Bloor 2004). The *interpersonal* metafunction encodes social relationships and interactions with people (Thompson 2004). In this sense, language can be used to understand and express opinions, attitudes etc. and to take on (and allocate) social roles (Bloor and Bloor 2004). Finally, the textual metafunction encodes the textual and contextual organization of messages (Thompson 2004). Of course, as Halliday ([1973] 2003) points out, none of these metafunctions is realized independently of the others: in any one clause, all functions may be present.

3.1.2.1 *Transitivity*

Affective states in the SFL sense are experiences of the social world, and such experiences are encoded in the ideational metafunction, and particularly in the experiential mode. In the clause, the ideational metafunction is represented by agents, processes and affected entities (Halliday [1973] 2003), in particular by a small set of process types. As Figure 3.1 shows, Halliday and Matthiessen (2004) distinguish between six process types in English: material, mental (sometimes called mental-affective), relational, behavioural, verbal and existential. The material and mental process types distinguish clearly between experience in the outer and the inner world. The outer experience is made up of events and actions that happen, or that people do or make happen. The inner experience, by contrast, is made up of 'reactions' (in a broad sense) to the outer experience (e.g. remembering it, thinking about it). The relational process type is used to identify and classify experiences in relation to each other. Halliday and Matthiessen (2004) suggest that these three are the main process types in English and are most clearly distinguishable from each other.There are also three 'minor' process types: the behavioural, the verbal and the existential. The behavioural process type represents 'the outer manifestations of inner workings, the acting out of

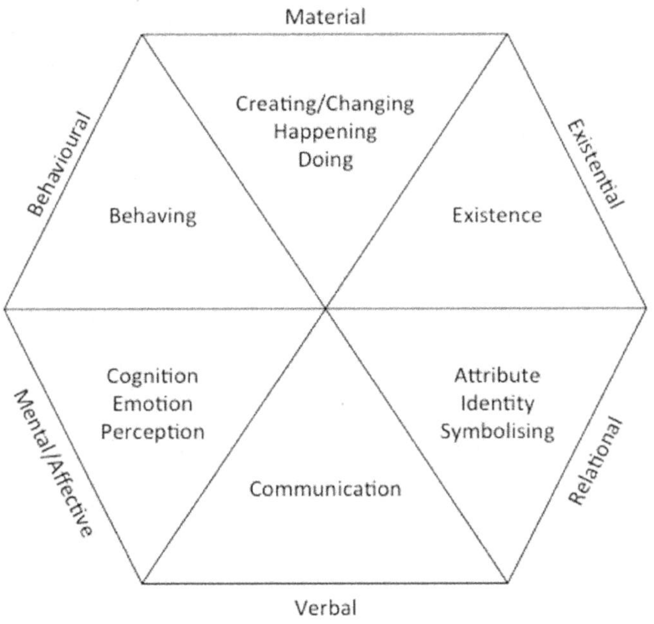

Figure 3.1 Types of processes in English.

processes of consciousness (e.g. *people are laughing*) and physiological states (e.g. *they were sleeping*)' (Halliday and Matthiessen 2004: 171). Verbal processes concretize symbolic relationships in language (e.g. saying and meaning). Finally, the existential process type reflects a simple recognition of existence – that something *is*.

Participants (enactors and receivers of the processes) are generally considered to be inherent in the processes, as all processes involve at least one (Halliday and Matthiessen 2004). Aside from participants and processes, clauses may also have added information in the form of *circumstances*. For example, in *birds are flying overhead, birds* are the participants, *flying* is the process and *overhead* is a circumstance. In this case there is only one participant, as no other entity is involved in the flight of the birds. In order to distinguish between the types of roles that participants can fulfil in various processes, Halliday (1994) provides a series of labels – these are reproduced below in diagrammatic form from Eggins (2004) (Figure 3.2). Distinguishing between process types in practice is not always straightforward. Halliday and Matthiessen (2004) acknowledge that processes can be more or less prototypical of any of the types, and therefore the boundaries between them can be rather fuzzy. For example, behavioural and mental process types generally have only one human participant – the behaver and the senser, respectively (see Figure 3.2). No entity other than the one experiencing or performing the process is involved. Differentiating between them requires attention to the semantics of the process itself. Similarly, material processes – although they usually involve

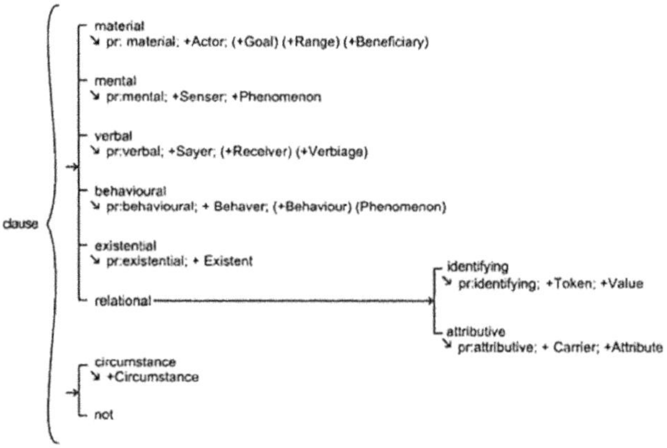

Figure 3.2 Transitivity (Eggins 2004: 214).

two or more participants – may also involve just one. However, semantically, material processes are normally *creative* or *transformative* in some way (Thompson 2004) – they bring entities into existence or change existing ones. Note how subcategorizing material processes in such a way already implies an entity that is affected.

Describing texts by identifying the processes and participants involved provides information about the way reality is understood and expressed by the originator of the text. It is in this sense that SFL, and particularly transitivity, will be useful for understanding how language conveys various aspects of affective states.

3.2 Language and psychology

Unsurprisingly, the link between language and affective states is not only of interest in linguistics but has also fruitfully been explored in the field of psychology. Narrative psychologists have focused on the role of life stories in therapy, while clinical social psychologists have explored the link between linguistic style and mental illness.

3.2.1 Linguistic indicators of mental illness

> *Word use can tell us far more than just the story; it is a window into the narrator's world.* (Pennebaker and Stone 2003: 291)

James Pennebaker and colleagues have done extensive work on whether language is characteristic of the person using it (e.g. Pennebaker and King 1999) and, if so, what can be deduced from it. Through numerous studies, they found that the use of function words (grammatical words/particles), along with emotion-related words, cognitive words and temporal words, can be indicative of sex, age and social class (e.g. Pennebaker and Stone 2003). The same words can also reveal social and personality processes, for example, they can be indicative of deception, dominance in conversation, depression, schizophrenia and some of the Big Five personality indicators (extraversion, agreeableness, conscientiousness, neuroticism and openness to experience), among other things (Chung and Pennebaker 2007, Ireland and Mehl 2014). This in itself is interesting, but the most significant feature of this body of research is its application of corpus-type, automated methodologies using the so-called Linguistic Inquiry and Word Count (LIWC) tool.

LIWC calculates the frequency with which people use types of words, such as emotion words (e.g. *love, nice, sweet, hurt, ugly, crying, grief, worried, hate, kill, annoyed*), self-references, words longer than six letters ('long' words), or words related to sex, eating or religion, across a range of texts. Some of these groups refer to function words (pronouns, modal verbs etc.), while others resemble semantic fields (for more details, see http://www.liwc.net/liwcdescription.php). The program works on the basis of a default set of word categories and a default dictionary that determines which words are counted in a text.

Using LIWC, Pennebaker and King (1999) tested which particular linguistic features were most reliable at indicating individual difference. They found that long words, the first-person singular pronoun, negation, articles, positive and negative emotion words, causation words (*because, effect*), insight words (*think, know, consider*), discrepancy words (*should, would, could*), tentative words (*perhaps, guess*), social processes (*mate, talk, they, child*), past tense, present tense and inclusive and exclusive word categories (*and, with, include, but, without*) were particularly reliable. Pennebaker, Mehl and Niederhoffer additionally found that for individuals, word use is stable across time and context and can therefore be used as a measure of individual difference (Pennebaker et al. 2003). Bearing this in mind, natural language use was found to be indicative of a number of psychological and social characteristics (and here the authors draw on various other research as well). Examples include

- neuroticism (high use of negative emotion words and the first-person singular)
- anxiety (high use of the first-person singular and explainers)
- anger (high use of negatives, rhetorical questions, direct references to others)
- deception (low use of the first-person singular, higher use of negative emotion words and lower cognitive complexity such as the use of exclusive words)
- emotional upheaval, depression and suicidality

The final point is most relevant to the current study. Stirman and Pennebaker (2001) found that poets with suicidal tendencies used more frequent first-person singular references and more references to death than did non-suicidal poets. In a case study, Baddeley et al. (2011) additionally describe an association between suicidal ideation and an increase in negative emotion words. This is taken as an indicator of decreased interest in social relationships coupled with increased focus on the self and death.

Rude et al. (2004) also found self-focus (as in an increase in the use of first-person singular pronouns) to be a key indicator of depression. They investigated the written language of depressed, depression vulnerable (formerly depressed) and never-depressed college students with the help of LIWC. The category that individuals belonged to was assessed using the Beck Depression Index (Beck et al. 1961) and the Inventory to Diagnose Depression–Lifetime (Zimmerman and Coryell 1987) prior to the study. In the study, students were asked to write an essay on the personal experience of starting college. Although there are potential methodological issues with this study (the precise essay question could have biased the students in a number of ways), Rude et al. (2004) found that the first-person singular pronoun was used significantly more frequently by both currently and formerly depressed students than by never-depressed students.

In a different study looking at the effect of collective trauma, Cohn, Mehl and Pennebaker (2004) investigated the language use of over 1,000 US users of livejournal.com – a blogging website – from two weeks prior to 11 September 2001 to six weeks after the attacks. After the upheaval of the 9/11 attacks, the language use of participants revealed more negative emotions and more cognitive and social engagement, as well as signs of psychological distancing,[1] when compared to their baselines. However, their emotional state and social referencing returned to baseline within two weeks, while the increase in indicators of psychological distancing persisted. In addition, after two weeks, the level of cognitive activity (as indicated by the language) dropped to significantly below the baseline. The increase in indicators of distancing lasted for the six weeks after 9/11 that the study included, and references to others continued to decrease during that time. Similar changes in tendencies were noted by Pennebaker and Lay (2002) in the speeches of Rudolph Giuliani, former mayor of New York, following a series of personal crises (prostate cancer, divorce, public scandal) and the collective crisis of 9/11.

These studies are innovative and exciting in many ways, but there are some limitations inherent in the methodology used. Computer programs in general cannot account for certain aspects of language use, such as context, irony and metaphor (Pennebaker and Stone 2003). This means that their results will, at best, be probabilistic (Chung and Pennebaker 2007), and it will require substantial manual work to make findings and interpretations reliable. In addition, Pennebaker et al. (2003) acknowledge that the differences between English and other languages, written and spoken data, intelligence, language proficiency etc. could all have effects on natural language use. For this reason, although these studies provide invaluable interpretative material, I do not use Pennebaker et al.'s methodology or the LIWC software in this book. Instead, as I discuss in the next chapter, Wmatrix (Rayson 2009), a linguistically more reliable corpus linguistic tool, is used for the quantitative analyses.

However, other clinical studies aimed at determining whether speech/writing pattern and style can be associated with various psychopathological states have also demonstrated 'that individuals sharing significant patterns of nonverbal behaviour express these tendencies in their manner of speaking' (Fekete 2002: 352). This means that people who are clinically depressed, for example, will share certain characteristics in their use of language that can be distinguished from linguistic characteristics of people who are not depressed or have other mental pathologies.

Diagnosing mental illnesses is notoriously difficult. The same physical symptoms can be indicative of a variety of illnesses, and many 'distinct' illnesses are, in fact, related (Appignanesi 2008). In an attempt at finding characteristic differences among three such (related) illnesses, Fekete (2002) conducted a study of language use in internet discussion groups on three self-help newsgroups: for suicidal, depressive and anxious people. These texts were compared to those of a control newsgroup (related to journalism) as well as to each other in order to better understand the underlying psychological mechanisms. Fekete (2002) found the following:

- The suicidal group was characterized by: higher use of personal references and *I*; higher use of feeling expressions (like-dislike, pleasure-displeasure, attraction-aversion) and adverbial intensifiers; higher dichotomies ('allness' terms or polarized expressions – *always*, *never*, *forever* etc.) scores than the other groups; high frequency of negation; low use of explainers (e.g. *because*, *therefore*, *since*).
- The depressive group was characterized by: higher use of personal references and *I*; higher use of 'emotional' categories, feeling expressions and adverbial intensifiers; frequency of the dichotomous structures higher than in the normal group, but much lower than in the suicidal group; frequent use of explainers and retractors (e.g. *but*, *however*, *although*, *except*).
- The anxiety group was characterized by: higher use of personal references and *I* and frequency of dichotomous structures comparable to the depressive group.

According to Fekete (2002), high frequency of self-references seems to reflect a self-preoccupation and an inability of such people to distance themselves from their personal concerns. An overuse of *me* in pathological groups (suicidal, depressive, anxiety disordered people) may be representative of passivity. On the other hand, a high frequency of retractors and explainers may be linked to ambivalence, indecision and impulsivity in self-preoccupied depressive persons. The fact that suicidal writers also used more polarized, dichotomous structures may reflect the psychological defence mechanism of mental/cognitive 'splitting' (i.e. severe dissociation) (Fekete 2002). The tendency to use negation more often than non-pathological writers can reflect denial, or more of the oppositional tendencies noted above. All of these together seem to concur with the psychopathology of the suicidal process where the 'archaic defence mechanisms of splitting and denial, the cognitive rigidity and dichotomous, partly stereotyped thinking' (Fekete 2002: 359) frequently occur. The progression from anxiety to suicidality (in terms of severity of the disorder) seems to be reflected in people's language use: the least different from the control group is the language use of people with anxiety, while the most different is that of the suicidal group.

Another way in which the link between language and mental illness has been explored in psychology is through patients' writing samples in the context of therapy. These can help psychologists understand patients' problems, since 'people's vocabulary reflects their mental preoccupations' (Vanheule et al. 2008: 1). In particular, personal documents such as letters and diaries are significant for psychological research (Allport 1942, cited in Fekete 2002) as these tend to reflect a freer and more personal form of expression. In addition, the content tends to focus on the individuals themselves, making them a valuable resource for investigating individual experience.

3.2.1.1 *Studies in narrative psychology*

Narrative psychology is a branch of traditional psychology that focuses on what narratives can reveal about the people producing them. A basic assumption is that 'systematic linguistic analysis of narrative discourse may lead to a scientific study of identity construction' (Lászlo et al. 2007: 1). This, again, is similar to the assumptions underpinning the concept of mind style outlined above. Identity, in this case, is taken to be malleable through time and circumstance, but to achieve overall wholeness and integrity in the individual's life story. In this way the story (narrative) becomes a representation of the more abstract and stable overall identity. Narratives are representative of identity because they involve a subjective point of view expressed in 'compositional devices such as time structure and time experience (the latter particularly in self-narratives), characters' agency, coherence, evaluation, spatial and interpersonal relations of the characters' (Lászlo et al. 2007: 10). In what follows I focus on two studies of such narrative features.

Hargitai et al. (2007) look at the psychological meaning of negation and self-reference 'based on the idea that the form and especially the extent of "saying no" often determines the relationship between the individual and the community' (Hargitai et al. 2007: 26). While, traditionally, a high rate of negation is associated with depreciation of the world or negativism, the potential for self-harm, psychological crises and suicidal tendencies, Hargitai et al.'s (2007) own study offers a more fine-grained examination of the results. The authors find that negation is significantly more frequent in narratives of negatively evaluated life experiences than in narratives of positive life experiences. There is still a difference between individuals – for some the rates are generally much higher than others – but the content of the narrative has a strong influence on the presence of the linguistic feature. As a consequence, the authors urge caution: 'The analysis of healthy people's words (sentences and stories) is only possible with a full knowledge of the aims and the content represented by the speaker' (Hargitai et al. 2007: 36).

The same principle seems to apply to findings related to the role of self-reference. While studies such as Rude et al.'s (2004) above link depression and anxiety with a high frequency of self-references regardless of context, Hargitai et al. (2007) note a difference in function between negative narratives – those of fear or anxiety – and positive ones (of achievement, for example).

> As far as the narratives of a good relation or the narratives of achievement are concerned, the statistical results confirm that high self-reference may link not only to the intrapsychic dynamics of depression, but it may refer to self-control, to conformity to reality and to autonomy as well. (Hargitai et al. 2007: 36)

The authors suggest that a similarity between the two types of writing in relation to the role of the self accounts for these divergent interpretations. In narratives of achievement, autonomy/the self is celebrated due to the positive association with acting individually. On the other hand, in narratives of negative life events, the self becomes increasingly important due to the desire to overcome difficulties alone. In both of these cases it is the importance of the self that is reflected in language. This means that the same phenomenon – a focus on the self – can be representative of different psychological processes depending on the type of story one is telling.

Rather than negation, Pólya et al. (2007) focus on the role of time references in narratives. They look at the relative spatio-temporal locations of the narrated event and the narration itself – that is, whether there is explicit distance between the events of the story and the events of the narrative time/situation. Based on this, the authors distinguish between three narrative forms: the retrospective, the experiencing and the metanarrative form:

> In the case of a *retrospective form*, the narrative content is located in the narrated events while the position [of the narrator] is located in the narration. In the case of an *experiencing form*, both the narrative content and the position are located in the narrated events. Finally, in the case of a *metanarrative form*, both the narrative content and the position are located in the narration. (Pólya et al., 2007: 51)

The various spatio-temporal locations can be determined by certain linguistic clues in the text:

- The narrator may state the location independently from his or her actual location (e.g. using specific terms referring to places or dates).
- The narrator may refer to his or her actual location, e.g. by using spatial (*there*, *here*) or temporal (*then*, *now*) deictic expressions; or verb tense (present tense suggesting proximity, while the past tense suggests distance).
- Interjections suggest a small distance between narration and narrative, that is, the experiencing mode.
- Some mental process verbs and some adjectives of modality (e.g. *probably*) are suggestive of metanarrative form.
- Clause types like questions, exclamations and optatives (i.e. wishes and hopes) are indicative of the experiencing or metanarrative modes. The retrospective mode can only consist of statements.

Earlier studies (e.g. Pólya et al. 2005) indicated that narrators speaking in the retrospective form were perceived as mentally and emotionally more coherent, more positively valued socially (thereby having higher self-esteem) than narrators using the experiencing form. Narrators taking the experiencing perspective were perceived as the opposite in these terms. The metanarrative form scored somewhere in between these two. The study conducted by Pólya et al. (2007) involved looking at the way various narrative forms represent a person's ability to regulate emotions (the ability to influence the types of emotions one has and how these are expressed, see Gross 2008). For this, participants were asked to write a series of stories and were then subjected to psychological tests for comparison. Pólya et al. (2007) found that the experiencing form indicated unstable emotion regulation, while the retrospective form indicated coherent regulation of emotions. The combined findings of Pólya et al. (2005 and 2007) suggest that the way readers perceive narrators based on the effects of narration correlates with the affective states experienced by the narrators in question.

As this overview demonstrates, a substantial amount of work has been done in order to understand the link between language use and affective states, both in linguistics and in psychology. The main limitation of the studies in psychology is their limited account of language. Pennebaker and colleagues, for example, have successfully mapped correlations between linguistic features and affective states and have created an automated tool for doing so. However, the dictionary that the LIWC software uses includes a finite number of words and cannot consider co-text. In this book, I use linguistically sound corpus tools to counteract these shortcomings. At the same time, linguistic approaches to affective states, including this one, necessarily suffer from a limited understanding of the psychological processes under discussion. Therefore, in what follows, every attempt is made to acknowledge the complexities involved and to hedge potential conclusions.

4

Linguistic Characteristics of the Smith Journal – Corpus Analysis I

Having so far covered some of the background to this study, this chapter begins the linguistic analysis of Sylvia Plath's Smith Journal. The role of corpus analysis in this book is twofold. To begin with, corpus analysis is used to gain a better understanding of the broad linguistic composition of the Smith Journal and to highlight those features of it that require detailed analysis. In a second stage, corpus analysis is used to compare sections of the data with each other in order to further investigate the potential significance of the key features identified previously. This twofold aim is mirrored in the general structure of the book: Part I and Part II.

The aim here is to establish the key linguistic characteristics of the Smith Journal by comparing it to a relevant norm using corpus linguistic tools and highlight the most salient characteristics for affective states and the self. Using Wmatrix (Rayson 2009), the Smith Journal is compared to the autobiography section of the Speech, Writing and Thought Presentation corpus (Semino and Short 2004) in terms of grammatical and semantic categories. The key grammatical and semantic categories are then considered for their relevance to affective states. In determining whether linguistic features potentially convey aspects of affective states, I refer to Biber (1988) and research in psychology. I begin with a very brief introduction to corpus linguistics, followed by a discussion of the methodology in this study.

4.1 Brief introduction to corpus linguistics

Corpus linguistics is the study of language through the, often automatic, searching and comparing of electronic versions of linguistic data (for an overview, see McEnery and Hardie 2012). A corpus is an often large body of such linguistic data and can be comprised of entire or sample written texts of all kinds, as well as transcribed versions of speech. In automated methods, these large bodied of text are loaded into corpus analysis software that can perform statistical comparisons between two or more corpora, or statistically analyse the composition of one, among others, for example, Wmatrix (Rayson 2009) and WordSmith Tools (Scott 2004).

Corpus analysis can be used to (a) investigate a particular linguistic feature, or (b) look at the characteristics of whole texts or trends in language varieties (Rayson 2008). The former requires a detailed investigation of the one linguistic feature within a corpus, while the latter requires a general comparison between two or more corpora of text and is used to establish characteristics of particular data sets, as in this study. There are two main types of corpus comparisons that can reveal key characteristics of texts (Rayson et al. 2004):

1. A comparison of a sample corpus with a large(r) standard corpus
2. A comparison of two similar sized corpora

The first of these methods refers to a situation where the larger corpus (called *normative* or *reference* corpus) is used as a frame of reference, representing a 'norm' of a certain type of text, or language in general. A (usually) smaller corpus comprised of the data under investigation is compared to this reference corpus in order to determine what features of language are under- or overused in it. The second type of comparison looks at two relatively equal sized corpora to discover features in both that distinguish them from each other – that is, what is over- or underused in each, relative to the other. Representativeness, homogeneity within the corpora, the comparability of the corpora, the independence of the corpora and the reliability of the statistical tests used are necessary preconditions for valid results, though some of these may be more important for one comparison than another (see Leech 1993 and Rayson et al. 2004 for more detail). Rayson (2008) additionally recommends that corpus analyses be data driven, that is, linguistic features to investigate should emerge from a combination of the two types of corpus comparison outlined above, rather than being preselected and actively searched for.

4.2 Corpus methodology

The Smith Journal was written in the United States between 1950 and 1953. It consists of 152 appropriate entries for analysis, amounting to approximately 77,900 words. This excludes Entries 20, 22, 32, 34, 57, 62, 65, 69, 71–7, 91, 100, 101, 110, 116, 119, 120, 122, 123, 135, 136, 140, 165 and 183, which are either works in progress or draft letters. The corpus and this word count include the numbering and dating of the entries, and the entries vary in length from about twenty-five to around 3,000 words. The Journal was not available in electronic format, so the paper copy was digitized using a scanner and text recognition software. The electronic copy was checked for inaccuracies and cleaned in terms of layout. It was then converted to a .txt file and uploaded to Wmatrix (Rayson 2009; http://ucrel.lancs.ac.uk/wmatrix).

As mentioned above, the reference corpus for this comparison is the autobiography section of the Speech Writing and Thought Presentation (SWTP) corpus (Semino and Short 2004). Semino and Short (2004) originally distinguish between *serious* and *popular* autobiography in their corpus, based primarily on the identity and status of the protagonist: 'Books on the lives of politicians, serious writers [...] and artists were considered serious, while the (auto)biographies of TV stars and sportspeople were considered popular' (Semino and Short 2004: 24). However, they acknowledge that the serious/popular distinction is not clear-cut in the case of this genre. As such, the reference corpus in this study (SWTPAuto) combines both serious and popular autobiographies.

SWTPAuto contains approximately 43,518 words (in twenty texts of about 2,000 words each) and consists of only first-person narratives. The texts represent British English from 1976–95. This would suggest a discrepancy in terms of language variety and era between the Smith Journal and the reference corpus, but this discrepancy is likely to be small. There is tentative evidence that British English lags behind American English by a few decades in terms of language development but appears to progress in a similar way (Leech 2004). This could mean that the fact that SWTP represents language use from later years is an advantage as this may actually diminish the difference between the language varieties.

SWTPAuto is also a more specific corpus than reference corpora tend to be, but there is good reason for this. The Smith Journal is not an example of general language use, but of a specific genre (that of personal journals) with some known linguistic characteristics, such as the use of the first-person pronoun. My interest in this study is not in discovering something about the genre, but about the data specifically. In this sense, it is an advantage if fewer of the linguistic features identified as key can simply be attributed to genre. The relatively smaller size of SWTPAuto (43,500 versus 77,900 words of the Smith Journal) is also offset by its comparability and homogeneity with the Smith Journal.

With all these caveats, one might wonder whether a reference corpus of diaries or online blogs might not have been more suitable. Unfortunately, diary data is difficult and ethically problematic to obtain, and it could be argued that the advantages of a corpus of blogs would not outweigh those of an autobiography corpus. Rodriguez et al. point out that

> blogs are increasingly becoming outlets to disclose personal information that is intended for, or at least not restricted from, public consumption. By contrast, personal diaries have remained an arena in which the expressed thoughts and feelings are truly private and inaccessible to others. (Rodriguez et al., 2010: 575)

Blogs, in this sense, would appear to be closer to autobiographies than to journals as they are both intended for an audience. In addition, blogs are a relatively recent phenomenon, making SWTPAuto at least chronologically closer to the Smith Journal.

The statistical test used to determine the significance of results is the Log-likelihood (LL) test. Rayson et al. (2004b) argue that the LL test is to be preferred to the more traditional chi-square test for low-frequency linguistic features. Given that both the data and the reference corpora are quite small in this study, it is reasonable to apply this method. In addition, instead of the more traditional keyword analyses, the analysis here focuses on the relative frequencies of parts-of-speech (POS) tags and semantic category (SEM) tags. Rayson (2008) suggests this as a way of reducing the amount of work a researcher has to do in looking at corpora. The tags represent groups of linguistic features (such as personal pronouns) as opposed to individual occurrences of words. A semantic field can include collocates, synonyms, antonyms and hyponyms of an item (Stubbs 2001). This allows the researcher to identify trends within a text much more quickly.

Wmatrix (Rayson 2009) automatically tags corpora for POS (using CLAWS[1]) and semantic category (using USAS[2]), and the results emerge in frequency tables similar to keyword lists showing the over- and underused POS and USAS categories, making overall trends are easier to identify:

> Collecting together words into their semantic fields allows us to see trends that are invisible at the word level. […] Two further advantages of the comparison at the semantic level are that multiword expressions are counted together and variants within a lemma are usually grouped together. (Rayson, 2008: 542)

Investigating key POS and SEM as opposed to keywords also increases the reliability of the LL statistic (Rayson and Garside 2000).

The accuracy of Wmatrix tagging is at 96–97 per cent for CLAWS (Rayson 2009) and 91 per cent for USAS (Rayson et al. 2004a). But Rayson argues that special care needs to be taken with the semantic tagging in particular: '[t]he sense distinctions marked by USAS are coarse-grained and may not match those required in specific studies, so care must be taken in interpreting the results' (Rayson 2008: 529).

There are various critical LL values (cut-off points) that can be used as measures of statistical significance: An LL value of 3.84 provides 95 per cent certainty that the results are not due to chance ($p < 0.05$); an LL value of 6.63 increases this certainty to 99 per cent ($p < 0.01$); when LL = 10.83 the certainty is 99.9 per cent ($p < 0.001$); and a critical value of LL = 15.13 provides 99.99 per cent certainty that the results are not due to chance ($p < 0.0001$) (Rayson 2009). However, especially for smaller sized corpora, it is important to also take into consideration the overall frequencies of the categories. There is little agreement among scholars as to what an appropriate cut-off point is, both for frequencies and for LL values. However, Rayson et al. (2004a) argue that the LL statistical test may yield reliable results for absolute frequencies of as little as 1, but only at a cut-off point (a critical value) of 15.13. For lower LL cut-off points, the frequency cut-off points need to be adjusted accordingly. After conducting reliability analyses for both the LL and the chi-square test, Rayson et al. (2004a) recommend the following frequencies cut-off points for the different LL values:

- At LL = 3.84 the cut-off frequency should be 13; ($p < 0.05$)
- At LL = 6.63 the cut-off frequency should be 11; ($p < 0.01$)
- At LL = 10.83 the cut-off frequency should be 8; ($p < 0.001$)
- And at LL = 15.13 the cut-off frequency should be 1; ($p < 0.0001$)

My analysis here follows these guidelines. In Part I, LL values of 6.63 are used as a cut-off point for significance combined with a frequency cut-off point of 11. In the corpus analysis of Part II of the book, the LL critical value is lowered to 3.84 and the minimum frequency adjusted accordingly to 13. As the corpus analyses in Part II are intra-textual (between sections of one text) (Adolphs 2006) even at this lower level, there may be differences that are important to consider.

Once the software calculates the LL values and produces a table of results, those that lie above the critical values (as outlined above) are investigated using concordancing. This second stage is particularly important in order to check the results provided by the software.

4.2.1 Interpreting corpus results – Biber (1988)

One drawback of a data-driven corpus exploration is the potentially high number of statistically significant differences that can sometimes be established between the data under investigation and any reference texts. Although corpus methods facilitate the analysis of large amounts of data, the output of any software still requires interpretation. Studies establishing norms for particular discourses, text types or genres can be useful in wading through the 'noise'. One such study is Biber's (1988) multidimensional (MD) approach to the linguistic composition of text types.

The MD approach searches for consistent patterns of co-occurrence between linguistic features using factor analysis, which derives smaller groups of variables (*factors*) from a much larger number of original variables. Individual linguistic features can be grouped into one factor for two reasons: first, if they systematically co-occur with high frequency (there is a high correlation between them); secondly, if they systematically do *not* co-occur with others in the group (i.e. are highly negatively correlated). Such factors can then be taken to represent linguistic dimensions. For example, Biber's (1988) Factor 2 consists of the positive correlation of past-tense verbs, third-person pronouns, perfect aspect verbs, public verbs (*assert, declare, mention*), synthetic negation (no *answer is good enough*) and present participial clauses and negatively correlates with present-tense verbs, attributive adjectives, past participial WHIZ deletions, also called past participial (passive) post-nominal clauses, and word length. This factor brings to light the 'Narrative versus Non-narrative Concerns' linguistic dimension (Biber 1988: 109).

Biber (1988) identifies the following six linguistic dimensions (to be understood as clines rather than discrete parameters) that are reliable in categorizing texts:

- Dimension 1: Informational versus Involved Production – this marks the informational content and density of texts, in contrast with affective, interactional, generalized content. The objectives of the speaker and the circumstances of production (i.e. time/editing constraints) influence this dimension.
- Dimension 2: Narrative versus Non-narrative Concerns – this dimension mainly distinguishes narrative discourse (focused on past events and activities) from other types (focused on description etc. and marked by immediate time).
- Dimension 3: Explicit versus Situation-Dependent Reference – this distinguishes between texts with high endophoric (explicit, context-independent) reference and high exophoric (non-specific, external situation-dependent) reference.

- Dimension 4: Overt Expression of Persuasion – marks whether a writer's/speaker's point of view shows subjective evaluation in order to persuade.
- Dimension 5: Abstract versus Non-Abstract Information – marks discourse that is technical and abstract.
- Dimension 6: Online Informational Elaboration – marks texts that are informational but are produced under real-time conditions, for example, unscripted speech.

Biber (1988) investigates how science fiction, adventure fiction, romantic fiction, humour, personal letters, professional letters, face-to-face conversations, telephone conversations, interviews, broadcasts, spontaneous speeches and prepared speeches score on each of these dimensions. He also looks at various text types such as biographies. Table 4.1 below summarizes the genres of general fiction, face-to-face conversation, personal letters and biographies, which are perhaps closest to the Smith Journal, according to their score on Biber's dimensions. H indicates a high score, M medium and L low; M+ indicates a 'high' medium, while M– indicates a 'low' medium score. This is a simplified version of Biber's results; for full details see Biber (1988, Chapter 7).

High scores on each of the dimensions mean the following in terms of linguistic characteristics (Biber 1988):

- Dimension 1: frequent use of mental process verbs, *that*-deletions, present tense, contractions, together with interactive features such as second-person pronouns, coupled with infrequent nouns, prepositions, long words, more varied vocabulary and attributive adjectives.
- Dimension 2: frequent use of past tense, public verbs and third-person pronouns.

Table 4.1 Genres and their relative scores on Biber's (1988) dimensions

Dimension	**1**	**2**	**3**	**4**	**5**	**6**
General fiction	M	H	M–	M+	L	L
Conversation	H+	L	M–	M	L	M
Personal letters	H	M	M–	M+	L	L
Biographies	L	M	M–	M	M	M–

- Dimension 3: frequent 'WH relative clauses, pied-piping constructions, phrasal coordination, and nominalizations, together with infrequent occurrences of place and time adverbials and other adverbs' (Biber 1988: 142).
- Dimension 4: frequent use of prediction, necessity and possibility modals, conditional clauses, suasive verbs, infinitives and split auxiliaries.
- Dimension 5: frequent use of conjuncts, passive constructions, past participle clauses and WHIZ deletions.
- Dimension 6: frequent use of *that* complements to verbs and adjectives, *that*-relatives in object positions (all for informational elaboration under real-time conditions, but it is also used to express opinions/attitudes) and demonstratives. This is coupled with the infrequent use of final prepositions, existential *there* and WH relatives in object positions.

Of course, Biber (1988) notes that genres are not necessarily internally consistent and can be made up of various text types. Table 4.1 above is simply representative of the general characteristics of the genres closest to Sylvia Plath's journals on each dimension and can be a useful guide in making sense of the results of the following corpus comparison.

4.3 Key features of the Smith Journal

In this section, I discuss the results of the comparison between the Smith Journal and the autobiography section of the SWTP corpus (SWTPAuto). The aims are to identify the key linguistic characteristics of the Smith Journal and to ascertain which of these need further (also qualitative) investigation because of their role in conveying aspects of Plath's affective states. While the analysis aims to be comprehensive, not all key features are discussed in equal detail. Instead, the focus is on the most relevant features for these aims as determined with reference to studies introduced in Chapter 3.

The analysis begins with a description of the results of a comparison of POS, before considering semantic differences between the Smith Journal and SWTPAuto. The final section provides some general conclusions and implications for Part II of the book, which will deal with selected linguistic features in more detail. The POS and semantic field (SEM) comparisons are carried out using the online application Wmatrix (Rayson 2009). The LL value of 6.63 is used as the cut-off point for significance ($p < 0.01$). Additionally, key linguistic features with a frequency of <11 in either corpus are excluded. This is in line with the recommendations of Rayson et al. (2004). Where concordances are presented, they are representative samples of complete concordances unless otherwise indicated. The total number of concordance lines from which the sample is taken is indicated in the title of the concordance. For example, in *VBM/331* the letters stand for the POS tag (see Section 4.3.1 below), and the number stands for the total number of concordance lines. While only sample concordances are presented, the statements and interpretations are based on an examination of all concordance lines unless stated otherwise.

4.3.1 Differences in parts-of-speech

POS analyses reveal something about the grammatical composition of a text. When two texts are compared in Wmatrix, a results table is produced, which lists the POS categories and is sorted by LL values, allowing the user to view

Table 4.2 Smith Journal versus SWTPAuto CLAWS

POS tag*	Freq. 1	% 1	Freq. 2	% 2	LL	Description	Example items
JJ	6997	9.42	2347	5.73	468.78	general adjective	*happy, strange, attractive, ignorant*
VVZ	705	0.95	87	0.21	250.93	s form of lexical verb	*hates, goes, hurts, likes, picks, cuts*
VV0	1820	2.45	481	1.17	234.49	base form of lexical verb	*hate, know, remember, dream*
VBZ	961	1.29	194	0.47	199.93	is	*is*
PPY	1080	1.45	243	0.59	189.52	second-person personal pronoun	*you*
CC	3335	4.49	1287	3.14	124.37	coordinating conjunction	*and, or*
VBM	331	0.45	49	0.12	100.01	am	*am*
VVG	1834	2.47	687	1.68	78.97	-ing participle of lexical verb	*speaking, pushing, looking, loving*
RRQ	349	0.47	99	0.24	38.16	wh- general adverb	*why, how, when, where*

Table 4.2 (Continued)

POS tag*	Freq. 1	% 1	Freq. 2	% 2	LL	Description	Example items
VBR	332	0.45	94	0.23	36.47	are	*are*
RT	634	0.85	222	0.54	36.29	quasi-nominal adverb of time	*then, now, tonight, someday, again*
VD0	246	0.33	61	0.15	36.16	do, base form (finite)	*do*
VH0	276	0.37	75	0.18	33.42	have, base form (finite)	*have*
RL	411	0.55	155	0.38	17.15	locative adverb	*home, here, there, upstairs, below*
PPIS1	2410	3.24	1149	2.8	16.79	first-person sing. subjective personal pronoun	*I*
IO	1883	2.53	880	2.15	16.78	of (as preposition)	*of*
PPX1	188	0.25	58	0.14	16.43	singular reflexive personal pronoun	*myself, yourself, herself*
DB	355	0.48	133	0.32	15.28	pre-determiner capable of pronominal function	*all, half*
VHZ	120	0.16	33	0.08	14.14	has	*has*
RR	2649	3.57	1290	3.15	13.64	general adverb	*never, suddenly, still, loudly, maybe*
VBI	450	0.61	187	0.46	10.98	be, infinitive	*be*
NN2	2893	3.89	1453	3.55	8.56	plural common noun	*parents, bones, opinions, boys*
NN1	9978	13.43	5265	12.85	6.78	singular common noun	*stick, room, hair, laughter, kiss*

*The complete CLAWS7 tagset is available at http://ucrel.lancs.ac.uk/claws7tags.html

the grammatical categories most to least characteristic of the data under investigation (Rayson and Garside 2000). Table 4.2 shows the results of the POS comparison between the Smith Journal and SWTPAuto. The Freq. 1 column shows the absolute frequency of an item in the text under examination (in this case, the Smith Journal), and % 1 shows the relative frequency. Freq. 2 shows the absolute frequency in the reference corpus, and % 2 shows the relative frequency. The LL column shows the LL value for an item, while the fifth column provides a descriptor for the POS tag. The final column includes a few linguistic examples from the data.

The most significantly overused item here is the general adjective. Concordance 1 below provides some examples of the types of adjectives used.

The keyness of 'general adjectives' seems to be related to descriptions of people and events in the Smith Journal. This is not entirely surprising, given that adjectives are generally 'descriptive, typically characterizing the referent of a nominal expression (e.g. **blue** and **white** flag, **unhappy** childhood)' (Biber et al. 1999: 506; emphasis in the original). Concordance 1 includes descriptions of people's accents (line 1–2), their physical features (line 3–7), their personality (line 18–20). There are also descriptions of inanimate things in lines 12–13 and an evaluation of events (line 17). In fact, lines 18–21, which show

:ion , speaking with his	thick	German accent . He straight
speaking with his thick	German	accent . He straightened up
aightened up , his tan ,	intelligent	face crinkling up with laug
g up with laughter . His	chunky	, muscular body was bronzed
laughter . His chunky ,	muscular	body was bronzed , and his
unky , muscular body was	bronzed	, and his blonde hair tucke
dy was bronzed , and his	blonde	hair tucked up under a whit
e hair tucked up under a	white	handkerchief around his hea
like Frank Sinatra ? So	sendimental	, so romantic , so moonligh
ra ? So sendimental , so	romantic	, so moonlight night , Ja ?
ight night , Ja ? 3. - A	sudden	slant of bluish light acros
? 3. - A sudden slant of	bluish	light across the floor of a
nt across the floor of a	vacant	room . And I knew it was no
the moon . What is more	wonderful	than to be a virgin , clean
ul than to be a virgin ,	clean	and sound and young , on su
in , clean and sound and	young	, on such a night ? (being
aped.) 4. - Tonight was	awful	. It was the combination of
the idea of being with a	stimulating	, brilliant , magnificent m
ing with a stimulating ,	brilliant	, magnificent male for thre
timulating , brilliant ,	magnificent	male for three days of conv
t male for three days of	conventional	and unconventional companio

Concordance 1 JJ/6997.

different sections of the same sentence in the data, exemplify a tendency of Plath to describe people (but also events and objects) in perhaps more than necessary detail. In these lines, she uses three different adjectives for someone denoted by the rather distant *male* and uses both *conventional* and *unconventional* to describe the potential companionship.

These concordance lines also include words and expressions that belong to other key POS categories. Items belonging to the categories of 'general adverbs' (*more*, line 14), 'quasi-nominal adverbs of time' (*tonight*, line 17), 'locative adverbs' (*under*, line 8; *across*, line 12) and *is* are evident, even in such a small concordance. These categories therefore seem to be related to the large amount of description (as defined in Section 2.1.1) in the Journal. In addition, 'common nouns' can also be linked to description, as they generally denote the things that are being described. In Concordance 1 there are common nouns in almost every line; examples include *accent*, *face*, *body*, *hair*, *handkerchief*, *room*.

The second most significant item in Table 4.2 is the '*s*-form of lexical verbs' (VVZ). Concordance 2 shows examples of the uses of this POS category.

It seems that the 's-form of lexical verbs' is used to narrate the actions of third parties and events in the surroundings. These verbs result from discussions of events but, more specifically, from more detailed description of various parts of events. For example, *dominates* and *penetrates* in Concordance 2 metaphorically ascribe agency to feelings and sensations triggered by events such as a drive with friends during Thanksgiving holidays.

and mankind . Yet , while America	dies	like the great Roman Empire die
icking clock , and the snow which	comes	too suddenly upon the summer . :
We all are on the brink , and it	takes	a lot of nerve , a lot of energ
is my date this weekend : someone	believes	I am a human being , not a name
staying here unless a blind date	turns up	. " Eventually my ignominy paid
nd I 'll be fine , no matter what	happens	. If character is fate , I sure
omentary loneliness , anyway . It	comes from	a vague core of the self - - li
y give to that sick feeling which	dominates	me now . I am alone in my room
n either side of me animal warmth	penetrates	regardless of sensibilities and
down in aimless little swoops and	spins	. All I need is to hear sleighb
etive . Girls bicycle by in brief	spurts	of color and motion , and the b
g , frozen ashes , of motion that	enhances	space behind . I can almost fan
ge fraternity parties where a boy	buries	his face in your neck or tries
merging my-self until his purpose	becomes	my purpose , his life , my life
disposed of only when desperation	sets in	. Now for jealousy . I can loop
nd admire . That 's where writing	comes in	. It is as necessary for the su
ty risky . Occupation ? teacher ,	comes	closest now - liesurely enough
ves , like dresses , to see which	fits	best and is most becoming ? The
t and is most becoming ? The fact	remains	, I have at best three years in

Concordance 2 VVZ/705.

1	love people . Everybody . I	love	them I think , as a stam
	. Everybody . I love them I	think	, as a stamp collector lc
	ng man , a whore , and then	come back	to write about my thought
	e present , and already , I	feel	the weight of centuries
5	. I am the present , but I	know	I , too , will pass . The
	oment , the burning flash ,	come	and are gone , continuou
	ething happens to you , you	go	to write it down , and e
	down , and either you over	dramatize	it or underplay it , exa
	er you over dramatize it or	underplay	it , exaggerate the wron
10	matize it or underplay it ,	exaggerate	the wrong parts or ignor
	aggerate the wrong parts or	ignore	the important ones . At
	s . At any rate , you never	write	it quite the way you want
	write it quite the way you	want	to . I 've just got to p

Concordance 3 VV0/1820.

The third item in Table 4.2 is the 'base form of lexical verbs'. In the Smith Journal, these types of verbs occur in conjunction with first- and second-person pronouns, but also with imperatives (see Concordance 3). This is not surprising, given that Plath writes not only about external events and others but also about her own actions (lines 7–10) and thoughts and emotions (lines 1–2, 4–5, 13).

About a third of these lexical verbs denote mental process types (Halliday and Matthiessen 2004). This can potentially be seen as a feature of journals that deal with the inner world of their writer. The co-occurrence of the base forms with the second-person pronouns as well as the imperatives are both a result of direct speech reporting as well as Plath's use of the second-person pronoun to refer to herself. In fact, the second-person pronoun is also statistically significantly overused in the Smith Journal, and the keyness of *are* can also be linked to this. Concordance 4 shows that the vast majority of the time, these are instances of the singular second-person pronoun (both in subject and object position).

Sometimes, Plath reproduces conversations or dialogues in her journals, and second-person pronouns occur there (e.g. lines 4, 6 and 10 in Concordance 4).

1	day . And Marcia , in tears , and	you	, somber , agreed to leave . Defin
	she pointed to a bag of peanuts .	You	gave her one . She ate it gravely
	aid hope-fully , reaching out for	you	to lift her down . " No , " you sa
	r you to lift her down . " No , "	you	said , sitting her down . " Daddy
5	dy " became a cry , then a wail .	You	lifted up the flailing bundle , th
	ver the screaming . " Poor baby ,	you	have n't had a nap today , no wond
	e n't had a nap today , no wonder	you	're tired . Does your arm hurt ? W
	mentarily , then began again . So	you	put her in the crib , sponge her h
	She cries fretfully and tiredly .	You	start to sing in your tuneless mon
10	otone , " Bye-bye baby , remember	you	're my baby . . . " Eyes open wide
	oop and slowly lift , and droop .	You	pull down the blinds . You shut th
	roop . You pull down the blinds .	You	shut the door after you , proud th
	blinds . You shut the door after	you	, proud that you sang her to sleep
	t the door after you , proud that	you	sang her to sleep , fond of her ba
15	, firm little body . That starts	you	feeling a little sorry . You wo n'
	arts you feeling a little sorry .	You	wo n't ever see her again . She wo
	again . She wo n't even remember	you	. Pinny has been put to bed , Mrs.
	been put to bed . Mrs. Mayo tells	you	in the kitchen . Two down , one to

Concordance 4 PPY/1080.

However, there are also occasions when the second-person pronoun is used to refer to Plath herself (lines 1, 2, 8 and 11–16), as noted above. In fact, there are entire entries in the journals that are written using the second-person pronoun to refer to the author herself. Using *you* to refer to oneself in this way is unusual in journals and is discussed in more detail in subsequent chapters.

In addition to the second-person pronoun, first-person singular pronouns and the first-person form of the verb *to be* are also key in the Smith Journal. VBM (am/'m) is the seventh most overused item in the Smith Journal and is strongly connected to the overuse of the first-person singular pronoun (I). Examples of the uses of *I am/I'm* can be found in Concordance 5.

Current copular verbs such as *to be* 'identify attributes that are in a continuing state of existence' (Biber et al. 1999: 436). The first line of Concordance 5 is an example of a metaphorical reference to an affective state (similar to line 9: *I'm*

ng embrace . 14. - This morning I	am	at low ebb . I did not sleep wel
liked me three years ago . Now I	'm	a wiseguy . " We sat together fo
ld you call him pipsqueak ? " " I	'm	not tan , " he continued . " It
an make a man someday . " Yes , I	'm	thinking , and so far it 's all
ords on paper ? How can he know I	am	justifying my life , my keen emo
rated hard . Man , I love you . I	'm	reaching out to you . I love you
e to learn someday 31 . Tonight I	am	ugly . I have lost all faith in
, here , and soon . Until then I	'm	lost . I think I am mad at times
Until then I 'm lost . I think I	am	mad at times . Tonight Bill and
, the world will not end , and I	am	somehow irrationally sure he wo
te " at this rate , cutie . (" I	'm	just a sentimentalist at heart ,
be a genius . let 's face it , I	am	in danger of wanting my personal
ght , oh god , (I think) that I	am	mortal , unthinking , unworthy a
ss , and though love be a day , I	am	afraid it will be only that ; an
at ; and though love be a day , I	am	afraid also that it will be more
o do anything more with because I	am	buying clothes because I love th
had whittled out for my life . I	am	lucky : I am at Smith because I

Concordance 5 VBM/331.

lost), while line 16 is an example of a literal reference to an emotion (fear). In this sense, the concordance lines for VBM ('m/am), as well as some instances of PPY (you) combined with *are*, directly express something about affective states and require more detailed investigation. The fact that both first-person references and second-person references that sometimes relate to the self are overused in the journals suggests a strong self-focus. Additionally, the singular reflexive pronouns can also be linked to this. Two-thirds of the 188 occurrences in this category are instances of *myself*, and some instances of *yourself* also refer to Plath.

The keyness of the '-ing form of the lexical verb' (VVG) can be explained by the presence of narration and description similar to the VVZ (is) and VV0 (base form of lexical verb) categories discussed above. Concordance 6 below is a small sample of the use of this feature.

From these concordance lines it seems that -ing forms are used in two main ways: to describe activities literally and to describe and inanimate objects figuratively. For example, in lines 2–4 and 9–16 the actions of people, and in line 5–7 the actions of natural elements, are described non-metaphorically. In line 8, on the other hand, an abstract construct – *the weight of centuries* – is metaphorically constructed as an agent (*smothering*). Using this verb aspect (-ing) makes such descriptions more vivid and immediate, which may be typical of journal writing.

tan , intelligent face	crinkling	up with laughter . His c
Mary . Jack and I were	pushing	out of the theater in a
of people , and she was	edging	the other way in a dark
ut beautiful . Ive been	looking	all over for you , I sai
steamy and wet . It is	raining	. I am tempted to write
er is always shifting ,	flowing	, melting . This second
ys shifting , flowing ,	melting	. This second is life .
the weight of centuries	smothering	me . Some girl a hundrec
room when I came home ,	fussing	with clothes , and she c
appened . She just kept	scolding	and chattering on and or
just kept scolding and	chattering	on and on . So I could r
e o'clock , people were	leaving	, and I was waiting besi
ere leaving , and I was	waiting	beside the cars for any
enough , there he was ,	coming	up the road in his old h
assurance . Now he was	working	on a sketch of one of th
ary Coffee . I felt her	looking at	me rather strangely . Sc

Concordance 6 VVG/1834.

Some examples of the finite forms of *do* and *have* are also involved in similar descriptions. It is worth noting however, that 60 per cent of *do*s are actually *do not*s, as the verb appears in its negated form (see Concordance 7).

Interestingly, the significance of the base form of *do* is also partly due to the presence of a large number of questions in the journals (see Concordance 7). Around 26 per cent of the concordance lines are a result of questions, which are associated with involved interactive discourse (Biber 1988). Sometimes, these questions in the data are part of the reproduced dialogues, but often they are rhetorical questions directed at Plath herself. The *have* (VH0) category is also mainly used for descriptive purposes, but also in expressions of obligation (have to) and in present perfect constructions.

in the strawberry field ,	Do	you like the Renaissance pa
nelangelo once . And what	do you think	of Picasso These painters w
and a little board going	do	for a leg ? We worked side
years ago once lived as I	do	. And she is dead . I am th
nuous , quicksand . And I	do	n't want to die . 9 . Some
My cheeks burned . " Why	do	they have to tease me ? " I
ohn 's head . " Why , how	do	you do it ? With the side o
eft for awhile . But what	do	I know of sorrow ? No one I
s , and a blas pout . How	do	I know ? I do n't ; I can o
" Still looking down : "	Do	you think you could dance ,
oout letters ... " " Oh ,	do	n't bother , if you 've got
, and think coolly : why	do	you react the way you are r
e my path after college ?	Do	I want to crawl into the gi
How will it work out ? I	do	n't know . In one year , tw
nd dislike ; but please ,	do	n't ask me who I am . " A p
joys : as I was saying :	do	you realize the illicit sen
. No soap ; no sir . What	do	I do ? Secretly try on dres

Concordance 7 VD0/246.

Another key linguistic feature of the Smith Journal is the 'pre-determiner' (DB). Determiners provide additional information by specifying the reference of nouns or noun phrases (Biber et al. 1999). Interestingly, approximately 97 per cent of the 'pre-determiner' (DB) category are instances of *all* – an expression of absoluteness (see Concordance 8).

A further item of interest is RRQ (wh- adverbs). As can be seen from Concordance 9, many of these adverbs are used to begin questions (lines 1–2, 6–7, 8 etc.), but they are also a way of explaining reasons for events and the manner in which they take place (e.g. lines 3, 5, 10–14 etc.).

A similar linking function is exhibited by the 'Coordinating conjunctions': 95 per cent of tokens consist of *and*. Coordinating conjunctions are also said to be characteristic of interactive or unplanned discourse (Biber 1988), when (usually) the speaker elaborates on statements and trains of thought.

. I had worked hard on beans	all afternoon	and picked over three bushels
tairs . " You live up there ?	All	these stairs ? " He kept walk
e nice , but they knew . They	all	must know . " There 's cutie
ridiculous pink . The books ,	all	that you would fill your rair
of nervous emotion and tears	all the time	. 25. - B. will be home , all
ime . 25. - B. will be home ,	all	mine , and I 'll be secure fc
ium on cars , superimposed on	all	we passed . There I was , tal
y by the wayside . So that is	all	for now . Perhaps someday som
night I am ugly . I have lost	all	faith in my ability to attrac
P.K. or Liota . God damn them	all	. I will bury my Perry , " Jc
at the boy beside me and feel	all	the hurting beauty go flat be
ttle , love me a little ? For	all	my despair , for all my ideal
le ? For all my despair , for	all	my ideals , for all that I lc
air , for all my ideals , for	all	that I love life . But it is

Concordance 8 DB/355.

, electric , shivering . " Why ,	why	, " he made sympathetic , depre
the cars . Bernie yelled out , "	Why	are you crying ? " I was n't cr
king up into a smile . So that 's	how	it was . . . so simple , and nc
. I had to write it , to describe	how	it was , before I went under .
s thinking . 12 . There are times	when	a feeling of expectancy comes t
I wish I hated you , " I said . "	Why	did you come ? " " Why ? I want
I said . " Why did you come ? " "	Why	? I wanted your company . Alby
girl meant in " Celia Amberley "	when	she said : " If he will kiss me
me spot . Lord , what will I be ?	Where	will the careless conglomeratic
my friends who had dates asked me	where	I was going . I decided to laug
all that the present is made of ,	why	then you may as well dispose of
ll blur and diminish , no doubt ,	when	tomorrow I plunge again into c
oking up at my window , wondering	how	it would feel to be on the othe
t describe it now . I do n't know	how	it will be . But I do know that
t to the bottom of his question :	Why	is he so afraid of my being sti
f my being strong and assertive ?	Why	has he found it necessary to be
ack . Bored , cross , all wrong .	Why	do I not wear heels . . . becau
e nonexistent , and wo n't matter	when	I rot underground . All want to
t , self-reviling , an imposter .	How	to justify myself , my bold , k
intellect and will . There is no	where	to go not home , where I would
l over me , drowning , drowning .	How	can I ever find that permanence
an artificial imposed solution ?	How	can I justify , how can I ratio
ed solution ? How can I justify ,	how	can I rationalize the rest of r
on or series of accomplishments .	Why	did Virginia Woolf commit suic

Concordance 9 RRQ/349.

The final linguistic feature that I would briefly like to mention is the 'general adverbs' (RR) category. It consists of items like *so, still, hardly, maybe, not enough, never,* which serve as a way of qualifying or modifying the verbs and adjectives that describe events (Biber et al. 1999). This can once again be linked to description. Such features introduce more subjectivity into a text as the modal expressions, at least, represent subjective judgements on the part of Plath. This qualifying of narration is also observable in some of the uses of the infinitive *be* that co-occur with modal verbs.

4.3.2 The semantic make-up of the Smith Journal

While a POS comparison can reveal something about the grammatical and linguistic composition of a text, a semantic comparison can reveal something about the content of a text (Hunston 2002). Wmatrix's USAS tagger automatically classifies the words in a text based on 'senses that are related by virtue of their being connected at some level of generality with the same mental concept' (Archer et al. 2002). Similar to the POS comparison, the LL value of 6.63 will be used as the cut-off point for significance ($p < 0.01$), and linguistic features with a frequency of < 11 in either corpus will be excluded. Table 4.3 below lists the

Table 4.3 Smith Journal versus SWTPAuto USAS

USAS tag*	Freq. 1	% 1	Freq. 2	% 2	LL	Description
O4.3	738	0.99	87	0.21	272.4	colour and colour patterns
B1	1436	1.93	337	0.82	234.1	anatomy and physiology
S3.2	297	0.4	52	0.13	74.7	relationship: Intimacy and sex
W4	163	0.22	14	0.03	74.3	weather
E2+	307	0.41	59	0.14	68.5	like
O4.2+	370	0.5	81	0.2	68.0	judgment of appearance: beautiful
W2	163	0.22	19	0.05	60.7	light
T1.1.3	518	0.7	146	0.36	57.5	time: future
S2.1	257	0.35	51	0.12	54.8	people: female
O4.5	161	0.22	22	0.05	52.5	texture
L3	194	0.26	33	0.08	50.5	plants
O4.4	265	0.36	57	0.14	50.1	shape
W1	183	0.25	32	0.08	46.1	the universe
O2	566	0.76	180	0.44	45.2	objects generally
T1.1.2	391	0.53	111	0.27	42.7	time: present; simultaneous
A7	106	0.14	13	0.03	37.9	probability
L1+	177	0.24	37	0.09	35.0	alive
O4.1	238	0.32	61	0.15	32.7	general appearance, physical properties
O1.1	229	0.31	58	0.14	32.3	substances and materials: solid
E4.1+	280	0.38	79	0.19	31.0	happy
X2	89	0.12	12	0.03	29.37	mental actions and processes
W3	244	0.33	67	0.16	28.84	geographical terms
N3.2+	138	0.19	28	0.07	28.50	size: big
Z4	527	0.71	190	0.46	26.84	discourse bin
K2	111	0.15	22	0.05	23.71	music and related activities

Table 4.3 (Continued)

USAS Tag*	Freq. 1	% 1	Freq. 2	% 2	LL	Description
B5	296	0.4	95	0.23	22.95	clothes and personal belongings
N3.2–	162	0.22	41	0.1	22.86	size: small
X2.1	675	0.91	269	0.66	21.21	thought, belief
S2	315	0.42	106	0.26	20.87	people
O1.2	159	0.21	42	0.1	20.51	substances and materials: liquids
X3.1	71	0.1	11	0.03	20.48	sensory: taste
E4.2+	87	0.12	17	0.04	18.96	content
X7+	451	0.61	173	0.42	17.33	wanted
Q3	242	0.33	80	0.2	17.04	language, speech and grammar
S1.2.3+	68	0.09	12	0.03	16.93	selfish
P1	186	0.25	57	0.14	16.57	education in general
X9.1+	117	0.16	30	0.07	16.07	able/intelligent
W2–	69	0.09	13	0.03	15.80	darkness
E3+	125	0.17	34	0.08	15.10	calm
S1.2.5+	67	0.09	13	0.03	14.74	tough/strong
O4.6–	95	0.13	23	0.06	14.62	temperature: cold
X2.3+	78	0.1	17	0.04	14.43	learning
O4.2–	141	0.19	43	0.1	12.73	judgment of appearance: ugly
A1.7–	85	0.11	21	0.05	12.58	no constraint
A5.1+ + +	83	0.11	21	0.05	11.72	evaluation: good
B4	110	0.15	32	0.08	11.29	cleaning and personal care
X5.2–	60	0.08	13	0.03	11.20	uninterested/bored/ unenergetic
N6+ + +	95	0.13	28	0.07	9.42	frequent
E6+	50	0.07	11	0.03	9.11	confident
T1.3+	65	0.09	17	0.04	8.57	time period: long
S5–	102	0.14	32	0.08	8.48	not part of a group

Table 4.3 (Continued)

USAS Tag*	Freq. 1	% 1	Freq. 2	% 2	LL	Description
A6.2–	97	0.13	30	0.07	8.41	comparing: unusual
X3.3	51	0.07	12	0.03	8.28	sensory: touch
N5.1+	502	0.68	222	0.54	7.71	entire; maximum
X1	46	0.06	11	0.03	7.25	psychological actions, states, processes
O4.6+	185	0.25	71	0.17	7.09	temperature: hot/on fire
N3.7+	123	0.17	43	0.1	7.08	long, tall and wide
F1	395	0.53	172	0.42	6.89	food
H4	194	0.26	76	0.19	6.69	residence

*The complete UCREL Semantic Analysis System (USAS) tagset is available at http://ucrel.lancs.ac.uk/usas/

substantial number of key semantic fields in the Smith Journal when compared to the autobiography section of the SWTP corpus.

The first column shows the USAS tag of the category in the last column. The second and third columns show the absolute and relative frequencies of the category in the data, while the fourth and fifth columns show the absolute and relative frequencies in the references corpus. The sixth column lists the LL values.

Table 4.3 lists fifty-nine semantic categories as key. Since a semantic analysis primarily reveals something about the content of a text, it can be assumed that the majority of these categories are a result of the topics discussed in the Smith Journal. A number of these semantic domains will also include expressions that occur in the context of description in the Smith Journal (see discussion below). For example, what falls under 'general adjectives' in the CLAWS results would here be classed as 'colour and colour patterns', 'general appearance', 'long, tall and wide' etc.

In fact, linguistic expressions belonging to different semantic fields occur in such close proximity that the same lines of text reappear in various concordances. Example 4 below is a representative section of the data including the USAS tags assigned to each lexical item and multiword expression. These lines reoccur in concordance lists as they include descriptive items that fall into a number of semantic categories.

Example 4

There_Z5 seemed_A8 to_Z5 be_A3+ no_Z6 wind_W4, but_Z5 the_Z5 leaves_L3 of_Z5 the_Z5 trees_L3 stirred_A1.1.1, **restless**_X5.2-, and_Z5 the_Z5 water_O1.2 fell_M1 from_Z5 them_Z8 in_Z5 great_A5.1+ drops_O1.2/N5 on_Z5 the_Z5 pavement_M3/H3, with_Z5 a_Z5

> sound_like_A6.1+ that_Z8 of_Z5 people_S2 walking_M1 down_Z5 the_Z5 street_M3/H3. There_Z5 was_A3+ the_Z5 peculiar_A6.2- smell_X3.5 of_Z5 mould_O2, dead_L1- leaves_L3, decay_O4.2-/A2.1, in_Z5 the_Z5 air_O1.3. The_Z5 two_N1 lights_W2 over_Z5 the_Z5 front_M6 steps_M1 were_Z5 haloed_S9 with_Z5 a_Z5 hazy_W4 nimbus_W4 of_Z5 mist_W4, and_Z5 strange_A6.2- insects_L2 fluttered_M1 up_against_Z5 the_Z5 screen_Y2, fragile_S1.2.5-/O4.1, wing-thin_Z99 and_Z5 blinded_X3.4-, dazed_E5-, numbed_B1 by_Z5 the_Z5 brilliance_A5.1+++. Lightning_W2/W4, heat_O4.6+ lightning_W2/W4 **flicked**_A1.1.1 off_and_on_N6, as_if_Z5 some_N5 stage_T1.2 hand_B1 were_Z5 toying_X2.1 with_Z5 the_Z5 light_W2 switch_O3. Two_N1 crickets_L2, deep_N3.7+ in_Z5 the_Z5 cracks_A1.1.2 in_Z5 the_Z5 granite_O1.1 steps_M1, **sang**_K2 a_Z5 **sweet**_X3.1, **haunting**-thin_Z99 trill_M2. And_Z5 because_Z5/A2.2 it_Z8 was_A3+ my_Z8 home_H4/H1c, I_Z8 loved_E2+ them_Z8. The_Z5 air_O1.3 flowed_M4 about_Z5 me_Z8 like_Z5 thick_N3.7+ molasses_O1.2, and_Z5 the_Z5 shadows_O4.3 from_Z5 the_Z5 moon_W1 and_Z5 street_M3/H3 lamp_O2/W2 **split**_A6.1- like_Z5 schizophrenic_B2-/X1 blue_O4.3 phantoms_S9, grotesque_A6.2- and_Z5 faintly_A11.2- repetitious_N6+. (Entry 15, USAS-tagged, my emphases)

This example includes items from the categories of 'colour and colour patterns' (e.g. *blue, shadows*), 'general objects' (e.g. *lamp, mould*), 'plants' (e.g. *leaves)*, 'sensory: smell' (e.g. *smell*), 'light' (e.g. *lights*), 'temperature: hot/on fire' (e.g. *heat*), 'weather' (e.g. *mist, nimbus*), 'the universe' (e.g. *moon*), 'substances and materials: solid' (e.g. *granite*), 'residence' (e.g. *home*) among others.

Of course this example already shows that description in Plath's writing is not simple. Similar to what was noted in the POS results, particularly towards the middle of Example 4, adjectives are compounded to create a more comprehensive description. In addition, there are a number of figuratively used expressions: interesting similes are underlined with dotted lines, and some obviously metaphorical expressions are in bold for exemplification. Another interesting element of this example is that, in the second line, the feelings of the narrator (Plath) are described in relation to a scene as well. This type of description occurs repeatedly in the Smith Journal (further examples will be considered in Section 4.3.3).

A close examination of Example 4, others like it and the USAS categories listed in Table 4.3 suggests that the following seventeen semantic fields (Table 4.4) are mainly used in such descriptions. Example types from the data are included in the final column.

Many of these correspond to the features of language that were noted as characteristic of the descriptive discourse type in Section 2.1.1. For example, 'colour and colour patterns', 'judgment of appearance: beautiful/ugly', 'general appearance and physical properties', 'long, tall and wide' etc., relate to visible characteristics of people, objects and surroundings, that differentiate the descriptive from the narrative discourse type, for example. However, some of these categories need to be examined in more detail, since descriptions can also be of the self. For example, Plath sometimes uses items from 'ugliness'; 'ability and intelligence' to describe herself.

Aside from descriptions, some of the semantic categories, as mentioned above, are key due to the topics that are discussed in the text (and that are discussed far

Table 4.4 Semantic fields used in description

USAS tag	LL	Description	Example items
O4.3	272.4	colour and colour patterns	*shadow, pallid, blue, coloured*
B1	234.1	anatomy and physiology	*leg, head, mouth, muscular, hands*
E2+	68.5	like	*love, like, fancied, popular*
O4.2+	68.0	judgment of appearance: beautiful	*clean, pretty, handsome, neat*
O4.5	52.5	texture	*hard, soft, smooth, greasy*
O4.4	50.1	shape	*arc, oval, round, sharp*
O4.1	32.7	general appearance, physical properties	*hard, moist, blurred, fertile*
O1.1	32.3	substances and materials: solid	*solid, metal, steel, soil, glass*
N3.2+	28.50	size: big	*big, grow, fat, colossal*
B5	22.95	clothes and personal belongings	*clothes, shirt, buttons, shoes*
N3.2–	22.86	size: small	*little, small, taut, negligible*
X3.1	20.48	sensory: taste	*sweet, bitter, taste, pungent*
S1.2.3+	16.93	selfish	*ego, selfish, patronizing, snooty*
E3+	15.10	calm	*rest, soothing, calm, tender*
O4.2–	12.73	judgment of appearance: ugly	*morbid, dirty, rotting, ugly, vile*
X5.2–	11.20	uninterested/bored/unenergetic	*dull, lazy, passive, banal, bored*
N6+ + +	9.42	frequent	*always*
T1.3+	8.57	time period: long	*long, all week, all year*
A6.2–	8.41	comparing: unusual	*strange, strangely, peculiar*
X3.3	8.28	sensory: touch	*smoothed, touch, rough*
N3.7+	7.08	long, tall and wide	*thick, deep, tall, long, high*

less in the reference corpus). Many of these topics reflect Plath's preoccupations, but some also indicate aspects of her environment. For example, the semantic field of 'relationships' (S3.2) is prominent, because Plath goes on a number of dates and reports on them, but also because she is preoccupied with the topic of relationships, men, sex and marriage, as in Example 5.

Example 5

> I_Z8 didn't_Z5/Z6 want_X7+ to_Z5 say_Q2.1 I_Z8 didnt_Z5/Z6 give_a_damn_E6+ about_Z5 him_Z8, but_Z5 just_A14 wanted_X7+ to_Z5 be_Z5 kissed_S3.2 good_A5.1+ and_Z5 hard_O4.1, and_Z5 that_Z8 he_Z8m wasn't_A3+/Z6 capable_X9.1+ of_Z5 satisfying_E4.2+ me_Z8 even_A13.1 in_that_Z5 way_X4.2. So_Z5 I_Z8 told_Q2.1 him_Z8 various_A6.3+ lies_A5.2- about_Z5 liking_E2+ him_Z8, and_Z5 he_Z8 told_Q2.1 me_Z8 about_Z5 his_Z8 girl_S2.1. From_now_on_T1.1.3 when_Z5 a_Z5 boy_S2.2 starts_T2+ telling_Q2.2 me_Z8 about_Z5 his_Z8 lost_X9.2- loves_S3.2 I_Z8 am_Z5 going_to_T1.1.3 run_M1/N3.8+ in_Z5 the_Z5 opposite_M6 direction_M6 screaming_Q2.2 loudly_X3.2+. It_Z8 is_A3+ a_Z5 bad_A5.1- sign_Q1.1. Somehow_X4.2 I_Z8 bring_out_M2 such_Z5 confidences_E6+, and_Z5 I'm_Z8/A3+ pretty_A13.5 sick_B2- of_Z5 hearing_about_X2.3+ Bobbe_Z99 or_Z5 Dorothy_Z1 or_Z5 P._K._Z1 or_Z5 Liota_Z99. (Entry 31, USAS-tagged)

Plath also discusses the effects of marriage and love on women. The preoccupation with the role of women in society is also reflected in the items that constitute the 'people: female category', but this category additionally includes items related to Plath's life in an all-female college at university.

The semantic fields 'plants', 'the universe', 'objects generally', and 'food', 'education', 'music and related activities' are a reflection of the variety of things that Plath talks about in her detailed descriptions. Similarly, the keyness of 'music and related activities', for example, partly stems from an extensive and detailed recounting of a concert that Plath attends one summer in Entry 137. Almost a third of the concordance lines for 'music and related activities' come from this entry. References to 'education' can similarly be explained by the fact that Plath attends university and therefore discusses it, including a botany class, which also contributes to the keyness of the semantic field of 'plants'.

The keyness of L1+ (alive) reflects the fact that Plath often writes about life and people in general in her journals. She muses about the nature/purpose of life, and about her own future life. The semantic category of 'residence' (H4) is also connected to this. It includes items such as *home, living, lived*. In fact, the most frequent item is *home* – which is one of the centres of Plath's activities. Example 6 is representative of this kind of contemplation of her own life – items from the semantic fields of L1+ and H4 are underlined.

Example 6

> At home I rested and played, here, where I work, the routine is momentarily suspended and I am lost. There is no living being on earth at this moment except myself. I could walk down the halls, and empty rooms would yawn mockingly at me from every side. God, but life is loneliness, despite all the opiates. (Entry 36; my emphasis)

Plath also often muses about freedom (semantic category of 'no constraint'), and faith ('confident'). In the process of these musings, many references are made to the internal workings of minds and her own mind in particular. The items in the categories 'mental actions and processes'; 'thought, belief'; and 'psychological actions, states and processes' reflect this. In addition to these general musings about life, repeated references to perfection/brilliance (e.g. 'evaluation: good') seem to reflect more grounded issues. Plath seems to focus very much on doing well and being adequate or more (Example 7). In a similar way, she seems to have a preoccupation with reading, writing and words in general ('language, speech and grammar'), with learning, and with intelligence (as a form of standard). In this sense she also aims to date 'brilliant' men who can inspire her.

Example 7

> There_Z5 is_A3+ the_Z5 hysteric_E1 and_Z5 persistent_T2++ fear_E5- that_Z8 I_Z8 do_Z5 not_Z6 understand_X2.5+ all_N5.1+ I_Z8 read_Q3, that_Z5 my_Z8 water-level_O1.2 of_Z5 comprehension_X2.5+ is_A3+ a_Z5 good_A5.1+ deal_N5 lower_M6 than_Z5 it_Z8 would_A7+ be_A3+ if_Z7 I_Z8 were_Z5 taking_A9+ the_Z5 course_M6 slowly_N3.8-, [...] Nothing_Z6/Z8 is_A3+ more_A13.3 difficult_A12- than_Z5 lashing_E3- a_Z5 vagrant_H4-/S2 mind_X1 suddenly_N3.8+ into_Z5 long_N3.7+ self-imposed_X7+/S6- stints_T1.3 of_Z5 concentration_X5.1+. But_Z5 I_Z8 will_T1.1.3 learn_X2.3+ a_Z5 few_N5- things_O2 from_Z5 this_M6 mass_N5+ of_Z5 material_O1. I_Z8 will_T1.1.3 read_Q3 and_Z5 ponder_X2.1 over_T2- my_Z8 70_N1 page_Q1.2 quota_N5 per_Z5 day_T1.3. (Entry 149, USAS-tagged)

Aside from the USAS categories discussed above, some of the most important results to emerge from Table 4.3 are semantic fields that potentially include references to affective states and the self, such as 'mental actions and processes'; 'confident'; 'thought, belief'; 'not part of a group'; and 'psychological actions states and processes'. These need to be explored further as they are directly relevant to affective states.

Concordance 10 below shows some concordance lines for just one of these key semantic fields: 'thought/belief'.

As can be seen from these concordance lines, the majority of items in this semantic category are versions of the lemma *feel*, which, unsurprisingly, is

1	except the present , and already , I	feel	the weight of centuries smothering me .
	n the way , we passed Mary Coffee . I	felt	her looking at me rather strangely . So
	ous and yellow , behind the trees . I	felt	suddenly breathless , stifled . I was t
	le dreams . I awoke , my head heavy ,	feeling	as if I had just emerged from a swim in
5	en they die contented - - - that they	feel	they have somehow transcended the wall
	torch and made you want to know , to	think	, to learn , to beat your head out agai
	and how sorry you were , and then you	felt	a sudden hardening and strange anger at
	e carnival . (Later years would have	found	you infinitely grateful for any of his
	a kiss was not as distasteful as once	imagined	. And so you could list the thirty or f
10	r love of someone beside yourself ? I	wonder	, sometimes .) You walked and you drov
	was talk , with boys especially . You	wondered	briefly if the Great God could stoop to
	could stoop to jealously and then you	felt	the lovely placating touch of hands on
	uld have been termed possessive . You	felt	very gay , very foolish , very cold and
	xing his mouth in little grimaces you	felt	a feeling of belonging to him curl cosi
15	s mouth in little grimaces you felt a	feeling	of belonging to him curl cosily inside
	ye , good-bye my love , goodbye . You	felt	no reality , no knife of sorrow cut you
	- must you wait till then before you	feel	the full impact of your loneliness ? 83
	of the lives of others all the tired	feelings	and emotional disturbances burst forth
	t spring - - - all that I thought and	felt	and said and recorded as reality , has
20	who is Dick ? Who am I ? My stubborn	unimaginative	self can not conceive of him as a flesh
	y stubborn unimaginative self can not	conceive	of him as a flesh-and-blood being any m
	e real hours were gone to find myself	believing	in him only in theory . Odd is the huma
	xity when examined and questioned . I	wonder	about all the roads not taken and am mo
	create ? No , I reproduce . I have no	imagination	. I am submerged in circling ego . I li
25	say I am interested in people . Am I	rationalizing	? God knows . Maybe he does n't . If he

Concordance 10 Thought, belief X2.1/675.

often used to express feelings (e.g. lines 13–15, 18 in Concordance 10). These are interesting from the point of view of direct references to affective states. In addition however, a number of expressions in the co-text of items in the semantic category seem to express affective states metaphorically and metonymically (see line 1 and 3, respectively). Lines 7, 17 and 20 also include metaphorical expressions that seem to be relevant to affective states and the self.

The following sections are dedicated to discussing the significance of these findings and elaborating on some of the interpretative comments already provided. Towards the end of the section, the implications of this analysis for the second part of the book are highlighted.

4.3.3 Discussion of quantitative results

To begin with, I want to elaborate on what I have noted repeatedly above: the Smith Journal contains a large amount of 'description'. As outlined in Section 2.1.1.1, this frequently occurs in various genres and communicates a 'vivid, often emotionally suggestive mental picture of factual phenomena, such as [specific] objects, people, and places in space' (Werlich 1976: 50). Its common linguistic features express an inherent subjectivity, as they portray the described situation from the perspective of the describer. This means that one can expect a descriptive text to contain many instances of features such as '-ing verbs', 'adjectives', 'adverbs' (of space and modality in particular), 'colour and colour patterns', 'texture', 'shape', 'size', 'judgment of appearance', 'light', 'darkness', 'temperature' etc. These can be used to describe visual (and other sensory) characteristics of objects and people. Grammatical markers of references to people and surroundings such as 's-form of verbs' and 'locative adverbs/nouns' should also be frequent. In addition, one would expect makers of subjectivity such as adverbials and emotive language. These linguistic features were shown to be key in the Smith Journal in the preceding discussions of results.

However, a number of other features were also associated with the notion of description, and I suggested that the keyness of these is due to the particular way in which Plath uses and adapts the descriptive discourse type. In order to specify what this means, I want to look at three short extracts from different parts of the Smith Journal and compare them to a 'norm' for the descriptive discourse type. I specifically selected these excerpts because their lines appear repeatedly in concordance lists – Example 4 and Example 8 in the 'weather' SEM concordance and Example 9 in the 'anatomy and physiology' SEM concordance.

The first extract, Example 4, can be found in Section 4.3.2 so I do not reproduce it here, but it includes items from the categories of 'colour and colour patterns' (e.g. *blue*, *shadows*), 'general objects' (e.g. *lamp*, *mould*), 'plants' (e.g. *leaves*), 'sensory: smell' (e.g. *smell*), 'light' (e.g. *lights*), 'temperature: hot/on fire' (e.g. *heat*), 'weather' (e.g. *mist*, *nimbus*), 'the universe' (e.g. *moon*), 'substances and materials: solid' (e.g. *granite*), 'residence' (e.g. *house*, *home*) among others. Example 8 and Example 9, with POS tags added, have not yet been introduced.

Example 8 is from the beginning of a relatively long (2,000-word) entry, which then proceeds in an introspective fashion depicting the writer's musings about life, the passage of time and a questioning of her place within these parameters.

Example 8

1 81. June 15, 1951 The_AT rain_NN1 comes_VVZ down_RP again_RT, on_II the_AT indecently_RR big_JJ green_NN1 leaves_NN2, and_CC

2 there_EX is_VBZ the_AT wet_JJ hiss_NN1 of_IO drops_NN2 splashing_VVG and_CC puckering_VVG the_AT flat_JJ veined_JJ vegetable_NN1 surfaces_NN2.

3 Although_CS the_AT rain_NN1 is_VBZ neutral_JJ, although_CS the_AT rain_NN1 is_VBZ impersonal_JJ, it_PPH1 becomes_VVZ for_IF me_PPIO1 a_AT1

4 haunting_JJ and_CC nostalgic_JJ sound_NN1. The_AT still_JJ air_NN1 of_IO the_AT house_NN1 smells_NN2 of_IO warm_JJ stagnant_JJ human_NN1

5 flesh_NN1 and_CC of_IO onions_NN2, and_CC I_PPIS1 sit_VV0, back_RP to_II the_AT radiator_NN1, the_AT metal_NN1 ribs_NN2 of_IO it_PPH1 pressing_VVG against_II

6 my_APPGE shoulders_NN2. I_PPIS1 am_VBM in_II my_APPGE old_JJ room_NN1 once_RR21 more_RR22, for_IF a_RR21 little_RR22, and_CC I_PPIS1 am_VBM caught_VVN in_II musing_VVG

7 – how_RRQ life_NN1 is_VBZ a_AT1 swift_JJ motion_NN1, a_AT1 continuous_JJ flowing_JJ, changing_VVG, and_CC how_RRQ one_MC1 is_VBZ always_RR saying_VVG
8 goodbye_NN1 and_CC going_VVG places_NN2, seeing_VVG people_NN, doing_VDG things_NN2. Only_RR in_II the_AT rain_NN1, sometimes_RT, only_RR
9 when_RRQ the_AT rain_NN1 comes_VVZ, closing_VVG in_II your_APPGE pitifully_RR small_JJ radius_NN1 of_IO activity_NN1, only_RR when_CS you_PPY sit_VV0
10 and_CC listen_VV0 by_II the_AT window_NN1, as_CSA the_AT cold_JJ wet_JJ air_NN1 blows_VVZ thinly_RR by_II the_AT back_NN1 of_IO your_APPGE neck_NN1 only_RR
11 then_RT do_VD0 you_PPY think_VVI and_CC feel_VVI sick_JJ. (Entry 81 – beginning, POS-tagged)

Example 9 shows the beginning of an entry with description occurring in the service of narration, that is, there is temporal progression in the text, but with a lot of descriptive detail. The rest of the entry proceeds in the same tone depicting the rest of the day.

Example 9

1 So_RR you_PPY walked_VVD in_RP to_II the_AT kitchen_NN1 that_CST saturday_NPD1 morning_NNT1, (it_PPH1 being_VBG cold_JJ bright_JJ blue_JJ August_NPM1,) lean_JJ,
2 a_RR21 little_RR22 stooped_VVD, in_II a_AT1 blue_JJ shirt_NN1, and_CC Mrs._NNB C._NP1 said_VVD, "Attila_NP1 this_DD1 is_VBZ Sylvia_NP1" while_CS you_PPY said_VVD ignoring_VVG,
3 "My_APPGE name_NN1 is_VBZ Attila_NP1", with_IW your_APPGE trace_NN1 of_IO accent_NN1, the_AT slight_JJ slur_NN1, the_AT nasal_JJ inflection_NN1. Breakfast_NN1,
4 then_RT, with_IW the_AT toast_NN1 and_CC jam_NN1, bacon_NN1 and_CC coffee_NN1, all_DB good-smelling_JJ and_CC warm_JJ, with_IW outside_II the_AT
5 sun-bright_JJ pieces_NN2 of_IO the_AT day_NNT1 waiting_VVG. You_PPY talking_VVG with_IW all_DB, and_CC I_PPIS1 listening_VVG, thinking_VVG, oh_UH, I_PPIS1 want_VV0 a_AT1
6 lot_NN1 to_TO grow_VVI to_TO know_VVI you_PPY. And_CC subsequently_RR, during_II day_NNT1 and_CC night_NNT1 and_CC day_NNT1 again_RT, talking_VVG,
7 looking_VVG, exchanging_VVG laughter_NN1. Your_APPGE hair_NN1 long_RR, black_JJ, combed_VVD back_RP, and_CC your_APPGE eyes_NN2, the_AT most_RGT
8 wonderful_JJ part_NN1 when_CS flashing_VVG back_RP a_AT1 look_NN1 of_IO appreciative_JJ understanding_NN1, dark_NN1 to_II blackness_NN1,
9 blazing_VVG laughter_NN1. There_EX is_VBZ the_AT indefinable_JJ alien_JJ air_NN1 about_II you_PPY not_XX just_RR your_APPGE deep_JJ voice_NN1 and_CC
10 uniquely_RR lovely_JJ inflections_NN2, but_CCB an_AT1 attitude_NN1 toward_II life_NN1, a_AT1 laughing_JJ wit_NN1, a_AT1 comprehension_NN1 of_IO
11 war_NN1, of_IO escape_NN1, deep_RR rooted_VVN your_APPGE graceful_JJ athletic_JJ build_NN1, strong_JJ, lean_JJ, resilient_JJ. The_AT muscles_NN2 in_II

12 your_APPGE thighs_NN2 and_CC calves_NN2 are_VBR taut_JJ, powerful_JJ. Behind_II our_APPGE playful_JJ beach_NN1 wrestling_NN1 there_EX was_VBDZ the_AT
13 leashed_JJ iron_NN1 fury_NN1 of_IO your_APPGE potential_JJ strength_NN1. (Entry 144 – beginning, POS-tagged, my emphasis)

Two out of three examples above are descriptions of scenes and thoughts (Example 4 and Example 8, respectively), while Example 9 is an instance of narration in the sense that there is temporal progression and changes in states, but includes substantial amounts of person description (the most prominent sections are underlined). All examples are written in a viewer/narrator centred perspective, which can be observed in the deixis and the narration of thoughts and feelings. Table 4.5 below summarizes the linguistic characteristics of the examples with reference to a general norm for description (cf. Werlich 1976,

Table 4.5 Descriptive characteristics of the examples

Characteristic	Norm	Example 4	Example 8	Example 9
Scene setting function	+	–	+–	–
Spatial locators	++	+	+	+
Lexis of vision	++	+	+	+
Hyperbole	+	+	+	+–
Metaphors	+	+	+	+
Comparisons	+	++	+	–
Evocative language	+	+	++	+
Atelic verbs	+	+	+	+
Lexis of other senses	+–	++	+	++
Modals	+	–	–	–
Adverbials	+	+	+–	+
Parentheticals	+–	–	–	+
Describes specific things, people, places	+	+	+–	+
First-person pronoun	+	+	–+	–
Other noteworthy characteristics:				
Mental-affective process types	n/a	+	++	+
Composite features	n/a	++	+	++

Merlini Barbaresi 2004). The '+' sign denotes a characteristic that is present in the text, '+ +' suggests that this is a dominant feature; while the '–' sign denotes an absence of a feature. The '+ –' signs are used when a feature is only present on a few occasions. The grey boxes highlight the main differences between the norm and the examples from the Smith Journal.

As Table 4.5 shows, the chosen passages contain most of the standard features of the descriptive discourse type as outlined by Werlich (1976) and Merlini Barbaresi (2004), among others. These excerpts can therefore be considered examples of description, or to contain large amounts of description in the case of Example 9. They contain spatial locators and often include progression in space (e.g. progression over a body as a person's features are described) in addition to

- lexis of vision (both in verbs such as *seem*; and in the descriptions of visible features, for example, lines 1–2 in Example 4; or lines 2, 11–12 in Example 9)
- atelic verbs (present tenses to denote actions that are incomplete)
- metaphors (the personification of the rain and lines 6–7 in Example 8)
- hyperbole (lines 6–7 in Example 4; line 9 in Example 9)
- evocative language (the adjectives in lines 9–11 in Example 8)
- parentheticals (e.g. line 1 in Example 9)
- adverbials (e.g. *faintly* in Example 4)

In general, the descriptive passages are also written in the first person; however, sometimes the second-person pronoun is used for the same referent (as in Example 8). This is due to the second-person narration that occurs at various points in the Smith Journal. In addition, like Attila in Example 9, other people are sometimes described using the second-person pronoun.

There are also important discrepancies. One clear difference between these examples and the general characteristics outlined above is the object of description. While the prototypical cases apparently refer to scenes, objects and people external to the describer, a large proportion of description in the Smith Journal refers to Plath and her inner thoughts (Example 8). Even when the description is of something/someone external, Plath not only describes their attributes but also discusses the effect of these on herself (e.g. lines 3–4 in Example 8). In this sense, there is a stronger sense of focalization through the narrator, and a stronger sense of subjectivity, than one would expect in prototypical description. This is further supported by the presence of mental processes performed by Plath and noted in the descriptions – see, for example, line 9 in Example 4; lines 10–11 in Example 8; line 5 in Example 9. These examples show how Plath introspects about even small experiences that she has, and these introspections form part of her descriptions of external entities.

In the Smith Journal, entire entries can be descriptions, and description can occur in the middle of entries, as well as throughout them. In fact, as Example 9 shows, description even forms a substantial proportion of narrative discourse types (although whether this conforms to the norm or not is difficult to judge). In addition, these descriptions are more complex than what seems to be the norm. There are references to sensory perceptions other than the visual (sound and smell in particular), and these are often more frequent than visual perceptions (see Example 4). The visual description is not absent, but is elaborated by referring to other senses such that the description becomes more comprehensive.

It seems that the type of description dominant in the Smith Journal is more detailed and stylistically more complex than prototypical description. It also reflects an additional level of subjectivity in that sensory perceptions are filtered through the mind of the narrator, and the mental reflections on/reaction to the object of description are also presented. This tendency seems to be part of Plath's mind style and may be connected to the fact that she was an aspiring writer and was training herself to be observant and expressive of details in her physical and social environment.

Of course, some of the POS and SEM categories that I discussed in the context of descriptions may also have other interpretations. According to Biber (1988), the use of spatio-temporal references and adverbs, for example, marks *online production* (Dimension 6), that is, the type of writing/speaking that is unedited and produced as the thoughts occur. The '-ing form of verbs' may also be a manifestation of this type of writing: 'The use of progressives indicates that a situation is incomplete or unstable' (Bockting 1995: 36). In fact, some of these features do occur in the context of speech presentation in the journals, and (direct) speech presentation can potentially be seen as 'mock' online production. However, as in Example 10 below, the features also concentrate in more descriptive and narrative passages in the Journal and could be evidence that the Smith Journal is less edited than autobiographies. Adverbs, spatio-temporal references and -ing forms are underlined in the following example.

Example 10

> but_CCB I_PPIS1 can_VM stop_VVI and_CC to_TO prove_VVI it_PPH1 I_PPIS1 will_VM ... there_RL ... there_RL ... I_PPIS1 am_VBM standing_VVG still_JJ and_CC my_APPGE feet_NN2 have_VH0 stopped_VVN clicking_VVG ... they_PPHS2 are_VBR waiting_VVG docily_RR

> in_II their_APPGE snail_NN1 like_II leather_NN1 houses_NN2 ... but_CCB I_PPIS1 could_VM not_XX turn_VVI and_CC walk_VVI back_RP ... no_UH ... but_CCB some_DD night_NNT1 I_PPIS1 will_VM break_VVI these_DD2 eighteen_MC years_NNT2 of_IO walking_VVG home_RL and_CC walk_VV0 all_DB night_NNT1, away_II21 from_II22 the_AT magnet_NN1 that_CST pulls_VVZ and_CC attracts_VVZ me_PPIO1 like_II a_AT1 scrap_NN1 of_IO metal_NN1 ... and_CC now_RT I_PPIS1 am_VBM walking_VVG again_RT ... but_CCB I_PPIS1 will_VM take_VVI this_DD1 road_NN1 instead_II21 of_II22 mine_NN1 ... I_PPIS1 will_VM assert_VVI myself_PPX1 feebly_RR and_CC approach_NN1 from_II a_AT1 less_RGR frequented_JJ path_NN1 ... (Entry 63, POS-tagged, my emphasis)

Although Biber's (1988) notion of online production may not be straightforwardly applicable to journals (and not all of its markers are present here), it is reasonable to say that there is a difference in the level of editing between journals and autobiographies. The latter are written with the intention of being sold and are therefore carefully edited. They need to appeal to a wider audience and are therefore potentially more general in their description of events – their function is both to inform and to entertain (Semino and Short 2004). In this latter function they most certainly differ from journals, in general, and particularly from private journals. Furthermore, autobiographies are, by definition, written in retrospect, in contrast to some journals. This may explain why there is an overuse of the present tense in the Smith Journal when compared to autobiographies.

Biber (1988) further suggests that features such as adverbs, questions, the present-tense, non-phrasal coordination (e.g. *and*) and the use of the second-person pronoun are markers of involvement. This is a more probable interpretation, as the Smith Journal exhibits all of these characteristics. As outlined in Chapter 3, in narrative psychology these features are associated with the *experiencing* narrative perspective (Pólya et al. 2007). In the Smith Journal, questions are represented in the 'wh- adverb' category, and some examples of *do*. According to Pólya et al., the experiencing narrative perspective 'reflects the instability of emotion regulation' (Pólya et al. 2007: 60). This makes these features relevant for affective states.

Another relevant finding is the overuse of *I am* in the journal (overuse of VBM and PPIS1 – 'I') (see Concordance 5). This suggests that there is a strong focus on the narrator – in this case Plath – in the data. This, in itself, would not be surprising, given that diaries are normally first-person narratives. However, the reference corpus also consists exclusively of first-person narratives (though not just present tense narratives). This makes the keyness more unusual. The combination of the first- and second-person pronouns with the copular *be* results in an attributive relational process type (Thompson 1996), indicating how the token – the entity whose attribute is being described – is categorized by the producer of the language. This creates a strong semantic connection between token and attribute. In the present case, the producer is Plath, and the token is also Plath. Given the importance of such descriptions for how Plath experiences her affective states, these are discussed in more detail in the subsequent chapter on self-descriptions and direct references to affective states.

In addition to considering the semantic content of such self-descriptions, evidence in the realm of clinical and narrative psychology suggests that unusual self-focus itself is important to consider. Possible interpretations of extreme self-focus can be 'egoism or egocentrism, moreover, it may denote narcissism and autism, where the transgression of the bounds of reality signals a real root of danger' (Hargitai et al. 2007: 27). Fekete (2002) claims that a high frequency of self-references seems to reflect a self-preoccupation and an inability to distance oneself from personal concerns. Rude et al. (2004) showed a link between excessive use of *I* with depression, which could be explained by the idea that emotional suffering encourages people to focus their attention on themselves (Pyszczynski and Greenberg 1987). In this sense, this particular characteristic of the data also deserves further attention.

Similarly, the fact that the second-person pronoun is key deserves attention. While some instances of this feature simply occur because of direct speech presentation, Plath also uses the second-person pronoun to refer to herself. In this sense, second-person pronouns represent additional self-references that need to be examined more closely. An examination of a random sample of 200 concordance lines (out of 1,080) suggested that about 50 per cent of *you* do not occur in speech presentation but do refer to Plath. Pennebaker and Lay (2002) suggest that second-person pronouns in particular indicate that speakers are creating a distance between themselves and their audiences. This has interesting implications when *you* is used to refer to the self.

As some of the excerpts above demonstrate (in particular Example 4), there is a considerable amount of figurative language in most of Plath's writing, and some of it is relevant to the experience of affective states. Potential semantic fields for such references include: 'happy'; 'thought, belief' (feeling); 'content'; 'wanted' (desires); 'greedy'; 'not part of a group' (loneliness); 'psychological actions, states and processes'. These semantic fields are primarily to do with the emotions and in some cases, may include conventional metaphorical expressions. However, in particular the 'thought, belief' category revealed a number of relevant metaphorical expressions in the co-text (as was noted in the context of Concordance 10). Table 4.6 below lists additional semantic fields where relevant figurative expressions were found. These categories revealed some interesting

Table 4.6 Potential Sources of figurative language

USAS tag	LL	Description	Example item
W4	74.3	weather	*I stood there, flooded with longing*
W2	60.7	light	*and black is death, with no light, no waking*
W3	28.84	geographical terms	*I am at low ebb*
N3.2+	28.50	size: big	*Time, experience: the colossal wave*
X2.1	21.21	thought, belief	*you wonder with quick fear*
O1.2	20.51	substances and materials: liquids	*fell in an epileptic froth of ecstasy*
X7+	17.33	wanted	*I no longer felt the desire flame up in me*
W2–	15.80	darkness	*the dark, warm, fetid escape from action*
O4.6–	14.62	temperature: cold	*you are frozen mentally*
A1.7–	12.58	no constraint	*Colossal desire to escape, retreat*
B4	11.29	cleaning and personal care	*Stop thinking selfishly of razors and self-wounds*
S5–	8.48	not part of a group	*a deep and pathetic loneliness*
X1	7.25	psychological actions, states, processes	*Stubborn, unimaginative state of mind*
O4.6+	7.09	temperature: hot/on fire	*I am warm, bubbling inside*

examples, as shown in the final column (lexical items that belong to given SEM category are underlined).

What is interesting to note is that the metaphorical expressions are not always the ones underlined. Similar to the 'thought, belief' category, metaphorical expressions are in the co-text of expressions belonging to these SEM categories. This means that these USAS tags, even if their items are not used metaphorically, may be useful in finding interesting metaphorical expressions via corpus methods (cf. Stefanowitsch 2006). This is explored further in Part II of the book.

The final linguistic features I would like to discuss are the semantic categories of 'evaluation: good'; 'entire; maximum'; and 'frequent' (N6+ + +) (and the 'pre-determiner' DB). As noted earlier, the first two of these reflect the extreme ends of two clines: perfection and eternity. The last category does this in a similar fashion, with prominent items being *very*, *all* and *full* (note: *all* is also in the 'pre-determiner' CLAWS category). Thinking in extremes is something that psychologists note as indicative of a potential affective state (in combination with other features): that of suicidality. Suicidal writers, for example, use more polarized, dichotomous structures (Fekete 2002). In this sense, these categories also need to be investigated further. In particular, it is essential to explore what other linguistic features they co-occur with.

4.3.4 Implications for Part II of the book

The previous section focused on the linguistic features that differentiate the Smith Journal from the reference corpus. This section summarizes the implications of key linguistic features for conveying Plath's experience of her affective states. These features emerged from the corpus comparison in combination with evidence from discourse type norms (cf. Werlich 1976, Biber 1988, Merlini Barbaresi 2004) and studies in clinical and narrative psychology.

First, potential metaphorical and non-metaphorical references to affective states and self-descriptions need to be considered. These emerge from both the POS and semantic comparisons. Metaphorical references are abundant in Plath's writing, but what I am concerned with here are those references that may be indicative of affective states. The USAS categories listed in the previous section are discussed in detail in Part II. Additionally, the CLAWS categories of VBM (*I'm*/*I am*); *are* and PPY (*you*) are also important in terms of affective states. These phrases, when they refer to Plath, are essentially descriptions of the self. Plath tells her journal how she sees herself. These direct references to affective states and self-descriptions are the subject of Chapter 5 in Part II of this book.

In addition to looking at VBM and PPY for references to the self in a semantic sense, the significance of the overuse of self-references in general also needs to be considered in more detail. Clinical and narrative psychologists have associated unusual self-focus with a variety of affective states including depression, suicidality and narcissism.

Finally, there seems to be an overuse of some features of language associated with dichotomous thinking in the Smith Journal. References to eternity, maximums and extremes in general ('evaluation: good' and 'entire, maximum', 'pre-determiner' *all*) are key in the SWTPAuto comparison. Dichotomous structures (polarized terms) can be a reflection of the psychological defence mechanism of mental/cognitive 'splitting' (Fekete 2002) and, in combination with negation, can also suggest suicidal ideation. These features of Plath's writing also need to be investigated further. While the 'negative' category did not come up as key in this initial comparison, I noted that about 60 per cent of *dos* are actually *don'ts*. In light of the link with suicidality (in combination with dichotomous structures), these may warrant further exploration as well.

The analyses in Part II of the book, therefore, focus on five elements in particular to gain a better understanding of how Plath's experience of affective states is conveyed through the language of the Smith Journal. These elements are: self-descriptions and direct (non-metaphorical) references to affective states; metaphorical references to the self and affective states; evidence of dichotomous thinking; the frequency of self-references in general; and the use of the second-person pronoun.

Part Two

Zooming In: Investigating Key Linguistic Features

5

Self-description and Direct References to Affective States

In this chapter, I discuss Sylvia Plath's self-descriptions and direct references to affective states in the Smith Journal, combining the qualitative results of a manual intensive analysis and quantitative results of a corpus analysis using Wmatrix (Rayson 2009). The term *direct* is, of course, not unambiguous. Steen et al. (2010) refers to expressions as direct or indirect, explaining that in indirect (but not in direct) metaphor, there is a conflict between the basic and contextual meanings of an expression. This relates to the Pragglejaz (2007) procedure for metaphor identification and highlights that, in technical terms, the line between metaphorical and literal is not always easy to draw. In this chapter, *direct* references to affective states are understood as words/phrases that express something about affective states, without a conflict between their basic and contextual meaning (e.g. *I am afraid*; *I feel happy*). In other contexts, these might be referred to as literal, or non-metaphoric, expressions.

The automated corpus analysis consists of investigating concordances of the verb *to be* in its first-person singular and second-person forms using Wmatrix. Concordances of VBM (*'m* and *am*) and VBDZ (*was*) capture instances of *I'm*, *I am*, *I was* in the Smith Journal. These concordance lines include relevant descriptions of Plath's self. *Relevant*, here, is to be understood as examples of *I am*, *I'm*, *I was* where *I* clearly refers to Plath. For example, *I am young, husky and eager to work* in Entry 152 of the Smith Journal occurs outside of speech reporting. It is part of the narration and contextually clear that *I* refers to Plath, making it an example of self-description. Similarly, the concordances of VBR (*'re*, *are*) and VBDR (*were*) are explored for entries written in the second person to investigate instances of *you're*, *you are* and *you were*, where *you* refers to Plath.

In addition to these grammatical structures, corpus methods help to explore the semantic fields that could include expressions that directly refer to affective states and the self. Some of these categories came up as key in the corpus analysis in Part I of the book, but some are not statistically significantly overused in the Smith Journal. They nevertheless warrant brief commentary, as they contribute to the overall composition of the Journal.

The analysis begins with the results of the automated corpus analyses, discussing the semantic fields (USAS tags) that explicitly include affective states and emotions. This is followed by a discussion of self-descriptions in both first-person and second-person entries. Finally, the analysis focuses on additional results from the manual intensive analysis of a set of sample entries.

5.1 Semantic fields relevant to affective states and the self

In this section, I discuss linguistic expressions found in relevant USAS categories in the Smith Journal. A semantic field was considered relevant if the tagset descriptors referred to emotions, affective states and self-evaluations. Self-evaluation is understood as valenced self-descriptions and is included here as such descriptions can be indirectly related to affective states (as discussed earlier).

Table 5.1 lists the semantic fields in the Smith Journal that are relevant to affective states and self-descriptions. The first column shows the USAS tag, the second column lists the category name. The third column shows the overall frequency with which items belonging to that category occur in the Smith Journal. Column four shows how many of these refer to Plath, either as agent (i.e. doing an action) or as object of her own description. The final column shows an adjusted frequency of references to Plath. This adjusting was necessary because in some cases the relevant references take on an opposite meaning (in terms of valence) due to negation. For example, under E5– ('fear'), one example is *I am not scared.* Wmatrix codes *scared* as an instance of E5– even though contextually it is an example of E5+ ('bravery'). The table is sorted according to the adjusted frequency column, in descending order. The final column includes some linguistic examples for the categories.

The categories in Table 5.1 generally include affective states and emotions ('fear', 'happy', 'sad', 'interested', 'worry', 'content', 'bored', 'angry/violent', 'calm', 'discontent'), descriptions of the self ('selfish', 'weak', 'able/intelligent', 'confident', 'unable/unintelligent', 'strong', 'bravery'), physical descriptions ('beautiful' and 'ugly') and descriptions of behaviour ('foolish', 'failure', 'success'). Highlighted

Table 5.1 A list of relevant semantic categories in the Smith Journal

USAS tag	Label	Overall frequency	Frequency references to Plath	Frequency adjusted	Examples
E5–	*Fear*	*130*	*71*	*69*	*afraid, fear, frightened*
E4.1+	Happy	280	52	52	*overjoyed, delight*
E4.1–	*Sad*	*158*	*43*	*43*	*jealous, sad, regret, jealousy*
X5.2+	Interested	188	51	39	*curious, excited, keen*
E6–	*Worry*	*85*	*34*	*33*	*uneasy, nervous, tense, anxious*
E4.2+	Content	87	24	22	*proud, glad, satisfied*
S1.2.3+	*Selfish*	*68*	*24*	*21*	*ego, vanity*
X5.2–	*Bored*	*60*	*9*	*21*	*wearily, banal, bored*
X9.2–	*Failure*	*61*	*13*	*20*	*failure, I am lost*
X9.1+	Able/intelligent	117	16	18	*not a cretin, capable, gifted*
O4.2+	Beautiful	370	16	17	*pretty, looked nice, lean, glowing*
S1.2.5–	*Weak*	*46*	*15*	*17*	*weak, not strong, vulnerable*
E3–	*Angry/violent*	*141*	*13*	*13*	*annoyed, morose, rage*
E3+	Calm	125	11	11	*hypnotized, tender, serene*
O4.2–	*Ugly*	*141*	*11*	*10*	*ugly, mess, horribly*
S1.2.6–	*Foolish*	*49*	*13*	*9*	*ridiculous, naive, stupidity*
E6+	Confident	50	9	9	*confidence, faith*

Table 5.1 (Continued)

USAS tag	Label	Overall frequency	Frequency references to Plath	Frequency adjusted	Examples
E4.2–	*Discontent*	*12*	*5*	*7*	*disgusted, frustrated*
X9.1–	*Unable/ unintelligent*	*13*	*7*	*5*	*unable, incapable*
X9.2+	Success	68	12	5	*live up to, success, make it*
S1.2.5+	Strong	67	5	3	*strong, invulnerable*
E5+	Bravery	12	1	3	*audacity, not scared*
TOTAL	***60%* – 40%**				

in italics are references to negative affective states or negative self-evaluations, while the positive ones are in normal font. I will focus here on the three most frequent affective states/emotions and the three most frequent descriptions of self. This is primarily to avoid repetition, as most of these categories reappear in the concordance lines of self-descriptions. Additionally, if expressions belonging to a particular semantic field are used in reference to Plath very infrequently (i.e. fewer than eleven times, as outlined in Section 4.2), then they are not considered major patterns.

The most frequently mentioned affective states/emotions in Table 5.1 are that of fear, happiness and sadness. In these top three, there are twice as many references to negative affective states as to positive ones, suggesting that Plath writes more about the former. This is echoed, though not as markedly, in the overall proportion of references to positive and negative affective states. Approximately 60 per cent of all references to affective states and self-descriptions identified in this automated search are negatively valenced.

Fear is an emotion that usually requires a trigger – something to be afraid of. However, Power and Dalgleish (1997) note that the trigger can be a mental event, for example, the belief that there is danger. In the Smith Journal the trigger of fear is sometimes specified. At various points in the Smith Journal Plath is afraid of:

- facing her housemates
- facing herself

- being dominated by a future spouse
- marriage and love
- being left by people around her
- responsibility
- letting her emotions show
- not having enough time to do all that she wants to
- failures both in the past and in the future

This list is quite extensive on its own, but it also seems to include all aspects of life. She fears social encounters but also solitude. She fears the future but also the present (responsibility) and the effect of past accomplishments and failures. In addition, there are several references to fear without a specified trigger, for example, *I am afraid*. Plath seems to be dominated by fear in a myriad of ways. References to happiness, although second in frequency, do not seem to be all-encompassing in the same way. Plath refers to being happy (usually temporarily) or finding delight in particular activities, events or people. For example, *I was so overjoyed by the fact I would save my face (what a flabby character I am) by being out of the house with a male on Saturday night*; or *There is a certain unique and strange delight about walking down an empty street alone*. A similar pattern can be seen for *glad*, which appears under the USAS category of 'content'.

Expressions in E4.1– ('sadness') include references to being sad, depressed, jealous, embarrassed, desperate and regretful. Jealousy often seems directed at those whom Plath perceives to have an easier life and more opportunities (*I am jealous of men*; *animal jealousy of other attractive women*). Regret, on the other hand, seems less specific. Aside from regretting being born, regret is presented as a persistent state rather than trigger specific.

The three most common self-ascribed traits in the Smith Journal are selfishness, intelligence and weakness. In the 'selfish' semantic field, Plath often refers explicitly to her ego or vanity (*and my ego was satiated*; *your vanity is hurt*). These examples are not necessarily negative, since most people are self-interested to some extent. However, Plath thinks that selfishness hinders her professionally. This is most marked in the following example (capitalization is in the original): *CAN A SELFISH EGOCENTRIC JEALOUS AND UNIMAGITIVE [sic] FEMALE WRITE A DAMN THING WORTH WHILE?*

In terms of a more positive self-image, Plath occasionally acknowledges her own intelligence and abilities. Under 'able/intelligent' there are examples such as *I am not a cretin*; *I know I am capable of getting good marks/attracting males*; *I have been gifted with five senses*; *I am capable of love again*; *use my intelligence and pragmatism*. Some of these examples, interestingly, refer to very basic abilities, which Plath nevertheless seems to consider worth mentioning (e.g. *capable of love/attracting males*; *gifted with five senses*). Plath also often considers herself weak, both in the physical and in the psychological sense: *I am not strong*; *I feel stifled, weak, pallid*; *I am weak*; *I felt too vulnerable*. This feeling sometimes stems from being a woman in opposition to men, but it sometimes does not have a specific trigger. Her weakness often prevents her from action similar to the fear discussed above.

Based on these examples, Plath seems to see herself in conflicting ways. She is sometimes strong, at other times weak; she is sad, but also happy; she is fearful, but also brave. This, in itself, seems intuitively normal. What is potentially unusual is the ratio of positive to negative affective states and self-descriptions. Plath feels and sees herself more negatively than positively.

I would like to briefly return to negation, which necessitated the adjusted frequency column in Table 5.1. Negation in examples such as *I am not a cretin*, implies that somebody somewhere expects the opposite of the statement to be true. After all, there are an infinite number of things that are not the case, so singling one of these out must be meaningful (Jeffries 2009). Negation is 'most frequently used to correct states of affairs assumed by the speaker to be either shared knowledge or to represent the commonest ones to be expected in the contextual situation' (Ramat 2006: 7114). Plath uses negation in a similar way in many of the semantic categories above. For example, *I am not strong enough* suggests weakness; *I am not stupid* means intelligent; *I will never quite fulfil* means failure. Hidalgo-Downing comments that, because of this, negation 'makes non-events and non-states more salient than events and states and is thus a natural foregrounding device' (Hidalgo-Downing 2003: 321). This means that all of these cases stand out and suggests that Plath assumes that the opposite of what she says is either true or contextually appropriate, that is, she should be strong but is not. These tendencies may indicate low self-esteem and are touched on again in Chapter 8.

5.2 Self-description: *I am* and *You are*

In this section, I turn to references to the self and its states in the form of the CLAWS categories VBM (*'m* and *am*) and VBDZ (*was*) in the Smith Journal. These capture instances of *I'm*, *I am*, *I was* where *I* refers to Plath. I also explore

:l spots .) So I will prove to him I	am	not the shy respectable naive fool he thi
, and I , drowsing on his shoulder ,	am	very glad to see the dark road and the le
k road and the leaves all around . I	am	sleepy and feel very sexy in my black vel
njoy being kissed for what it is . I	am	growing quite warm and desiring , and his
d n't think you would be . I guess I	am	trying to prove something . We have n't g
s I wanted to . To hell with him . I	am	not a tease , nor a whore he could go hom
course , just a halfway deal . But I	am	not yet the smart woman who can keep her
address) I listened to him say : I	am	not just going to sit here and watch you
e are scholarships , fellowships ; I	am	young , husky , and eager to work . Probl
l do graduate work in Philosophy . I	am	going to do it . Main fear , nagging : me
do it . Main fear , nagging : men I	am	in love with two brothers , embarrassingl
ssingly so . I will leave . Unless I	am	lucky , both may give way to marrying whi
oth may give way to marrying while I	am	gone so I will come back to a big void .
tonight , oh god , (I think) that I	am	mortal , unthinking , unworthy and that the
thless , and though love be a day , I	am	afraid it will be only that ; and though lc
y that ; and though love be a day , I	am	afraid also that it will be more . what to
ey to do anything more with because I	am	buying clothes because I love them and they
se I had whittled out for my life . I	am	lucky : I am at Smith because I wanted it e
tled out for my life . I am lucky : I	am	at Smith because I wanted it and worked for
cause I wanted it and worked for it I	am	going to be a Guest Editor on Mlle in June
use I wanted it and worked for it . I	am	being published in Harper 's because I want
ty by the work . But now , although I	am	a pragmatic machiavellian at heart , I finc
eath of the wheels I will be safe . I	am	very tired , very banal , very confused . I
, very confused . I do not know who I	am	tonight . I wanted to walk until I dropped
acrifice the time . People know who I	am	, and the harder I try to know who they are
sentences , let me someday see who I	am	and why I accept 4 years of food , shelter
ithout questioning more than I do . I	am	tired , banal , and now I am getting not or
I do . I am tired , banal , and now I	am	getting not only monosyllabic but also taut
hich can never happen to me because I	am	I which spells invulnerable .) Over orange
desire to retreat into not caring . I	am	incapable of loving or feeling now : self-i

Concordance 11 VBM in the whole of the Smith Journal/331.

the tags VBR (*'re, are*) and VBDR (*were*) in entries that are written using the second-person pronoun to refer to Plath.

Concordance 11 above shows 30 randomly selected instances of *I am* out of 331 in the Smith Journal, while Concordance 12 shows a random 17/76 instances of *you are* in second-person entries. The verb *to be* combined with the relevant pronouns in these cases results in self-descriptions. Note that some of the concordance lines (in particular for *you are*) include interesting metaphorical references to the self. These are discussed in Chapter 6.

Over 85 per cent of the 331 concordance lines for VBM refer to Plath and about a third of these uses of VBM are relational process types (i.e. do not occur as part of compound verbs), as in *I am scared*. Of these, approximately 55 per cent are negative self-descriptions, while fewer than 40 per cent are positive. There are also some neutral descriptions such as *I am young* (line 9 above) where the attribute does not have an obvious valence. Examples of positive self-descriptions include: I am … *content, gay, lucky, not scared, worthwhile, active, glad, maternal, not a tease or a whore, entranced.* Examples of negative self-descriptions are: I am … *jealous, not content, naïve, weak, obsessed, not sure, ugly, lost, frightened,*

1	mutual wounds . More often you	are	too sickened to fight back , because you
	g as she . More so , since you	are	so small that you ca n't be magnanimous b
	nnocence wo n't help you ; you	're	done . But then you 're on top , shaking
	. So you try to be basic . You	are	such a basic character yourself , anyway
5	you 're eighteen , because you	're	still vulnerable , because you still do n
	le for all your fat nose , you	're	quite a presentable long and lithe piece
	later and later . . . and you	are	n't the sort of human being that can writ
	hild Hemingway , but God , you	are	growing up . In other words , you 've com
	ur grip on creative life . You	are	becoming a neuter machine . You can not l
10	, and secretarial files . You	are	an inconsistent and very frightened hypoc
	months of god-awful time , you	are	paralyzed , shocked , thrown into a nause
	rse after course : when if you	are	anybody , which you are no doubt not , yo
	if you are anybody , which you	are	no doubt not , you should not be bored ,
	ds and ideas on your own . You	are	frozen mentally scared to get going , eag
15	rice of getting to know if you	are	clever enough to write &; improvise anyho
	for that . a.m . Right now you	are	sick in your head . You have called Narci
	talk &; friends . You fool you	are	afraid of being alone with you own mind .

Concordance 12 VBR/76.

not yet the smart woman. The use of negation mentioned in the previous section is also apparent in some of these examples.

For the CLAWS tag VBDZ (was), only about 25 per cent of 448 instances referred to Plath and, of these, even fewer are self-descriptions. Just under 50 per cent of these were positive self-descriptions such as: I was ... *all right, tall, light-haired, sure of my looks, overjoyed, gay and tanned and glowing, happier, so ecstatic*. Just over 50 per cent were negative self-descriptions (e.g. I was ... *still weak, alone, jealous, nauseated, glum, morose, critical, afraid*). This is similar to the proportions described for VBM (I am) above.

The proportion of negative and positive self-descriptions in second-person entries is markedly different from the proportion in the Smith Journal overall. As Concordance 12 shows, almost all self-references using *you* are negative in some way. Focusing only on the direct (albeit slightly hyperbolic ones): you are ... *vulnerable*; *a hypocrite*; *afraid*; *if you are anybody which you are no doubt not*. In second-person entries (which constitute 10 per cent of the Smith Journal), over 75 per cent of *you are/you're* that refer to Plath express something negative or at least self-doubting/questioning (e.g. line 15). Additionally, only one of the self-descriptions in these entries suggests anything explicitly positive (line 6 above). This pattern is also apparent in the CLAWS category VBDR (you were).

This is a strong contrast to the proportions described for the whole Smith Journal (about 55 per cent of self-descriptions are negative; approximately 40 per cent are positive) and suggests that when Plath refers to herself in the second person, she has a more negative self-image than when she writes about herself in the first person. This is investigated further in Chapter 7.

5.3 Qualitative analysis of a set of sample entries

In this section, I build on the results of the quantitative analysis above by discussing a manual intensive analysis of eighteen sample entries. I begin with a description of the sample selection before addressing the findings.

5.3.1 The sample

I selected the sample entries for manual intensive analysis in this chapter (and in Chapter 6 on metaphorical references) through a slightly unorthodox process, in order to avoid any bias that I may have developed as a result of familiarity with the text. I used the index of *The Unabridged Journals of Sylvia Plath* as a source of information for deciding which entries of the Smith Journal to focus on in detail. The index contains almost 100 entries under the general heading *Plath, Sylvia* such as *adolescence of*; *clothes of*; *emotions of*; *sexual experiences of* etc., listing those pages where these topics are discussed in the journal (see Figure 5.1).

A number of these index entries allude to, or explicitly mention, moods, feelings, affective states and self-descriptions (e.g. introspection, personality traits). I matched page numbers suggested by the index entries to journal entries. For instance, the index reflected that 'suicidal thoughts' occur on page 186 of the text. This corresponds to Entry July 6, so I tagged Entry July 6 with *suicidality*. The process was repeated for any other relevant index headings that also pointed to July 6. Any journal entries with more than one tag (e.g. Entry 188 was tagged for *depression, introspection* and *suicidality* based on the index) were contenders for the sample.

The relevant index entries under the general heading *Plath, Sylvia* are

- depression, feelings of;
- emotions of;
- fears of;
- introspection of;
- loneliness of;
- madness, feelings of;
- panic, feelings of;
- personality traits (introversion, negativism, sensitivity);
- self-confidence;
- self-perception; and
- suicidal feelings and fantasies of.

Plath, Sylvia
abortions of, *see* Pregnancies and childbirths of SP
adolescence of, 65–6
airplane rides of, 156
appendectomy of, 530, 531, 599–608
archives of: at Indiana University, 676n, 698, 699; at Smith College, 689, 695, 703

[...]

emotions of
anger, 176, 226, 233–4, 243, 250, 285, 292, 307, 309–10, 317–18, 339, 392, 394–5, 399, 413–15, 420, 437–8, 444, 447, 462, 484, 558, 583, 616, 635, 642, 646, 651; *see also* Plath, Aurelia (SP's anger at)
crying, 11, 18–19, 21, 70, 84–5, 130, 149–51, 152–3, 176, 195, 223–4, 226, 227, 230, 360, 372, 397, 403, 405, 446, 448, 459–60, 467, 473, 475, 501, 515, 553, 559, 561, 566–7, 600, 636, 673
happiness, 8, 51, 59, 67, 70, 91, 96, 132, 140–2, 148, 158–60, 177–8, 179–80, 198, 204, 226, 230–2, 249, 271, 290, 310, 331–2, 366, 371, 413, 422–3, 441, 455, 463, 466–7, 486–7, 491, 525, 527, 528–9, 554, 557, 601–2, 605
jealousy and envy, 20, 34, 98–101, 144–5, 149–50, 152, 185, 187, 199, 215, 295, 315, 317–18, 334, 390–1, 446, 454, 464, 484, 519, 520, 543, 544, 545, 620

Figure 5.1 Excerpt from the index of *The Unabridged Journals of Sylvia Plath.*

The eighteen entries selected for analysis on this basis are numbers 33, 36, 38, 46, 82, 104, 117, 118, 128, 138, 154, 155, 157, 181, 186, 188, July 6 and July 14. The following events take place in these journal entries:

- Entry 33: Plath sits in the library and muses about who she is.
- Entry 36: Plath drives back to university with friends after Thanksgiving.
- Entry 38: She thinks that she should be happy.
- Entry 46: She muses on the nature of life and wishes to live more than one.
- Entry 82: She describes an afternoon at the Cape with friends.
- Entry 104: She describes feeling blocked and trapped.
- Entry 117: She reflects on her experience of working as a mother's helper over the summer.
- Entry 118: She talks about the quick passage of time and saying goodbye to people.

- Entry 128: She is recovering from an illness and gets herself out of her summer job (but regrets it later).
- Entry 138: Plath lists past achievements.
- Entry 154: She seems to express frustration, fear and despair.
- Entry 155: Plath rationalizes her breakdown and appears to be taking control of her life with concrete plans of how to tackle the tasks at hand.
- Entry 157: Plath reflects on a past emotional crisis and her relationship with Dick.
- Entry 181: She describes waiting for and finally meeting Myron – descriptions of passionate kissing.
- Entry 186: Myron has kissed another girl. This prompts some unflattering descriptions of marriage.
- Entry 188: She mentions how lucky she is and muses on love, exhaustion, identity and her reasons for writing.
- Entries July 6, 1953 and July 14: These final two entries are in close chronological proximity to each other and only a month before Plath tried to commit suicide. Plath describes *running away* from herself, in order to escape responsibility. She contemplates suicide explicitly.

5.3.2 Findings

What seems apparent from the corpus analysis above is that, in general, Plath writes about negative affective states slightly more than positive ones, and her self-descriptions are also more often negative. The proportions vary across the Smith Journal, but this is the general trend. The manual analysis confirmed these initial findings. In fact, in the eighteen entries, only about 20 per cent of the identified references to affective states and the self are positive. Examples include:

- *I have been gifted with five senses and an attractive exterior*
- *Tan, tall, blondish, not half bad*
- *I feel a new eagerness*
- *reasonably healthy and attractive, alive, thinking, tall, sensuous, powerful, colourful white woman, age 21*

Some of these have already been mentioned in the corpus-based investigation. The final example here is interesting as it reads almost like a personal ad – albeit a very modest one. Similar to what was noted above, the positive characteristics mentioned seem to be quite basic, for example, *alive*, *thinking*. *Alive* in particular seems to function akin to negation in the sense that mentioning it only makes sense if the opposite was assumed. This could also be interpreted in terms of the Gricean (1975) conversational maxims. Mentioning *alive* and *thinking* flouts the maxim of relation: it would only be relevant to point these out if somebody assumed/stated that the opposite was true. Given that they are mentioned, one has to assume precisely this conversational implicature. In some ways, a similar argument can be made for *five senses* in the first point in the list above.

The vast majority of self-descriptions and direct references to affective states in the eighteen sample entries, however, are negative. There are references to Plath being *scared*, *alone*, *exhausted*, *angry*, *glum*, *jealous*, *bored*, *ugly* etc. In addition, there are several references to self-directed hatred. These did not stand out in the corpus analysis but seem to recur in the sample entries.

- *I hate myself for not being able to go downstairs naturally*
- *despising yourself for your tremulous sensitivity*
- *I cursed myself*
- *I am drowning in negativism, self-hate, doubt, madness*

As these examples did not stand out in the corpus analysis, the semantic category E2– 'Dislike' was additionally explored. Of fifty-eight concordance lines, twenty-one referred to Plath – she hates someone or something. Of these twenty-one, in six (almost a third) cases she describes hating herself.

Of course, the disproportionately frequent references to negative affective states and self-perceptions in these eighteen entries might be due to the methodology for selection outlined above. It was generally the case that when an entry was tagged for more than one affective state, then at least one of those tags was for something negatively valenced. Whenever 'happy' occurred as an index entry, it was always the only tag for that particular journal entry, and these were excluded from the sample. In terms of relative proportions of positive and negative references, this suggests that the proportions identified in the corpus analysis are more accurate. While the manual intensive analysis suggests that only 20 per cent of references to affective states and the self are positive, the overall proportion in the Smith Journal is actually around 40 per cent.

Although the manual intensive analysis may be misleading in terms of proportions, it was useful in highlighting one other type of reference that may be relevant to affective states: self-questioning.

5.3.3 Questions about the self

Questions in general are not significantly overused in the Smith Journal – they do not come up as key in the corpus comparison with the SWTP corpus (an LL calculation was performed for the number of question marks in both corpora). However, some types of questions stood out in the manual intensive analysis:

- *God, who am I?*
- *Have you a capacity for love of someone beside yourself? I wonder, sometimes.*
- *Where is the girl that I was last year?*
- *How to justify myself, my bold, brave humanitarian faith?*
- *how many different deaths I can die?) How am I a child? An adult? A woman?*
- *How can I ever find that permanence, that continuity with past and future, that communication with other human beings that I crave?*
- *Will I be a secretary – a self-rationalizing, uninspired housewife, secretly jealous of my husband's ability to grow intellectually & professionally while I am impeded.*

These questions seem to be about the self, as well as directed at the self. In terms of their relevance for affective states, questioning oneself is, at least, a sign of insecurity. This is particularly evident in questions about identity (*who am I?*). Although these types of questions are not necessarily unusual for a person in his or her early twenties, combined with the number of references to fear, they could indicate certain affective tendencies. In addition, questions normally occur within an interaction, where an interlocutor can provide a response. When questions are directed at the self, a dialogic situation is set up which implies two entities where there is only one. The implications of this are elaborated in Chapter 6 and Chapter 7 on metaphor and the personal pronouns, respectively.

5.3.4 Conclusions

This short chapter dealt with direct references to affective states and self-descriptions. In the expressions discussed here, Plath effectively tells her journal how she feels and how she sees herself. Throughout the Smith Journal, there are more negative self-descriptions and references to negative affective states than positive ones. Overall, this suggests a tendency for Plath to perceive herself negatively – self-doubt and even self-hatred seem to be dominant affective states. This trend was more pronounced in second-person entries than in the Smith Journal overall.

While these direct descriptions do not provide a substantial amount of analytic material, they do provide an important frame of reference within which subsequent analyses can be contextualized. With this in mind, the next chapter focuses on metaphorical reference to affective states in the Smith Journal.

6

Affective States and Metaphor

In this chapter, I investigate Plath's experience of her affective states through detailed discussions of metaphorical expressions, as in *My mind is, to use a disgustingly obvious simile, like a wastebasket full of waste paper; bits of hair, and rotting apple cores. I am feeling depressed.* (Entry 38). I also explore the link between the patterns and entailments of Plath's metaphor use and metaphors commonly associated with depression and related mental health problems. There is a substantial amount of literature on the link between emotions, mental health issues etc. and metaphorical language (see, for example, Kövecses 2000, McMullen and Conway 2002, Schoeneman et al. 2004). Emotions and the experience of mental health issues are precisely the types of abstract, subjective, sensitive and sometimes taboo subjects that tend to elicit the use of metaphor (Semino 2008). It is no surprise, then, that the corpus analysis in Chapter 4 revealed that metaphors do indeed occur in relation to the expression of affective states in the Smith Journal.

I begin this chapter with a necessarily brief overview of the literature on figurative language, especially in relation to mental phenomena. This will be followed by a section (6.2) outlining the methodological approaches taken and an investigation of the types of metaphorical expressions and patterns identified in the Smith Journal.

6.1 Introduction to metaphor theory

People do not normally use literal OR figurative language to describe emotions, but tend to use BOTH in order to detail the complexity and intensity associated with them (Gibbs et al. 2002). In fact, it has been noted (Gibbs et al. 2002) that figurative language is particularly important in expressing *nuances* of emotion.

Different types of figurative language, or tropes, can be broadly described as 'lexical or semantic deviations of some kind' (Wales 2001: 398). Prominent examples of tropes include metaphor, metonymy and simile but also hyperbole and irony. Similes are, perhaps, the easiest to identify in language. They can be defined as 'an explicit statement of comparison between two different things, conveyed through expressions such as "like", "as if" and so on' (Semino 2008: 16). The most interesting types of tropes for the present purposes, however, are metaphors and metonymies.

Metaphor, in general, is a 'pervasive linguistic phenomenon, which is varied in its textual manifestations, versatile in the functions it may perform, and central to many different types of communication' (Semino 2008: 1). Ortony (1975) notes that metaphors compactly, efficiently and vividly convey a large amount of information that would be inexpressible literally due to the gap between the discreteness of language as a set of symbols and the continuity/fluidity of experience, which is what needs to be conveyed (Ortony 1975). A prototypical metaphor takes the form of *A is B* as in Plath's *Hell was the Grand Central subway on Sunday morning*. Here, the reference to *the Grand Central subway* is understood as conveying some of the characteristics (presumably, crowded, loud, smelly, unpleasant etc.) that Plath attributes to hell.

In a more recent approach, linguistic metaphors have been defined – and subsequently identified – by the Metaphor Identification Procedure (MIP) (Pragglejaz 2007); for more details, see Section 6.2. In this approach, a metaphor occurs when the contextual meaning of a word or phrase is different from and to be understood in comparison to the basic meaning of the same word or phrase. This definition highlights that metaphors in this context are not necessarily only what ordinary listeners or readers would judge as metaphorical. They also include conventional expressions (see discussion below) used in everyday language that may or may not be understood metaphorically by a lay audience (Steen 2008).

Metonymy is similar to metaphor, but 'metonymy, unlike metaphor, is a "stand-for" relation (i.e. a part stands for the whole or a part stands for another part) within a single domain' (Kövecses 2002b: 5). For example, a car could be described metonymically as *a set of wheels*. However, this should be understood loosely: a metonymic relationship can also arise when something is referred to by an attribute or a semantically related entity (Wales 2001).

Although, at first glance, it appears possible to make clear distinctions between various forms of figurative language, it has repeatedly been noted that such differentiation cannot be discrete and precise (e.g. Goatly 1997, Deignan

2005, Partington 2006). For a start, boundaries between semantic domains are not fixed or clear-cut, making this basis of differentiation between metaphor and metonymy rather imperfect (Steen 2007, Barnden 2010). Barnden (2010) and Steen (2007) also argue that where, traditionally, metaphor was assumed to be based on similarity and metonymy on contiguity, the distinction between contiguity and similarity is actually a matter of degree. In addition, as Goossens (1990) and Deignan (2005) point out, metaphor and metonymy can interact in various ways. Deignan (2005), for example, suggests that many metaphors that have the human body as basis (i.e. something is described in terms of the human body) are based in metonymy. An example is *get back on one's feet* when used to describe recovery after illness. Rather than describing recovery in terms of something else, this expression describes it in terms of a physical manifestation of itself. Ill or infirm people are often weak and have to lie down. Once they are better and regain their strength, they can stand on their feet again.

Bearing this in mind, any subsequent distinctions in this book between primarily metaphorical and primarily metonymic language should be understood as a matter of degree. Where a distinction between metaphor and metonymy is pointed out, it should be understood as a shorthand way of denoting tendencies rather than a strict differentiation.

6.1.1 Cognitive metaphor theory – an approach to metaphor

One of the most influential theories of metaphor towards the end of the twentieth century was CMT. Broadly speaking, CMT focuses on frequent and ubiquitous patterns of metaphorical language and assumes that these reflect patterns of thought. The frequent and ubiquitous patterns in language are known as linguistic metaphors, and the supposed underlying thought patterns are called conceptual metaphors. The fundamental difference between CMT and more traditional approaches to metaphor is this focus on thought patterns rather than language. In fact, linguistic manifestations are seen as secondary. The definition of metaphor that CMT adopts reflects this approach: metaphor is a way of '*understanding* one conceptual domain in terms of another conceptual domain' (Kövecses 2002b: 4, my emphasis).

The leap from language to thought was popularized primarily by Lakoff and Johnson's *Metaphors We Live By* (1980), but it has been adopted as an operational framework by many (e.g. Goatly 1997, Deignan 2005, Semino 2008, Kövecses 2010 etc.). In simplified terms, CMT assumes that only a few basic concrete concepts can be understood in a literal way. These are generally concepts that can be learnt through sensorimotor experience (Lakoff and Johnson 1980, 1999) such as spatial orientation (up, down, to the side etc.), motion (forwards, backwards, fast, slow etc.) and containment (in, out). Abstract concepts are then understood in terms of these basic literal categories, for example, progress in life is understood as motion forwards. Although CMT is aimed at understanding thought, it relies on linguistic examples for evidence. CMT, therefore, is mainly interested in what it calls *conventional* metaphors – ones that have frequent linguistic manifestations. Only these can be taken to represent underlying conceptual structures.

Linguistic examples are usually grouped according to the semantic fields evoked by their non-metaphorical meanings (the source domain). For example, the abstract concept *time* (target domain) is often described in terms of the more concrete *money* (source domain). Linguistic examples of this phenomenon are aplenty:

Example 11

- This gadget will *save* you hours.
- How do you *spend* your time these days?
- That flat tire *cost* me an hour.
- I have *invested* a lot of time in her.
  (adapted from Lakoff and Johnson 1980)

These expressions are said to realize the conceptual metaphor (denoted by small capitals) TIME IS MONEY (Lakoff and Johnson 1980). Lakoff and Johnson (1980), Kövecses (2010) and others provide helpful lists of frequently cited conceptual metaphors.[1]

Conventional conceptual metaphors are thought to come about by two main means: through perceived similarity (resemblance) and experiential correlation (Grady 1999). For example, parental love may be described in terms of warmth, because an infant's experience of being cuddled coincides with an increase in experienced temperature (Grady 1997a). LOVE IS WARM, then, is a conceptual metaphor based on experiential correlation, which can occur in a number of linguistic forms (linguistic metaphors). On the other hand, Grady (1999) cites *Achilles is a lion* as an example of a metaphor that cannot be motivated by experience (since most people do not have much experience with lions). Examples such as this can be explained by some perceived similarity (Grady calls this the *resemblance hypothesis*) in the characteristics or behaviour of the two entities. In this case, the perceived similarity could be in the way dangers are confronted (which can be interpreted as courage).

Because CMT assumes that metaphors are central to thought, it also postulates that they are used to reason with (Lakoff and Johnson 1999). This notion is particularly relevant for the analysis of metaphors of affective states. If metaphors are indeed used for reasoning, then the entailments of metaphors used to convey such states and their various aspects may also influence reactions and behaviours.

The basic tenets of CMT undoubtedly have intuitive appeal. Nevertheless, various aspects of the theory have been criticized, not least due to a strong need for mitigation in some of its assertions. For example, while it is CMT's focus on conventional metaphorical expressions, as in Example 11, that constitute its originality (Semino 2008), it has repeatedly been pointed out that its examples were elicited from informants or constructed by the researcher and not taken from naturally occurring data (Deignan 2005, Semino 2008). Such personal intuitions about language are known to be unreliable, and informants have a tendency to produce examples that are rare (Deignan 2005).

It has also been pointed out that the relationship between linguistic manifestations of metaphors and the thought processes these are said to represent is not straightforward (Steen 1999, Deignan 2005, Semino 2008). There is no widely accepted methodology for moving from the linguistic to the conceptual level (see Steen 1999, for one attempt). Casasanto (2008b), like Steen and Gibbs (1999), argues that cognitive linguists have to be careful with how far they can interpret and generalize from examining linguistic manifestations of conceptual metaphors. In fact, Crawford states that one of the main issues in cognitive psychology and linguistics continues to be whether linguistic metaphors reflect a 'deeper principle of cognition' at all (Crawford 2009: 129). While corpus studies in linguistics (e.g. Deignan 2005, Stefanowitsch 2006) have contributed greatly to this debate, this means that the question Lakoff and Johnson purport to have answered almost thirty years earlier is still being asked.

While these critiques still stand to some extent, CMT has also benefited from developments in cognitive linguistics over the last few decades. Tolaas (1991), for example, has suggested an evolutionary basis for spatial metaphors (near-far; up-down). Spatial concepts stem from the fact that the human body has a central nervous system (which perceives) and is located in a gravitational field (which serves for spatial orientation), so, for an infant, certain basic experiences correlate with certain spatial locations. For example,

- light comes from above (giving rise to the LIGHT IS UP conceptual mapping);

- parents – the source of food, love and care – are higher up than the child (leading to GOOD IS UP and putting the two together, GOOD IS LIGHT);
- parents can only give love when they are physically close (EMOTIONAL CLOSENESS IS SPATIAL NEARNESS); etc.

In addition, Tolaas suggests that the positive associations of light and the negative associations of dark may have an evolutionary basis because humans depend on vision for survival: vision only functions in the light.

In another important contribution, Grady (1997b) notes that not all metaphors are grounded in sensorimotor experience. Instead, he proposes a distinction between what he calls *primary* and *compound* metaphors. The former are based on sensorimotor experience, and the latter are said to be made up of a combination of primary ones. Compound metaphors (such as TIME IS MONEY discussed above), therefore, do not have to be explained in terms of identifiable sensorimotor experiences if their constituent parts (primary metaphors) can be. This distinction contributes to explaining how one can arrive from linguistic to conceptual metaphors.

But perhaps the strongest support for the validity of certain claims in CMT comes from the work of Daniel Casasanto. For example, at least a weak version of linguistic relativity is involved in CMT's claim that language is central to thought. Linguistic relativity (also called *Sapir-Whorf* or *Whorfian Hypothesis*) states that 'the structure and lexicon of one's language influences how one perceives and conceptualizes the world, and they do so in a systematic way' (Swoyer 2008). Casasanto (2008b) tests this underlying assumption by comparing the time perception of Greek and English speakers. The English language strongly prefers to express time in terms of distance, while Greek has a preference for expressing time in terms of volume. In order to test whether English and Greek speakers think about time differently, candidates were asked to estimate the duration of short events, while being presented with potentially distracting visual information about linear distance or amount/volume (for more detailed information, see Casasanto 2008b).

The results showed that distractions of volume interfered with Greek speakers' temporal estimation accuracy, but not with English speakers'. The same was true vice versa for the distance distraction. This indicated that people's mental representation of time covaries with the way it is expressed in their native language. However, Casasanto conducted another experiment where some English native speakers were 'primed' for conceptualizations in terms of volume. After such priming, their performance 'was statistically indistinguishable from the performance of the native Greek speakers' (Casasanto 2008b: 75), demonstrating that while the way people think may reflect the way they speak, this link is not fixed, or 'hard-wired'.

Given these developments, in this book a certain link between language use and thought is assumed to exist. However, I acknowledge that the precise nature of this link is not yet entirely understood. It also follows that the nature of the connection between linguistic and conceptual metaphors cannot be determined with certainty. I therefore move on to a framework that allows one to claim a more modest position and proposes a more explicit methodology.

6.1.2 Systematic metaphor – an alternative approach

Cameron's 'systematic metaphor' approach acknowledges the necessarily tentative nature of inferences drawn about thought from language (Cameron 2008b). 'A "systematic metaphor" is a set of linguistic metaphors in which connected vehicle words or phrases are used metaphorically about a particular topic' (Cameron et al. 2010: 127). In other words, systematic metaphors describe more or less persistent patterns of vehicles and topics (what in CMT are source and target domains) in a particular discourse. Although systematic metaphors often resemble conceptual metaphors, they do not make claims about the cognitive reality of metaphorical patterns. They only suggest that there may be a cognitive basis for them. Cameron recommends that systematic metaphors be used as 'a discourse alternative to "conceptual metaphor"' (Cameron 2008b: 57). She also notes that they may be useful in distinguishing between established conceptual mappings and mappings that seem to be the product of a specific individual (Cameron 2008a).

Broadly speaking, systematic metaphors are based on the identification of individual metaphors via the MIP (Pragglejaz 2007). Once individual metaphors are identified in a particular discourse, they are grouped according to broad vehicle domains. They are then also grouped according to topics (or target domains). The authors note that metaphor topics are not always easy to identify (sometimes they may be explicit in the discourse, but not normally). However, they suggest that a potential way of rationalizing this process is to use a reduced/predefined set of topics (so-called key discourse topics) that emerge from research questions. The co-text of metaphorical expressions is seen as helpful in identifying metaphor topics.

Labels chosen for systematic metaphors aim to reflect the actual words in the discourse as closely as possible and are denoted by *SMALL ITALIC CAPITALS*.

This demonstrates their link to, but also their difference from, traditional CMT conceptual metaphors. Cameron et al. (2010) acknowledge that this interpretative process is necessarily subjective, and therefore they urge flexibility and repeated review of the connections/labels identified. They argue that categories of vehicle domains may and should be allowed to evolve with increasing numbers of linguistic examples.

Systematic metaphors rather than conceptual metaphors seem particularly appropriate for this book. As discussed previously, the Smith Journal can in no way be seen as a broad, heterogeneous data set. While this has some advantages (for corpus methods, for example), it makes any results less generalizable. As such, the metaphorical patterns described in the subsequent analysis are best understood as systematic metaphors specific to the discourse at hand.

I now turn to a discussion of figurative language conventionally used to convey affective states and emotions.

6.1.3 Metaphor and affective states

One of the most important studies in this area is Kövecses' (2000) *Metaphor and Emotion*. Kövecses (2000) argues that emotions are mainly expressed and understood in terms of comparisons to other domains or in terms of stand-for relationships of their physical characteristics, or both. He divides emotion language in English into the following categories:

- Expressive words such as *yuk!* (in disgust), *wow!* (in surprise) *shit!* (in anger) that express an emotion without naming it
- Words like *happiness, joy, frustration, shame* etc. that actually give names to or label emotions, are therefore descriptive and non-figurative (although certain descriptive terms may also be expressive, e.g. *I love you*)
- Figurative language

Figurative language can be seen as another type of descriptive language, which expresses not only the emotion, but something about it as well – it describes emotions in their various aspects such as intensity, cause, control and duration. Kövecses (2000) argues that there is a group of conceptual metaphors generically associated with a number of 'basic'[2] emotions such as anger, love, sadness, happiness, fear, shame etc. (albeit, the conceptual metaphors may not be unique to emotions):

> The generic metaphor [of emotion] speakers of English (and other languages as well) most heavily rely on in understanding what the emotions are is EMOTION IS A FORCE. [...] This particular conceptualization goes with a certain logic. For ordinary people emotions are FORCES that emerge independently of a rational and conscious self as a result of certain causes, and that, in most cases, have to be kept under control. (Kövecses 2002a: 112)

Other conventional conceptual metaphors for emotions generally include EMOTION AS

- SOMETHING IN A CONTAINER (*the sight filled her with fear*)
- LIVING ORGANISM[3] (*he drowned his sorrow in drink*)
- NATURAL/PHYSICAL FORCE (*to be swept off ones feet; to be burning with love*)
- SOCIAL SUPERIOR (*to be ruled by love*)
- an OPPONENT (*to struggle with depression*)
- a CAPTIVE ANIMAL (*his joy broke loose*) – the last three are, of course, also manifestations of the FORCE concept
- INSANITY (*the man was insane with rage*)
- a DIVIDED SELF (*to be beside oneself*)
- BURDEN (*he staggered under the pain*) and
- an ILLNESS (*to be sick with fright*) (examples adapted from Kövecses, 2000).

Kövecses (2000) also identifies mappings that are more specific to individual emotions. For example, emotion-specific metaphors for fear appear to be FEAR IS A HIDDEN ENEMY (*fear slowly crept up on him*) and FEAR IS A SUPERNATURAL BEING (*she was haunted by fear*), while the most specific metaphors of happiness seem to be ANIMAL THAT LIVES WELL (*he looks like the cat that got the cream*) and PLEASURABLE PHYSICAL SENSATION (*I was tickled pink*) and LIGHT and UP (*so see the bright side; to cheer someone up*) (Kövecses 2000). By contrast, the specific metaphors of sadness are the same as those for happiness, but in the opposite form. For example, *I'm feeling down today* (SADNESS IS DOWN) and *to be in a dark mood* (DARKNESS).

In addition to identifying general and specific mappings associated with these (and other) emotions, Kövecses (2000) also discusses some mappings/metaphors that are used to express the various aspects of emotions. Kövecses (2000) makes explicit that emotion concepts tend to be considered in terms of a sequence of events. They make use of the EVENT STRUCTURE metaphor, which in general progresses from the cause of an emotion, to the emotion (with all its physical and psychological elements), to an attempt to control emotion and, finally, to a loss of control, and retribution (or reaction). These different aspects of emotions tend to have their own typical conceptual metaphors. For example, control can be expressed via the NATURAL/PHYSICAL FORCE, OPPONENT, CAPTIVE ANIMAL, FLUID IN A CONTAINER, INSANITY, MAGIC, SUPERIOR, INCOMPLETE OBJECT, RAPTURE/HIGH metaphors (e.g. *she kept her emotions in check*; *his emotions ran away with him*; *she could not hold back her feelings*; *he was overwhelmed*). Intensity, on the other hand, is usually expressed via the CONTAINER (something safely in, or about to burst out of a container), HEAT/FIRE (is something just warm, or burning), NATURAL/PHYSICAL FORCE metaphors.

The relative frequency and novelty of metaphorical expressions for affective states can also be indicative of various aspects of the emotions described. Gibbs et al. (2002) note that metaphors (in particular novel ones) are more frequently used to describe intense emotions than mild ones. Similarly, Ortony and Fainsilber (1987) found that a higher percentage of novel metaphors were used to describe intense emotions than mild ones. They conclude that 'when people are experiencing intense feeling states, they are more likely to generate striking and complex metaphors to explain how they feel' (Ortony and Fainsilber 1987: 183). This suggests that metaphoricity itself could be an indicator of emotional intensity.

Of course, Kövecses (2000) is not alone in having paid special attention to metaphors of affect. Lakoff and Johnson (1980 and 1999), for example, suggest that people's understanding of emotions is also structured by basic metaphorical constructs created through sensorimotor experience. In fact, one could say that metaphors of emotion will often be considered metonymically based. For example, it is generally accepted that the conceptual metaphor EMOTIONS ARE TEMPERATURES is grounded in the physical sensations that accompany various emotions. But, if the temperature rise is essentially part of the experience of an emotion, then conceptualizing emotion in terms of temperature can be seen as the general metonymy A PART FOR THE WHOLE. This metonymy can be seen as informing metaphorical expressions of the EMOTIONS ARE TEMPERATURES concept.

6.1.3.1 Typical metaphors of depression and suicidality

Potential metaphors used to convey depression and suicidal tendencies are also of particular interest, because Sylvia Plath was a diagnosed sufferer of depression and attempted suicide on more than one occasion. As such, her lived experience potentially bears relevance for the experience of depression more broadly. Examples of common metaphors include DEPRESSION AS PAIN/SUFFERING/ILLNESS (Schoeneman et al. 2004); DEPRESSION AS DESCENT; DEPRESSION AS A BOUNDED SPACE (McMullen and Conway 2002).

McMullen and Conway (2002) and Charteris-Black (2012) found that DEPRESSION IS DESCENT was the most frequent metaphor for depression. The metaphor was linked to DEPRESSION AS FEELING DOWN, but it included entailments of descent, such as the idea that going down is easy, effortless and uncontrollable, but going back up is hard and strenuous. Specific examples included *I just really do not want to backslide into the dreary, dismal pit that I was wallowing around in when I first came here*; *down in the catacombs* (McMullen and Conway 2002: 171). McMullen and Conway (2002) point out that the DEPRESSION IS DOWN/DESCENT metaphor (descent implies lack of control as well) is so often used colloquially that even experienced therapists fail to pick up on even evocative manifestations of it (e.g. *dreary, dismal pit*) in therapy sessions.

Another common metaphor for emotions and depression, in particular, is DARKNESS (McMullen and Conway 2002, Charteris-Black 2012). Linguistic manifestations of this source domain often also hide an element of uncontrollability in the way the disease autonomously descends on the sufferer, for example, *It is really like a black cloud* (McMullen and Conway 2002). Metaphors of being weighed down and even slowed down (although this is less often used) are also common, according to the authors. These seem to represent physical changes that happen to people's appearance/body when they are depressed (McMullen and Conway 2002). Another metaphor that McMullen and Conway identified in their study is that of DEPRESSION IS CAPTOR, for example, *when I get depressed, I just am immobilized*; *I feel trapped*; *I want to break out.*

Of course, some of these metaphors of depression are similar to those of emotions in general. The presence or existence of any emotion, for example, is often conceptualized as being in a bounded space – EXISTENCE OF EMOTION IS BEING IN A BOUNDED SPACE (Kövecses 2000). However, Semino (2008) notes that when the emotion or affective state concerned is depression, the figurative space is often unpleasant or difficult to get out of. Charteris-Black (2012) notes that in his data, this metaphor tended to come from a combination of CONTAINMENT and CONSTRAINT metaphors and was actually the second most frequent way patients conceptualized their depression.

In many ways, metaphors of suicide have been found to be similar to those of depression, but they show an absolute lack of control and a lack of energy. Examples provided by Reeves et al. include *can't move forward – really stuck*; *It just feels like I'm stuck in it and it's gone on for ages and it's going to go on for ages – there doesn't feel like there' s any ... any way out of it* (Reeves et al. 2004: 65).

6.1.4 Accounting for metaphorical patterns in language

Aside from the fundamentals of metaphor theory and studies of different metaphors for particular topics or target domains, one also has to account for the ways in which systematic patterns are established and maintained. This requires an account of novelty/creativity and textual patterning.

The conceptual account of creativity states that the most common devices for transforming conventional metaphors into creative ones are extension, elaboration, questioning and composing (Lakoff and Turner 1989). Extension is the expression of a conventional metaphor by 'extending the metaphor to map additional slots' (Lakoff and Turner 1989: 67). Lakoff and Turner (1989) argue that conventional mappings are partial – not every element of the source domain gets mapped onto the target domain. Extension, therefore, is when a normally unused element of the source domain is mapped onto the target domain:

> Two roads diverged in a wood, and I –
> I took the one less travelled by.
> And that has made all the difference. (R. Frost 1916)

Here, the standard metaphor is LIFE IS A JOURNEY, but the extension consists of asserting that any one road can be more or less travelled. This suggests that choices one makes in life can be more or less common.

Elaboration, on the other hand, involves (as the name suggests) elaborating on the source domain in an unusual way and capturing it in a new way or 'filling in slots in an unusual way' (Lakoff and Turner 1989: 67). Usually, this takes the form of specifying an element of the source domain. Lakoff and Turner (1989) provide Horace's description of death as *eternal exile of the raft* as an example of elaboration. This linguistic metaphor makes use of the DEATH IS DEPARTURE conventional mapping but elaborates on it by specifying both the type of departure (exile) and the vehicle (raft) adding 'considerable conceptual content to the metaphor' (Lakoff and Turner 1989: 68).

Questioning transforms conventional metaphors by calling into question their appropriateness and pointing out their limitations (Lakoff and Turner 1989).

Finally, composing (or Combining, in Kövecses 2010) involves adding a number of standard conceptual metaphors to one another to express one concept in a 'composite metaphor' (Lakoff and Turner 1989). For example, *life* or *death* can be expressed using more than one source domain; composing would involve combining two or more of these (in ways that they would not normally be) to produce a richer metaphor.

In addition, Semino (2008) points out that conceptual creativity may also be produced by introducing novel source domains for a particular target domain (which may partly rely on conventional mappings). For this, Semino provides Ian McEwan's *Atonement* (in particular Chapter 6) as an example, where a migraine is described in terms of a dark animal moving inside the head of a character (see Semino (2008) for an extensive discussion of this). She notes that this is 'the linguistic expression of a novel and highly original conceptual metaphor, which is *consistent* with conventional conceptual metaphors, but cannot easily be subsumed under any of them' (Semino 2008: 50).

While Lakoff and Turner (1989) suggest a typology for describing how an expression may be novel/creative, what they do not provide is a 'benchmark' of conventionality, that is, a quantitative way of differentiating between what is conventional and what is novel. Deignan (2005) does precisely this. Deignan (2005) defines metaphor novelty mainly on the basis of corpus frequencies and suggests four points on a cline of metaphoricity:

1. Innovative (or novel) metaphors are ones that are rare (less than once in every 1,000 citations of the word).
2. Conventionalized metaphors are ones where the metaphorical meaning will already be in dictionaries, but the metaphorical meaning is still dependent on the literal (the boundary between these and innovative ones is unclear, and often innovative metaphors eventually become conventionalized).
3. Dead metaphors are where speakers are no longer prompted to think of the literal meaning when they hear these (e.g. *crane* for the machine).
4. Historical metaphors are where the original literal sense of the word has dropped out of usage.

Semino (2011) proposes that a comprehensive account of creativity in metaphor needs to take into account various aspects of context. She proposes three different dimensions that need to be taken into consideration: '(a) the uses of the individual word or multi-word expression, (b) the co-text, and (c) broader patterns of systematicity in the relevant language, which may reflect conventional conceptual metaphors' (Semino 2011: 85). While creativity at the word/multi-word level can be accounted for using Lakoff and Turner's (1989) and Deignan's (2005) frameworks, establishing creativity on the level of co-text requires a different approach.

Accounting for creativity in terms of the dimension of co-text (Semino's point (b) above) can most reasonably be done using Semino's (2008) own framework of textual patterning. Semino argues that creativity in metaphorical language may also stem from 'the establishment of salient patterns of metaphorical expressions within and across texts, involving repetition, recurrence, textual extension, intertextual references and so on' (Semino 2008: 219). She proposes the following framework to describe how metaphorical patterns occur in texts:

- *Repetition* occurs when a particular metaphorical expression is used in a text repeatedly and in the same or similar contextual sense.
- *Recurrence* is defined as 'the use of different expressions relating to the same broad source domain in different parts of a text' (Semino 2008: 23) but not with a similar contextual meaning. Semino provides the examples of <u>*battle*</u> *of metaphors*, <u>*army*</u> *of charity workers* and <u>*combating*</u> *climate change*, where the underlined metaphorical expressions can all be related to the source domain of war, but they are used in different contextual senses (although, broadly speaking, they all refer to difficult enterprises). Such recurrences may be scattered throughout a text.
- *Clustering* occurs when metaphorical expressions from different source domains are close together in a text. This definition is somewhat open to interpretation as identifying 'normal' metaphor density or the number of linguistic metaphors per 1,000 words (Cameron and Low 2004) is not straightforward. It can vary between fifteen and approximately 100 metaphorical words per 1,000.
- *Extension*[4] can be seen as a type of cluster, where at least two metaphorical expressions in close proximity to each other stem from the same broad source domain and relate to the same broad target domain or scenario.

Semino (2008) also discusses *combinations* and *mixing*. The former denotes different metaphorical expressions relating to different target domains occurring close together in a text. The latter refers to instances where contradictory source domains are used to refer to the same target domain. While not all of these patterns necessarily involve creativity, Semino's

(2008) framework can be used to account for systematicity, similar to the methodology of Cameron et al.'s (2010) methodology. However, while Cameron et al. (2010) focus mainly on the existence of patterns, Semino (2008) describes the types of patterns more comprehensively.

6.2 Methods of metaphor analysis

The broad method of metaphor analysis in this book is a combination of quantitative and qualitative techniques. There is an emphasis on the manual/qualitative to enable a thorough and in-depth analysis of the nuances of the metaphorical expressions in the data, but corpus methods are used to substantiate and further explore any findings. A quantitative corpus analysis has three main advantages that allow for a more reliable account of language:

1. A corpus will include words that the researcher may not know.
2. A computer can sort and store large amounts of data that a researcher cannot.
3. Researcher intuitions about language are unreliable (adapted from Deignan 2005).

There are two stages in the procedure: first, a sample of the Smith Journal is analysed manually to identify metaphorical expressions referring to affective states and the self. This is the same sample of eighteen entries that were discussed in Chapter 5. Metaphors are identified using the MIP (Pragglejaz 2007), and the relevant expressions are grouped into broad semantic fields (or source/vehicle domains). In the second stage, the discussion is augmented with quantitative data from corpus explorations of the relevant semantic fields and key terms across the Smith Journal using Wmatrix (Rayson 2009). The automatic search uses a semantic tagger ensuring that the relevant semantic fields, as opposed to just key words, are examined. Any metaphorical expressions discovered during analyses for other parts of this study are also reported on.

6.2.1 Identifying figurative language

Any discussion of metaphor needs to present a clear methodology for identifying metaphorical expressions. For this, I adopt the MIP (Pragglejaz 2007). The Pragglejaz Group proposes the following method to provide analysts with an explicit, systematic and reliable tool for metaphor identification:

1. 'Read the entire text–discourse to establish a general understanding of the meaning.
2. Determine the lexical units in the text–discourse
3.
    a. For each lexical unit in the text, establish its meaning in context, that is, how it applies to an entity, relation or attribute in the situation evoked by the text (contextual meaning). Take into account what comes before and after the lexical unit.
    b. For each lexical unit, determine if it has a more basic contemporary meaning in other contexts than the one in the given context. For our purposes, basic meanings tend to be
        i. More concrete [what they evoke is easier to imagine, see, hear, feel, smell, and taste];
        ii. Related to bodily action;
        iii. More precise (as opposed to vague);
        iv. Historically older;

Basic meanings are not necessarily the most frequent meanings of the lexical unit.

    c. If the lexical unit has a more basic current–contemporary meaning in other contexts than the given context, decide whether the contextual meaning contrasts with the basic meaning but can be understood in comparison with it.
4. If yes, mark the lexical unit as metaphorical.' (Pragglejaz 2007: 3)

As this procedure does not explicitly allow for the identification of metonymies, a slight modification to steps 3c and 4 will be employed. The final two steps will be:

3.
    c. If the lexical unit has a more basic current–contemporary meaning in other contexts than the given context, decide whether the contextual meaning contrasts with the basic meaning but
        i. can be understood in comparison with it; or
        ii. can be understood/explained in terms of association with it

4. If 3c i, mark as metaphorical; if 3c ii, mark as metonymical.

It should also be noted that 3c i and 3c ii are not mutually exclusive – in some examples, both could be true. In such cases, a linguistic expression can be understood as both metaphorical and metonymical. Barnden (n.d.) provides a good example of this. He suggests that *The U.S. believes that* can be understood as metonymical, where *the U.S.* stands for the people of the country – that is understood in association with its basic meaning. However, he argues that the example can also be analysed as metaphorical, where the country is metaphorically regarded as a cognitive agent. In such cases, categorizing something as metaphor or metonymy is not always straightforward.

The MIP involves certain decisions about how to code various metaphorical expressions and what resources can be used for the identification of basic meanings, and the advice is to make such decisions explicit. In this spirit, the identification of basic meanings relies on the online version of the *Oxford English Dictionary* (*OED*) (http://dictionary.oed.com, accessed via MetaLib). This dictionary is updated regularly and includes information about when expressions were first used in particular senses.

A lexical unit is understood as one word or inseparable compound. Such compounds are auxiliary + main verb, personal names/proper nouns, phrasal verbs, fixed collocations and idioms. In an attempt at limiting and somewhat simplifying the analysis of metaphorical expressions, I focus only on lexical words (open-class words) rather than function words. Although Semino notes that prepositions are an exception to this, she states that

> 'Closed-class' words (also known as 'function' or 'grammatical' words) vary in their potential for metaphorical uses […] depending on whether they have enough semantic content to establish a distinction between contextual and basic meanings. (Semino 2008: 18)

As the case may be, investigating only lexical words does not result in too much of an omission, since the majority of metaphorical expressions are nouns or verbs (Goatly 1997, Cameron 2003, Semino 2008). In the same vein, I exclude delexicalized/grammaticalized (Hopper and Traugott 2003) words such as *have*, *do*, *give*, *take*, *make*, *get*, *put* and *like* (Deignan 2005). These verbs arguably also lack sufficient semantic content to be able to establish basic and contextual meanings. A similar difficulty is also apparent in dead and historic metaphors (Deignan 2005) where the original literal sense is no longer in use. MIP requires the basic meanings to be in current use, so these types of metaphors are also excluded. Prepositional adverbs such as *up*, *down*, *back*, *forward* etc. are coded, however. They are different from prepositions in that they have more clearly identifiable basic meanings and have been shown to be important, specifically in the expression of emotions (Kövecses 2000).

These coding decisions, to some extent, reflect an interest in more creative/novel metaphorical expressions. This can be justified in two ways. First, it enables me to do justice to the data at hand, which is rich in complex and novel metaphorical patterns. Secondly, the aim of the analysis is to investigate specifically what Plath's metaphorical language use conveys about her affective states and experience and how it does so. With most highly conventional metaphorical expressions (such as 'felt' in *I felt sad* or 'in' in *she is in love*), it is difficult to even imagine a different way of expressing the same affective state. As such, these expressions may be less representative of particular topics and more representative of standard conceptualizations in a particular language and culture. There is little or no element of choice. On the other hand, with less conventional metaphorical expressions the linguistic options are more open. Therefore, the actual choices that have been made can be taken as more of a reflection of the topic at hand.

6.2.1.1 Metaphor analysis and corpus methods

At the time of writing, no single corpus software exists that can automatically perform metaphor analysis. Metaphorical expressions, after all, do not have a specific linguistic form and are extremely context dependent. Nevertheless, corpus linguistic tools can be used and adapted effectively for investigating metaphor, in particular for identifying the presence of conceptual mappings. 'The first problem that any corpus-based analysis faces is that of identifying and extracting the relevant data from the corpus' (Stefanowitsch 2006: 1). Stefanowitsch suggests that a combination of the following strategies is likely to yield the best results:

a. searching for source domain vocabulary
b. then searching for target domain vocabulary

This combination adheres to the data-driven approach advocated by Rayson (2008). In the case of a search for source domain vocabulary, the choice of key lexis can be based on a priori decisions, pre-existing lists, a preliminary keyword analysis of texts dealing with target domain topics, or indeed a qualitative/manual intensive analysis of a sample data set. Searching for target domain lexis is particularly useful when research is focused on a particular target domain (Stefanowitsch 2006). In such cases, source domain searches are less likely to be successful, as they require a priori knowledge about what is likely to be in the source domain vocabulary. Successful target domain searches begin by selecting and searching for lexical items directly related to the target domain concepts (Stefanowitsch 2006). In the case of the Wmatrix software (Rayson 2009), this can be achieved by exploring relevant semantic fields and identifying examples that contain metaphorical expressions using MIP.

6.2.2 Which metaphors are relevant for affective states?

Broadly speaking, almost any example of language (e.g. description of physical appearance or behaviour) can lead to inferences about affective states (Palmer 2004). However, what I am particularly interested in here are expressions more explicitly related to these states. For the current purposes, metaphorical expressions can be taken to be relevant to affective states if they describe feelings or valenced perceptions of the environment and their effects on the self. These expressions can be preceded/indicated by the use of mental process verbs as well as relational processes (Halliday 1994). For example, the underlined words in *I look at the hell I am wallowing in, nerves paralyzed, action nullified*, can be understood to refer to affective states. Furthermore, metaphorical expressions can be taken to relate to affective states if they include references to physical actions and states where, contextually, it is clear that the actions and states are mental (this, incidentally, is what makes them metaphorical) (e.g. *shutting yourself up in a numb defensive vacuum*). Metaphorical self-descriptions will also be considered. This rests on the assumption that a person's view of themselves is dependent, at least to some extent, on their state of mind (Rodriguez et al. 2010).

6.3 Metaphors of affective states in the Smith Journal

In this section of the chapter, I zoom in on the metaphorical expressions and patterns in the Smith Journal and discuss what they reveal about how Plath experienced her affective states. I also comment on connections between her patterns of metaphor use and metaphors commonly associated with depression and related disorders such as suicidal ideation. As Plath was diagnosed with depression, her lived experience potentially bears relevance for the experience of depression more broadly.

Although I explore all patterns related to affective states, it is apparent from even a passing glance at the data that the focus is mainly on negative states. This is not incidental: the vast majority of metaphorical expressions in the Smith Journal are used to express negative affective states. Positive affective states are discussed metaphorically to a lesser degree, and the figurative language itself tends to be less elaborate. To demonstrate this, I begin with a section on the (less frequent) metaphors of positive affective states before moving on to the more frequent and varied metaphors for negative states. The patterns describing negative affective states are organized by vehicle meanings and fall into the following broad systematic groups:

- *MOTION* metaphors: including examples of metaphors expressing external and internal physical confinement/immobility, that is, a lack of motion, due to imprisonment and paralysis, for example, as well as examples where there is mobility, but it is not under the control of the self and/or there is no progress as a result (e.g. as with a vicious cycle for instance).
- *AFFECTIVE STATE AS FRAGMENTATION OF ENVIRONMENT OR THE SELF* metaphors: including metaphors where various elements of a self are referred to as separate entities, often in the sense of independent selves with potentially opposing interests. They also include examples where the immediate environment is described as disintegrating.
- *AFFECTIVE STATE AS PHYSICAL PAIN* metaphors: including metaphors that concretize (mental illness is referred to as a physical illness) and/or construct an affective state as an internal aggressor.

As outlined in Section 6.2, most of the analysis is devoted to more unconventional (though still salient) metaphorical patterns, as these are more representative of the affective states described. These patterns are therefore best seen as systematic (Cameron et al. 2010) rather than conceptual metaphors (Lakoff and Johnson 1980) and are therefore denoted by *ITALIC SMALL CAPITALS*. In accounting for creativity, however, I do also refer to conventional conceptual metaphors for comparison, which are denoted in the usual way using SMALL CAPITALS. Where appropriate, I support the mostly qualitative discussion with quantitative evidence from corpus analysis.

6.3.1 A preliminary example

There are over 400 metaphorically used expressions referring to affective states in 14,630 words in the eighteen entries selected for qualitative analysis. That is approximately twenty-seven metaphorical expressions relevant for affective states per 1,000 words. Though this figure is on the lower end of metaphor density scales (see, for example, Cameron and Stelma 2004 and Steen et al. 2010), it represents only a subset of all metaphorical expressions in the data, suggesting that the text is reasonably metaphor rich. The precise nature and complexity of these metaphors is best introduced by two representative examples demonstrating how figurative expressions from various semantic fields interact and pattern. Parts of this analysis are also discussed in Demjén (2011a).

The passages below are both taken from Entry 154, written on 3 November 1952 (one of the few entries that are dated), when Plath is in her second year at Smith College, and the possibility of going to England for graduate study has arisen. Aside from debating the advantages and disadvantages of leaving the United States, most of the entries that year detail aspects of Plath's summer jobs and her romantic dates. Entry 154 itself details personal frustration and despair and begins with an arguable culmination of these feelings in *God, if ever I have come close to wanting to commit suicide, it is now*. There is little indication of the cause of this negative state, but Plath alludes to the burden of duties, the uncertainty of the future and the unfulfilled need to talk to somebody. Later in the entry, Plath recognizes that she is privileged and has no rational reason for feeling the way she does. In subsequent entries, the tensions appear to find release in conversation with a good friend.

In the examples below, the metaphorical words or phrases relevant for affective states are underlined; any similes are underlined with a dotted line. Overall, Entry 154 is 1,401 words long, and 127 words are used metaphorically to refer to affective states.

Example 12

> I_Z8 am_A3+ afraid_E5- I_Z8 am_A3+ not_Z6 solid_O1.1, but_Z5 hollow_O4.1. I_Z8 feel_X2.1 behind_Z5 my_Z8 eyes_B1 a_Z5 numb_B1, paralyzed_B2- cavern_W3, a_Z5 pit_O2 of_Z5 hell_S9, a_Z5 mimicking_Z99 nothingness_A3-. I_Z8 never_T1/Z6 thought_X2.1, I_Z8 never_T1/Z6 wrote_Q1.2, I_Z8 never_T1/Z6 suffered_E4.1-. I_Z8 want_X7+ to_Z5 kill_L1- myself_Z8, to_Z5 escape_A1.7- from_Z5 responsibility_S6+, to_Z5 crawl back_M1 abjectly_Z99 into_Z5 the_Z5 womb_B1. I_Z8 do_Z5 not_Z6 know_X2.2+ who_Z8 I_Z8 am_A3+, where_M6 I_Z8 am_Z5 going_M1 – and_Z5 I_Z8 am_A3+ the_Z5 one_Z8 who_Z8 has_to_S6+ decide_X6+ the_Z5 answers_Q2.2 to_Z5 these_Z5 hideous_O4.2- questions_Q2.2. I_Z8 long_X7+ for_Z5 a_Z5 noble_G2.2+ escape_A1.7- from_Z5 freedom_A1.7- – I_Z8 am_A3+ weak_S1.2.5-, tired_B1, in_Z5 revolt_G2.1- from_Z5 the_Z5 strong_S1.2.5+ constructive_S8+ humanitarian_S8+ faith_E6+ which_Z8 presupposes_X2.1 a_Z5 healthy_B2+, active_X5.2+ intellect_X2 and_Z5 will_X7+. There_Z5 is_A3+ no_Z6 where_M6 to_Z5 go_M1. (Entry 154, USAS-tagged, my emphasis)

Example 12 repeats (Semino 2008) linguistic expressions denoting some form of emptiness: *not solid*, *hollow*, *cavern*, *pit*, as well as, possibly, *nothingness* and *womb*. These vehicles arguably belong to the semantic field of *empty container* (*hollow* suggests that there is a boundary to the space) and refer to a negative affective state (topic). These and similar linguistic expressions in the Smith Journal suggest the systematic metaphor of *NEGATIVE AFFECTIVE STATE AS AN EMPTY CONTAINER*, which is related to conventional metaphors for emotions such as EMOTION IS FLUID IN A CONTAINER and/or THE BODY IS A CONTAINER FOR EMOTIONS (Kövecses 2000). Both of these are also part of the broader CONTAINER schema (they have an inside/outside, can be full/empty etc.), but *EMPTY CONTAINER* vehicles are less conventional for emotions/affective states. These have negative associations and imply that the state is immaterial and intangible. The examples here also include creative elaboration (Lakoff and Turner 1989), for instance, the *EMPTY CONTAINER* metaphor is specified as a *cavern* rather than a generic container and has a specific location: *behind my eyes*. This adds to the sense of emptiness as it implicitly contrasts with the normal state of that particular location. Reeves et al. (2004) associate similar examples with suicidal ideation, which resonates with the statement *I want to kill myself* in lines 2–3 of the example.

Womb and *nothingness* are slightly different from the other examples of EMPTY CONTAINER, and a useful notion for making the case for their inclusion is 'attraction'. According to Cameron and Low (2004), metaphor clusters such as Example 12 (numerous metaphorical expressions occuring in very close proximity to one another) seem to have two main effects:

a. words that may not be interpreted as metaphoric on their own can acquire metaphoric 'resonance' due to the main metaphor in the cluster (such words can occur before or after the main metaphor); and
b. 'the "base" metaphor can "attract" different metaphors which just happen to be on the same topic' (Cameron and Low 2004: 367; also noted in Low 1997).

The second point, in other words, states that metaphorical expressions that might otherwise be interpreted as belonging to different source domains can be interpreted as part of the 'base' metaphor's source domain due to close textual proximity. While *nothingness* would not normally be part of the *empty container* semantic field – it implies no boundaries – in Example 12 it occurs in a cluster with several other expressions that are more obviously CONTAINER metaphors, so it is attracted in. Metaphor attraction can also operate in what Cameron and Low (2004) call 'loose clusters', which would apply in the case of *womb* above. As most metaphors in the eighteen qualitatively analysed entries occur in more or less dense clusters, such cross-fertilization between vehicles is quite characteristic. Though metaphor clustering may be a result of Plath's talent as an articulate, aspiring writer, it can also indicate points of significance, such as particularly emotional topics, in a text (Low 1997).

Linguistic expressions such as *numb* and *paralyzed* express physical states where perceptions are subdued or non-existent. Paralysis also denotes an illness but, although both interpretations are nested (Charteris-Black and Musolff 2003) in the vehicle, metaphor attraction results in the lack of sensation meaning being more salient here. In this way, both expressions relate to the broad semantic field of *lacking sensations* or *not feeling*. Emotions are, of course, conventionally conceptualized as physical sensations (Kövecses 2000), so references to the absence of these in an affective state can be considered a subtype of the conventional mapping. In fact, the contextual meaning of *numb* even appears in the *OED*. However, in Example 12, the target concept of the negative affective state is expressed creatively by combining the *LACK OF SENSATION* with CONTAINER metaphors. In this creative combination, they provide a more comprehensive impression of the target: it is not only a state where there is a lack of perceptions, thoughts and other 'mental content' (*nothingness*) but also a state where external stimuli are not perceived (*numb*, *paralyzed*).

The EMPTY CONTAINER metaphor is creatively exploited further using *mimicking*. Mimicking can be interpreted as conceptual extension (Lakoff and Turner 1989) or as an example of compounding (Goatly 1997): one metaphorical expression (nothingness) is referred to metaphorically again by means of personification. In either case, it implies a certain agency on the part of the affective state, making it a participant in the (mental) events: it imitates in order to ridicule (*OED*). With such participants and events, this example, and others like it, can also be understood as metaphor scenarios rather than simple clusters. Metaphor scenarios are 'mini-narratives' involving participants, actions/events and goals (Musolff 2006, Semino 2008), which carry implied meanings and associations beyond the individual vehicle terms. Such scenarios and their various elements can (and in the case of the Smith Journal do) recur at different points in the text (cf. Gibbs et al. 2013) creating underlying themes and contributing to coherence.

The phrase *no where* [sic] *to go* contains two examples of *movement* expressions associated with the conventional CHANGES ARE MOVEMENTS and PURPOSES ARE DESTINATIONS sub-mappings of the event structure metaphor (Lakoff 1993; see also Lakoff and Johnson 1999 and Kövecses 2010). They also relate to the more specific LIFE IS A JOURNEY mapping: the first part of the expression relates to life choices, while the latter part expresses the notion that destinations are reached through movement. However, in combination and negated, the phrase signifies precisely a lack of progress, thereby becoming part of the semantic field of *no movement* or *lack of movement*. This carries a negative evaluation in terms of LIFE IS A JOURNEY, since it is movement in a forward direction that brings a person closer to desirable goals. With similar effect, Example 12 also includes related expressions that denote movement away from somewhere: *escape* (repeated twice) and *crawl back* can be grouped in an *escape/retreat* semantic field. Although *escape* and *retreat* are not strictly synonyms, they both involve movement away from something that is unpleasant (e.g. danger or conflict/war). *Back*, in *crawl back*, emphasizes the unpleasantness, as it is also negatively evaluated in terms of LIFE IS A JOURNEY, where movement forward is desirable.

Though the semantic fields of *lack of movement* and *escape/retreat* are subgroups of a broad MOTION metaphor, there is creativity involved in these examples too. Framed by *I want to kill myself*, these expressions move from a more generic topic to a specific one. According to the *OED*, *escape* is used figuratively to mean 'avoid or retreat from the realities of life', but it is not recorded in reference to suicide: it is conventional in reference to the more generic topic but not the specific one. The contextual meaning of *womb* also does not appear in the *OED*, and neither of these terms seems to be captured in conventional conceptual metaphors to do with emotions. As such, they are creative in Semino's (2008) sense of using a new source domain to refer to a particular target domain. Additionally, *escape* and *womb* are combined in a scenario where *womb* becomes a destination, the end of the escape route. The co-textually more remote combination with *no where to go* adds a sense of inevitability that makes suicide seem like the only option. This is a rich and complex conceptualization of this negative affective state.

In addition to the aforementioned patterns, there are also two textually isolated metaphorical expressions in Example 12: *hell* and *revolt*. The latter appears to be a manifestation of some form of struggle or conflict, but because it stands alone in the example, it is difficult to categorize definitively. *Hell* is a conventional religious metaphor to denote something that is unpleasant, as recorded in the *OED*: a 'place, state, or situation of wickedness, suffering, or misery'. In this example it is isolated, but in the entire Smith Journal the lemma *hell** is repeated nine times in this highly conventional metaphorical sense.

Example 12 also contains potential hyperbole (*I never thought, I never wrote, I never suffered*; *I do not know who I am*; and, to some extent, *I want to kill myself*) and direct references to affective states (*I am afraid*). These inevitably also interact with the metaphorical expressions, increasing the intensity of affective states and enabling a specification of the target concepts. A similar interaction can also be seen in Example 13, where the descriptive labels (Kövecses 2000) *fear*, *envy*, *hate* occur within another cluster of metaphorical references to affective states. In fact, there seems to be a general pattern in the eighteen sample entries for direct references and hyperbole to co-occur with metaphorical references to affective states.

Example 13

> Reality_A3+ is_A3+ what_Z8 I_Z8 make_it_X9.2+. That_Z8 is_A3+ what_Z8 I_Z8 have_Z5 said_Q2.1 I_Z8 believed_X2.1. Then_N4 I_Z8 look_at_X3.4 the_hell_Z4 I_Z8 am_Z5 wallowing_M1 in_M6, nerves_B1 paralyzed_B2-, action_A1.1.1 nullified_T2-/G2.1 – fear_E5-, envy_S1.2.2+, hate_E2-: all_N5.1+ the_Z5 corrosive_A1.1.2 emotions_E1 of_Z5 insecurity_A7- biting_B1 away_M6 at_Z5 my_Z8 sensitive_X2.5+/E1 guts_B1. Time_T1, experience_A2.1+/A3+: the_Z5 colossal_N3.2+ wave_W3/M4 sweeping_O4.4 tidal_W3/M4 over_Z5 me_Z8, drowning_L1-, drowning_L1-. (Entry 154, USAS-tagged, my emphasis)

In Example 13, the target affective state is again clearly a negative one, and some expressions noted in the previous example are repeated (e.g. *hell*, *paralyzed)*. This repetition creates a cohesive link between Example 12 and Example 13, even though they are used to express slightly different target concepts ('multivalence' in Goatly's (2007) terms) and occur approximately 300 words apart.

Wallowing in implies another form of motion and belongs to the *movement* semantic field mentioned above, albeit as a new subtype thereof. The movement is circular so is 'unproductive' in the sense of the LIFE IS A JOURNEY conceptual metaphor: it also does not progress forwards. Example 13 also includes additional vehicle terms from the *lack of movement* semantic field: *paralyzed* and *action* nullified. In this case, the classification of *paralyzed* is less ambiguous than in the previous example. Although the expression remains polysemous, the fact that it is followed by *action nullified* arguably foregrounds its physical restriction meaning. Similar to Example 12, combination plays a significant role in this cluster. The target concept of Plath's affective state is expressed by combining *hell* with *wallowing in*: the connotations of *hell* ensure that the space is perceived as negative or unpleasant, while the various *MOVEMENT* metaphors construct it as a space that is difficult to get out of.

The expressions *corrosive* and *biting away* – although normally used in slightly different contexts – share the characteristic of destruction. Corrosion destroys or breaks down metal, while the flesh of a dead animal is normally bitten away at by predators or scavengers. *Corrosive* activates, or primes (Charteris-Black 2012), a particular metaphorical interpretation of *biting away*, allowing both to be grouped under the semantic field of *aggression* or *destruction*. However, as both of these terms animate the affective state and the 'actions' are specifically located in the *guts*, they are more accurately described as part of an *internal aggressor* semantic field. The personification of the emotions denoted by descriptive labels (*fear*, *envy*, *hate*), constructs these emotions as participants with agency in a metaphor scenario.

A further new semantic field is evoked by *wave*, *sweeping* and *tidal*. These expressions refer to natural forces with a destructive element. There is also an implication of a downward movement, in particular in the wave that sweeps over Plath, thereby pushing her down. These examples could form another subgroup of the *motion* semantic field already discussed. However, motion is an entailment of the type of force being referred to in these expressions, rather than a main meaning. As such, I find it more useful to group these in a *forces* semantic field, which is conventional in reference to emotions: 'For ordinary people emotions are FORCES that emerge independently of a rational and conscious self as a result of certain causes, and that, in most cases, have to be kept under control' (Kövecses 2002a: 112). Specification of the type of force and a description of what it does elaborates on the conventional conceptualization. In addition, the element of attempted control is not referenced in these expressions. As such, the most accurate semantic field to encompass these expressions is *uncontrollable kinetic force*.

Drowning may also be linked to this group, as it involves downward movement and happens in water. It can even be a consequence of a tidal wave. Conventionally, metaphorical drowning refers to a general inability to 'function' normally in society/life (often used to express being overwhelmed). At the same time, Kövecses (2000) notes that FORCE metaphors can be indicative of passivity, as there is nothing one can do when faced with such forces. In this particular case, the repetition of *drowning* combined with metaphors drawing on the *uncontrollable kinetic force semantic field* intensifies this perceived passivity.

Example 12 and Example 13 both corroborate what has been suggested about the conceptualization of negative affective states such as depression: they are unpleasant spaces to be in (Semino 2008, Charteris-Black 2012) and are difficult to get out of (McMullen and Conway 2002). However, the examples here also go beyond that. The recurring themes of emptiness and passivity and the various ways in which the notion of unpleasantness is repeated also suggest that Plath experienced these aspects very intensely. The discussion of these two examples illustrates the linguistic style of the Smith Journal and the complexity embedded in interactions between different metaphorical expressions. It also introduces some of the key source domains that are discussed as systematic metaphors in the next sections.

The rest of this chapter looks at broad groups of metaphorical expressions individually. This is a challenging task for two reasons. As the previous two examples demonstrated, accounting for metaphorical patterns involves looking at textual and conceptual patterning, and this can only be done by considering vehicle terms in context. However, in order to do justice to the data, it is also necessary to discuss a wide range of metaphorical expressions. In the interests of clarity and rigour, each grouping or subsection below begins with a bulleted outline of the various types of expressions that are discussed in it. Contextualized examples are then presented with more detailed discussions. All metaphorical expressions that refer to affective states are underlined, but the ones I focus on at any given point are in bold.

6.3.2 Positive affective states

There are two main groups of expressions that can be linked with positive affective states in the eighteen sample entries. First, expressions such as *self-integrality, integrated, whole person, integrating* can be grouped in the semantic domain of *wholeness*. Second, words like *born, fertilization, conceived* and *gestation* all have something to do with coming into existence in a broad sense, so they can be grouped under the semantic domain of *coming into existence*. Linguistic expressions belonging to these two groups account for only 4 per cent of all metaphorical expressions related to affective states in the eighteen entries. Considering that these are the main ways of metaphorically referring to positive affective states in the Smith Journal, this relatively low percentage consisting of just two broad types is a reflection of the fact that positive affective states are portrayed metaphorically less frequently and less variedly than negative ones.

6.3.2.1 Wholeness

Positive affective states in the eighteen entries are described in terms of integrity or wholeness, as in Example 14 and Example 15.

Example 14

> Complete physical well-being, exalted environment, a sense of capability and **self-integrality** never before felt. (Entry 117)

Example 15

> I remembered how I was before, how **integrated**, how positive (Entry 155)

Both examples refer to a relatively undifferentiated positive state or general well-being, as can be inferred from the co-text. Example 14 clearly shows how well-being is described as *self-integrality* and suggests that this is, in fact, a rare experience. The term *integrity* and its various lexemes are repeated in this same sense three times in the eighteen entries analysed manually. In addition, other linguistic expressions (e.g. *whole person, bundle*) belonging to broadly the same semantic domain recur five more times in eighteen entries. These expressions can be subsumed under the systematic metaphor *POSITIVE AFFECTIVE STATE IS WHOLENESS*.

This pattern is interesting for two reasons. First, it can be seen as the counterpart to the metaphors drawing on fragmentation and disintegration that are associated with negative affective states (to be discussed later). Second, while the metaphorical use of *integration* for psychological well-being is not entirely novel – according to the *OED*, in psychology it can mean 'the harmonious combination of the different elements in a personality' – other linguistic manifestations such as *self-integrality* are not noted in the *OED*. This suggests creativity at the word level (Semino 2011). The process of integration or integrating is not given an agent – it is not known who integrates, or what makes integration come about – it is simply conceptualized as present or absent. This suggests that while *AFFECTIVE STATE AS WHOLENESS* metaphors express a positive state, achieving such a state is not a matter of will and so not in Plath's control.

6.3.2.2 Coming into existence

References to the semantic field of *coming into existence*, as in the examples below, also express positive affective states. While the expressions in Example 16 suggest a human conception, expressions in Example 17 and Example 18 are more associated with plants.

Example 16

> Now a love, a faith, an affirmation is **conceived** in me like an **embryo**. The **gestation** may be a while in producing, but the **fertilization** has come to pass (Entry 155)

Example 17

> All of life is not lost, merely an eighteeth [sic] summer. And perhaps something good has been **sprouting** in the small numb darkness all this while. (Entry 104)

Example 18

> there was that **germ** of positive creativeness (Entry 155)

A life form coming into existence is usually seen as something positive, so it is not surprising that linguistic expressions relating to this event are used to express positive affective states. Such metaphorical references are repeated seven times in the eighteen entries and can be subsumed under *POSITIVE AFFECTIVE STATE IS LIFE FORM COMING INTO EXISTENCE* (*COMING INTO EXISTENCE* for short). Of course, *sprouting* and *germ* also belong to the semantic domain of *plants*, but in the current co-text the meaning signifying the beginning of life seems to predominate. In the case of Entry 155 (Example 16 and Example 18), this can be explained by metaphor attraction. A corpus exploration of the semantic fields 'Life and Living Things' (L1) and 'Alive' (L1+) in Wmatrix USAS yielded no additional results. However, lexical searches for 'born' and 'birth' revealed that *born* is used 6/19 times to refer to the coming into existence of an affective state in the Smith Journal.

A state of mind described as 'being born' is a manifestation of conventional mapping of EXISTENCE IS BEING BORN; however, the present examples extend this conventional concept. In Example 15, for instance, the reference to the various stages before birth (*gestation*, *fertilization*) maps normally unused elements of the source domain implying the difficulty involved in the process. This suggests that, for Plath, 'being positive' involves all these elements of difficulty as well. In fact, the positive state is not actually in existence yet in any of these examples – the metaphors merely suggest a potential for it. Although Plath, again, is not represented in an active role as causing the 'conception', it is at least presented as taking place within her. She is the one responsible for nurturing (*gestation*) and thereby has some role to play in the coming about of a positive affective state.

6.3.3 Negative affective states

The rest of this discussion addresses a large amount of material. In order to both do justice to the data and allow for a comprehensive and comprehensible discussion of the results, the analysis is subdivided into three groups of the most frequent metaphorical expressions in the eighteen entries selected for manual intensive analysis. Each subsection begins with a bulleted outline of the various subtypes of expressions from the Smith Journal that it includes. I present the results in this decontextualized way, initially, in order to provide preliminary linguistic evidence for the groupings that structure the analysis. Within each subsection, I then consider contextualized examples in more detail. A slightly briefer discussion of metaphorical patterns that are less frequent, but nevertheless salient in some way, concludes this section on negative affective states.

6.3.3.1 Metaphors related to motion or lack of motion

About 28 per cent of metaphorical expressions referring to affective states are related to movements of some sort, or to a marked lack of movement – some of these were discussed in the context of the preliminary examples above. The following groups of linguistic expressions constitute this category:

- Expressions such as *retreat*, *withdraw* and *escape* suggest movement away from some, usually unpleasant, thing.
- Expressions such as *thrown*, *plunged*, *whirlpool*, *sweeping*, *tidal*, *overthrown*, *ricochet* etc. suggest a physical force that moves, possibly against the will of the entity being moved.
- Expressions such as *paralyzed*, *shocked*, *stasis* etc. suggest an internal, physical inability to move.
- Expressions such as *cage* and *prison* denote external confinements preventing movement.

The first two groups are classed as *AFFECTIVE STATE AS MOVEMENT AWAY* and *AFFECTIVE STATE AS UNCONTROLLABLE KINETIC FORCE* systematic metaphors, while the last two suggest the systematic metaphors of *AFFECTIVE STATE AS IMMOBILITY* and *AFFECTIVE STATE AS CONFINEMENT*. I discuss these groups in reverse order, as the first three have already been mentioned in the context of the preliminary examples.

6.3.3.1.1 Confinement metaphors

In the examples below, words such as *caged* and *prison* metaphorically refer to aspects of a negative affective state. These expressions normally denote objects or spaces that are used to confine animals and people, respectively. Additionally, Example 21 mentions a process of confining in *shutting up* and refers to a *vacuum* as the container or space within which confinement takes place.

Example 19

> to feel his mind soaring, reaching, and mine **caged**, (Entry 154)

Example 20

> Stop thinking selfishly of razors & self-wounds & going out and ending it all. Your room is not your **prison**. You are. (Entry July 6)

Example 21

> don't ignore all the people you could know, **shutting** yourself **up** in a numb defensive vacuum (Entry July 6)

As they mention the space of confinement, these examples could also be seen as linguistic manifestations of the conventional EMOTION AS BEING IN A BOUNDED SPACE metaphor. Linguistic examples of this metaphor are commonly used in the expression of emotions, especially using the preposition *in* (e.g. *she was in ecstasy*) (Kövecses 2000: 36). However, the examples here go beyond this conventional conceptualization. The figurative space is not denoted by a preposition and is elaborated into specific spaces. Prisons, cages and vacuums can generally be considered unpleasant or disconcerting 'places', and the first two, at least, are designed to confine. In fact, the negativity of the relevant affective state in these examples is conveyed by the connotations of being locked up. Prisons and cages are, by default, designed to be difficult to get out of, and there is also no freedom of movement in or out of the spaces.

Although *prison* is negated in its own clause, it is referred to without negation in the subsequent elliptical sentence – the implication is that Plath is her own prison. The most interesting difference between these two examples is the role of the self. In Example 19, the cage seems externally imposed, while in Example 20 the self is the prison. Similarly, *shutting up* in Example 21 is done by the self. Confinement that is self-created is potentially more difficult to get out of than one that is externally imposed. These expressions are closely related to examples that Semino (2008) and Charteris-Black (2012) noted in the context of descriptions of depression. In Charteris-Black's (2012) data, examples such as *you have a sort of bubble round you. It's a thick, Perspex bubble that you cannot break* also combine elements of containment and constraint. BOUNDED SPACE metaphors, in the context of the negative affective state of depression, are also discussed by McMullen and Conway (2002). In fact, one could say that the *CONFINEMENT* group metaphors in these examples can be seen as a creative elaboration on the conventional BOUNDED SPACE metaphor. The BOUNDED SPACE is specified as a particular type of space that highlights the elements of unwilling confinement. In addition, the element of agency in two of these examples can be seen as a form of extension.

In Example 19, Plath's mind is presented as not free to act, juxtaposed with *his* mind: his (Plath's boyfriend at the time) mind is free and active, while hers is confined. The contrast intensifies the metaphor. A corpus search for *cage* and *caged* revealed that this expression recurs three more times in the Smith Journal in a metaphorical sense. However, it is used slightly differently, to refer to the restriction imposed by routine or society on people in general. A key word search for *prison* revealed eight instances in the Smith Journal. Three of these are repetitions of the metaphorical sense in Example 20, but only one of these involves agency on the part of Plath. There are also twenty-six occurrences of the lemma *shut** in the Smith Journal with various prepositions. Of those, five are repetitions of Example 21, including the self-imposed nature of the imprisonment. An additional exploration of the semantic field of 'Constraint' (A1.7+) revealed that of the eighty-three concordance lines in A1.7+, twelve lines overall carried the metaphorical meanings referring to negative affective states. Vehicle terms included *trapped, limited, tightens, sealed, tense, caged* and *pent up*. These can be interpreted as recurrences (Semino 2008), as they do not refer to exactly the same target domain. These figures suggest relatively persistent patterns.

Some of the metaphors I discussed in this section are similar to ones that McMullen and Conway (2002) identified as DEPRESSION IS A CAPTOR. However, I have opted for a broader label to highlight differences among the types of metaphors that belong in this grouping. In addition, the linguistic examples discussed above do not animate affective states in the way that CAPTOR suggests. An alternative interpretation for some of these examples (e.g. Example 19) could see them as versions of Barnden's (n.d.) MIND AS ANIMATE BEING or LIVING BODY. The ATT-Meta Databank (Barnden n.d.) includes examples such as *Sit at your desk and allow your mind to wander to a great night of sex in the past*. In these metaphors, a person's mind is viewed as a complete animate being, which can therefore be *caged* or 'given permission' separately from the rest of the person. Barnden (n.d.) notes that such metaphors can be seen as a special case of the broader MIND AS PHYSICAL OBJECT metaphor.

6.3.3.1.2 *Immobility metaphors*

The expressions highlighted in the following examples suggest a restriction on movement that comes from an internal physical inability, instead of being externally imposed. This is most obvious in *paralyzed*, but also applied for the basic meanings of *shocked, nullified* action and *stasis*.

Example 22

> look at the hell I am wallowing in, nerves **paralyzed**, action **nullified** (Entry 154)

Example 23

> you are **paralyzed, shocked**, thrown into a nausea, a **stasis**. (Entry July 6)

Paralyzed is particularly interesting in these examples, as it seems to have two meanings. As noted earlier, the term refers to a type of illness or disability that has the effect of both restricting mobility and restricting sensations. In this sense, it is an example of what Charteris-Black and Musolff (2003) call a *nested metaphor*. It has the potential to activate more than one semantic domain (in this case, *immobility* and *lack of sensations*), leading to a double metaphor effect. Even when one meaning predominates, all are carried and can add entailments to the overall metaphor. This is also true of other expressions that have meanings additional to that of motion (e.g. *shocked*). There is also evidence of creativity in these examples. While the *OED* includes a figurative meaning for *paralysis* that refers to an affective state, the use of *stasis* in this sense is not included, suggesting creativity at the word level. Example 22 and Example 23 can also be seen as clusters that include some repetition: expressions belonging to the *IMMOBILITY* domain are repeated and are in close proximity to metaphorical expressions related to other domains. Repetition also occurs on a wider scale. In the eighteen entries, expressions linked to immobility are repeated eighteen times. Such textual patterning provides potential evidence for underlying conceptual patterns and for an *AFFECTIVE STATE AS IMMOBILITY* systematic metaphor.

The type of immobility in these examples is potentially more difficult to overcome than the confinement described in the previous section. The possibility of overcoming physical confinement is entirely dependent on the ability to move and on strength. In paralysis, it is precisely this ability that is absent, suggesting that the negative affective state itself is more difficult to overcome. Metaphors of 'being stuck' are additionally associated with suicidal ideation (Reeves et al. 2004: 68): 'The client does not see themselves engaged with this otherwise dynamic process [life]: while others move and negotiate, they "stand still" and therefore "get in the way"'. Because clients are unable to progress, Reeves et al. (2004) suggest, they see suicide as the only way of removing themselves as obstacles.

6.3.3.1.3 Uncontrollable Kinetic Force metaphors

I now turn to expressions where movement does occur, but it is in some way out of the moving entity's control.

Example 24

> you are paralyzed, shocked **thrown** into a nausea a stasis. You are **plunged** so deep in your own very private little **whirlpool** of negativism that you can't do more than force yourself into a rote (July 6, 1953)

Example 24 is an extended version of Example 23 discussed above, but with a focus on different metaphorical expressions. The highlighted words refer to movements that are imposed on Plath. There is no known agent for *thrown* or *plunged*, but both express an externally caused involuntary downward movement. *Whirlpool* also entails involuntary downward motion, but the named entity itself exerts the force that causes the movement, and there is an element of circularity. These expressions have in common the lack of agency and control on the part of the moving entity and an element of force that causes the movement. As such, they fall under *AFFECTIVE STATE AS AN UNCONTROLLABLE KINETIC FORCE*. As Example 24 includes metaphorical expressions relating to different domains in close textual proximity, it is also an example of a metaphor cluster, with repetition of the FORCE source domain.

Semantic fields that might contain expressions similar to the ones discussed here were explored across the Smith Journal using the USAS categories in Wmatrix. The relevant categories were W3 'Geographical Terms'; W4 'Weather'; M1 'Moving'; M2 'Pushing, Pulling etc.'; and L1 - 'Death' (for *drowning*). This exploration resulted, overall, in almost 2,000 concordance lines, of which only eighteen expressions belonged to *AFFECTIVE STATE AS UNCONTROLLABLE KINETIC FORCE*. Examples of linguistic expressions included those in the examples above, as well as *submerge, yank, ricochet*. Note that over two-thirds of these entailed a downward movement. In addition, eight expressions (e.g. *whirlpool, tide, flood, drowning*) were identified where FORCES expressed a positive affective state, namely lust.

McMullen and Conway (2002) noted that tied in with DEPRESSION IS DESCENT was the idea that going down was easy, effortless and uncontrollable, but going back up was difficult and strenuous. This can be applied to the examples outlined here as well and linked to the *CONFINEMENT* and *IMMOBILITY* groups discussed above. Once again, a negative affective state is conceptualized as something that is difficult to get out of for multiple reasons. FORCE metaphors in reference to emotions are quite conventional (Kövecses 2002a). However, the expressions presented here appear to go beyond the conventional EMOTIONS ARE FORCES, and beyond McMullen and Conway's DEPRESSION IS DESCENT: they are more specific than the former (the force moves in particular directions) and are differentiated by the added element of force from the latter. The combined effect appears to be a somewhat violent affective state.

6.3.3.1.4 Movement away metaphors

There are two groups of expressions that I would like to discuss as 'movement away': expressions such as *retreat, withdraw, crawl back* and expressions such as *escape*. These all involve movement away from a place of conflict or discomfort but are nevertheless slightly different. *Retreat*, *withdraw* and *crawl back* (also in the context of Example 12) can all be understood as synonyms of each other. In their basic meaning, they describe a movement backwards or away from a place of conflict to a safer place (*OED*). These expressions refer to negative affective states and give rise to the systematic metaphor *AFFECTIVE STATE AS RETREAT* in the Smith Journal.

Example 25

begging for sleep, **withdrawing** into the dark, warm, fetid escape from action (Entry 154)

Example 26

Perverse desire to **retreat** into not caring. (Entry July 14)

The two excerpts above and the instance of *crawl back* in Example 12 exemplify the main manifestations of the *RETREAT* vehicle group. Although these expressions are to do with movement away from somewhere, another basic meaning of *retreat* and *withdraw* is related to a general *war* domain in the sense that retreating is what the losing side does in order not to incur further losses (*OED*). As a result of this nested meaning (Charteris-Black and Musolff 2003), Plath is positioned on the losing side of a conflict, and in the process of moving away from a source of distress (potentially aggression). The source of distress itself is never explicitly mentioned in these examples but is merely evoked by the activation of the *RETREAT* scenario. *Crawl back* could also be seen as a nested metaphor: it implies movement away from somewhere but also an animal-like movement that is often very slow (*OED*).

Lexical items belonging to *RETREAT* in this sense occur fourteen times in the Smith Journal, with the lexeme *retreat* (always in reference to Plath) repeated eight times (see Concordance 13), *withdraw* three times and *crawl back* twice. Additionally, there is an isolated example of *return* used in a similar sense. An exploration of the USAS tag 'Warfare' (G3) (which *retreat* falls into) showed no

of time , race of time , speed of time , I	retreat	into non-thought merely into Epicurean sens
will not let myself get sick , go mad , or	retreat	, like a child into blubbering on someone e
character . I had been withdrawing' into a	retreat	of numbness : it is so much safer not to fe
around to absolve me of my burdens , so I	retreat	, in a numb womb of purposeless business wi
sciously manufacture my own . and then , I	retreat	and revel in poetry and literature where th
be able to think , accept , affirm and not	retreat	into a masochistic mental hell where jealou
ective humor . Colossal desire to escape ,	retreat	, not talk to anybody . Thesis panic lack c
kind of creative life . Perverse desire to	retreat	into not caring . I am incapable of loving

Concordance 13 All instances of 'Retreat' in Smith Journal.

further lexical manifestations of this metaphor. *Retreat* in the sense outlined here is quite conventional. This figurative meaning, to remove oneself from emotions, is recorded in the *OED*. However, *withdraw* and *crawl back* are not, so they can be seen as less conventional at the word level.

McMullen and Conway (2002) as well as Schoeneman et al. (2004) note that depression can be conceptualized as a struggle, while Kövecses (2000) notes that emotions in general can be conceptualized as opponents in a struggle. However, I would argue that the expressions discussed here extend the conventional EMOTION IS A STRUGGLE metaphor. They focus on a different element of the STRUGGLE scenario – namely the movement away from it. They suggest a lost battle in the case of Plath. In terms of the experience of the negative affective state, this could be interesting: the examples suggest that Plath *retreats* before a struggle even takes place. There is an element of helplessness and dejection in this: *retreat*, *withdrawal* and *crawling* imply resignation and inevitability. The sense of exhaustion evoked by *crawl* seems to reinforce the sense of helplessness, while the animal scenario may suggest distancing or dehumanization.

Another way of looking at *AFFECTIVE STATES AS RETREAT* metaphors is in terms of LIFE IS A JOURNEY. As discussed above, conventionally the LIFE IS A JOURNEY conceptual metaphor involves movement forwards, evaluated as positive and representing progress in life. However, in all these examples the movement is backwards. In the frame of LIFE IS A JOURNEY, this is undesirable and unproductive movement, as there is no progress towards objectives and goals.

ink they may have been relieved at my narrow	escape	; they may have expected me to cry . They kne
n't yet - - - not yet . No , I wo n't try to	escape	myself by losing myself in artificial chatter
by getting manuscripts published ? Is it an	escape	an excuse for any social failure so I can say
se ideal standalds ? Good for you . The only	escape	(do I sound Freudian ?) from the present se
he need to write as I would lose the need to	escape	. Very simple . If all my writing (once , I
icism from mother to girlfriend) and yet to	escape	the subtle feminine snare and be free of the
hal dominance which he is probably trying to	escape	from . He would then be selfish admitting als
s showed , and mentally , as I was trying to	escape	from something) I wanted to withdraw from al
a laughing wit , a comprehension of war , of	escape	, deep rooted your graceful athletic build ,
or . There is the urge to procrastinate , to	escape	from the rigid cage of study routine I have m
le waking up in tomorrow . Another device of	escape	. It seems that every year I wince and grovel
p , withdrawing into the dark , warm , fetid	escape	from action , from responsibility . No good .
never suffered . I want to kill myself , to	escape	from responsibility , to crawl back abjectly
these hideous questions . I long for a noble	escape	from freedom I am weak , tired , in revolt fr
country : you are not sure whether it is an	escape	or a refreshing cure from cooping yourself in
soul . ") Well , yes , the leg has been an	escape	. All the pamperings given to the tuberculosi
do n't want , to use higher education as an	escape	from responsibility , but I feel there is so
upon me : hoping I do not want primarily to	escape	dick and " show " perry , to merely conquer t
neither a glamorous gamble nor an ephemeral	escape	. I know none of these three boys well enough
ss of perspective humor . Colossal desire to	escape	, retreat , not talk to anybody . Thesis pani
you and love and mankind . You must not seek	escape	like this . You must think .

Concordance 14 All instances of 'Escape' in the Smith Journal.

Escape also occurs in Example 25 and in Example 12. Although, admittedly, it is linked to RETREAT in the sense that it implies movement away from somewhere, I consider it separately here to highlight potential differences. The most common linguistic realization of this group of metaphorical expressions is the word *escape* as in Example 12 and Example 25 above. As such, I refer to these as a systematic metaphor of *AFFECTIVE STATE IS ESCAPE*.

Overall, the word *escape* occurs twenty-four times in the Smith Journal, eleven of which are repetitions of the sense described here. Concordance 14 shows all twenty-one instances of the word *escape* in the Smith Journal. The expressions *run away*, *hide away*, *go where I will be safe* account for the other three instances of the same concept.

The figurative use of *escape* described here is also quite conventional. The *OED* records the meaning as 'to avoid or retreat from the realities of life' (note that the definition includes the word *retreat*, supporting the proposed link between these two expressions). However, the co-text makes these examples somewhat unusual. In the concordance lines, *escape* is seen as something *dark* (cf. BAD IS DARK) and *fetid* (foul smelling), which both have negative connotations. Interestingly, *warm*, which normally has positive prosody (like emotional proximity), also characterizes *escape*. In the given context, however, it also becomes something negative: warmth is conducive to rotting, so a foul smell would be exacerbated by it. *Escape* is also sometimes used as a euphemism for suicide, and in the preliminary example in this section (Example 12) this connotation is made explicit. In this context, it is significant that over half of *AFFECTIVE STATE IS ESCAPE* metaphors in the eighteen entries are in the final two entries, before Plath's suicide attempt.

The examples in Concordance 14 are also interesting because of various 'destinations' that they imply. As I outlined in Demjén (2011a), the co-text of the words in both Concordance 13 and Concordance 14 show that *retreat* is always in*to* something, for example, *non-thought*, *blubbering*, *numbness*, *womb*, *masochistic mental hell*, *not caring*. *Escape*, on the other hand, is always *away from* somewhere, for example, *myself*, *something*, *rigid cage of routine*, *action*, *responsibility*, *freedom*. The co-text of other relevant terms such as *withdraw* and *crawl back* also corroborates this pattern. Plath appears to want to retreat to places that, most people would agree, should be avoided, while she wants to escape from things that most people would consider normal parts of everyday life. In this sense, there seems to be a conflict between 'normal' perceptions and how reality is perceived by Plath. In Entry 121 she makes this contrast explicit by asking: *Why am I so perturbed by what others rejoice in?* One is supposed to embrace *freedom*, *action* and *responsibility* and not move away from it. Similarly, one should avoid *non-thought* and *mental hell*, not move towards it. This pattern seems to be characteristic of Plath's experience of the affective state that is described here.

6.3.3.2 Affective state as fragmentation

In this section, I turn to the second most frequent group of metaphors in the Smith Journal. Approximately 12 per cent of metaphorical expressions related to affective states in the eighteen sample entries can be grouped in the following way:

- Expressions such as *falls apart, crumbles, no integrating force, disintegration* etc. that suggest a coming apart of some sort.
- Expressions such as *loose ends, fragments, mask* etc. are similar to the expressions above, but the fragmentation remains contained within the self. In some of these cases, the context suggests some sort of inner conflict.
- Expressions that endow the relevant affective state or parts of the body with an independent identity, thereby personifying them. Examples include the mind being described as *crying* or *self-reviling*. As these examples suggest, the personified body/mind parts are often in conflict.

The first group suggests the systematic metaphor *AFFECTIVE STATE AS A COMING APART*, while the last two groups can broadly be subsumed under *AFFECTIVE STATE AS INNER DIVISION* (I discuss the latter in Demjén 2011a). All three, in turn, could potentially be subsumed under the broader category *negative affective state as fragmentation*.

6.3.3.2.1 Metaphors of coming apart

Expressions such as those highlighted in Example 27 and Example 28 make reference to some aspect of the environment or the self becoming separated into parts instead of remaining whole.

Example 27

> My world **falls apart crumbles**. **'The center does not hold.'** There is no **integrating** force (Entry 154)

Example 27 repeats the idea of *coming apart* four times, including one intertextual metaphor (Zinken 2003). '*The center does not hold*' is an allusion to Yeats's 'The Second Coming':

Things fall apart; the centre cannot hold;
Mere anarchy is loosed upon the world,

The poem itself was written in reaction to World War I and contains images of cycles and references to the cyclical nature of events (Lakoff and Turner 1989). However, in Plath's case it is not the entire world that is coming apart, but only *my* world. *World* here can be understood as a synecdoche standing for Plath's sense of self. Alluding to the phrase from Yeats in this context (where the actual world, larger than anybody's own world, is falling apart) intensifies the metaphor and potentially increases the significance of the affective state being referred to.

The final expression in Example 27 makes explicit reference to a lack of integration. This is repeated in Example 28, suggesting an *AFFECTIVE STATE AS COMING APART* systematic metaphor.

Example 28

frozen into **disintegration** I was (Entry 155)

An entry in the *OED* suggests that *I am falling apart* is a relatively conventional expression for negative affective states. However, other linguistic manifestations of the same broad semantic domain (e.g. *disintegration*) are not recorded in the *OED*, suggesting creativity at the word level. Lexical searches for *fragment, crumble, dis/no integration, fall/break apart, loose end, burst* in Wmatrix revealed seventeen (out of thirty-four) references to coming apart as repetitions of the examples here. Together with the four examples above, this persistence is potentially indicative of an underlying conceptual pattern.

Kövecses (2000) records the comparable conventional metaphors A PERSON OUT OF CONTROL IS A DIVIDED SELF and its 'counterpart' ATTEMPT AT EMOTIONAL CONTROL IS TRYING TO KEEP A COMPLETE OBJECT TOGETHER. However, the examples here are different in that the 'keeping together' is expected from a force, rather than the self. Similarly, Example 28 does not imply a loss of control but rather suggests an inability to influence the situation. In these *AFFECTIVE STATE AS COMING APART* metaphors, there is a sense that the experiencer of the affective state is passive. Both *falling apart* and *disintegration* suggest a multitude of parts, which cannot be held together by the experiencer. In Example 28, this is enhanced by the combination with *frozen*. Although it, perhaps, primarily belongs to the semantic field of temperature, in the present context the immobility and inflexibility meanings of *frozen* are foregrounded through attraction. It also sets up a contrast in the juxtapositioning with *disintegration*, since one implies lack of movement, while the other implies movement apart.

The importance of these metaphors is partly highlighted by the presence of the *WHOLENESS* vehicle group for positive affective states, as discussed above. This suggests two underlying systematic metaphors – *MENTAL WELL-BEING IS WHOLENESS* and *NEGATIVE AFFECTIVE STATE AS FRAGMENTATION* – which can be understood as counterparts to one another, providing further evidence for a conceptual pattern.

6.3.3.2.2 Inner division metaphors

In some parts of the Smith Journal, Plath writes about different selves within her, separating out various parts and writing about them as if they were independent. This effect does not always come about solely through metaphorically used words. For example, in *[m]y stubborn unimaginative self cannot conceive of him* (Entry 117) and *[but] my honest self revolted at this, hated me for doing this* (Entry 155), *self* is potentially used metonymically (as it refers only to a part of the whole). However, the sense of split is achieved more by the fact that a part of the self is being contrasted, via the adjectives, with another part of the self: an honest self implies a dishonest one; an unimaginative self implies an imaginative one. Such ways of talking about different 'selves' are quite common, especially in reference to social roles (e.g. *this is my teacher-self speaking*), and have been discussed in detail (e.g. Lakoff and Johnson 1999). In fact, even in the Smith Journal, eight out of twenty instances of *self* are repetitions of this type of reference. Adjectives used to denote the various selves include *vibrant, radical, limited, selfless*. What I focus on in this section are more explicitly metaphorical examples, such as the uses of *conceive, revolted* and *hated* in the examples above.

There are two broad groups of expressions that are discussed in this subsection:

- Expressions such as *loose ends, fragments, split* used to denote multiple parts that are contained within the self
- Expressions such as *conceive, revolted* and *hated* in the examples above that endow a part of the self with an independent opinion, will or identity

The first group could be seen as a variation on the *AFFECTIVE STATE AS COMING APART* metaphor discussed above. There is a similar sort of fragmentation, however; crucially, the parts remain contained within the self. The second group of expressions involve personification, and could be understood as a reference to multiple selves, sometimes in conflict.

In the first expressions in this section (Example 29 and Example 30), there is an element of apartness (as opposed to wholeness) but in a more static way. There is no ongoing process of coming apart, and the various parts remain somehow contained. Overall, this type of fragmentation occurs eight times in eighteen entries.

Example 29

I am a conglomerate garbage heap of **loose ends** (Entry 154)

Example 30

it was good to let go let the tight mask fall off, and the bewildered, chaotic **fragments** pour out (Entry 155)

In these examples, *loose ends* and *fragments* connote a self in separate parts. In addition, *conglomerate* in Example 29 suggests that the separate parts are still held together in some way. Similarly, the potential to *pour out* in Example 30 suggests that the parts are contained to begin with. While these expressions could be seen as a subgroup of the *COMING APART* group above, the separate parts are here being held together until they are willingly let out (Example 30). For this reason, they are more accurately subsumed under *AFFECTIVE STATE AS INNER DIVISION/SEPARATION*. There is an element of control that is not present in the *AFFECTIVE STATE AS COMING APART*.

The two examples here form metaphor clusters, where the various expressions interact. For example, references to *INNER SEPARATION* and *garbage heap* in Example 29 combine to suggest that the separate parts are also useless or something to throw away. This may imply that parts of the self are perceived as useless. Similarly, *bewildered* in Example 30 combines with the *INNER SEPARATION* vehicle and endows the separate parts with a cognitive capacity (see next subsection for further discussion). Although fragmentation metaphors such as *COMING APART* and *INNER SEPARATION* groups are not particularly well documented in the psychology literature, Goatly et al. (2002–5) have some comparable examples under MENTAL DISTURBANCE IS DIVISION/INCOMPLETENESS in the Metalude databank. In fact, it is this conceptual category that inspired the label and title of this section.

6.3.3.2.3 Multiple selves metaphors

The examples in this section and *my honest self* and *my stubborn unimaginative self*, mentioned earlier, imply the existence of two selves. Although the self as an entity tends to elude definition, Ramachandran (2003) argues that it has four defining characteristics:

1. Continuity – that is, a sense of time, past and future. It is like a thread running through the personality.
2. Unity or coherence – this is closely related to the above in that, despite the diversity of sensory experiences, memories, beliefs and thoughts, one experiences oneself as one person, as a unity.
3. A sense of embodiment or ownership – the self as anchored to the body.
4. A sense of agency or free will – this is the sense of being in charge of one's own destiny.

These characteristics imply the potential for splitting in the following ways: in terms of continuity there can be a split between time 1 and time 2; in terms of unity there can be split between two entire selves or two states of mind; in terms of embodiment there can be an implied split between mind and body or between various parts of the body. In terms of agency, there can possibly be a difference/separation between two different wills. For example, *my honest self* and *my stubborn unimaginative self* could imply splits in unity and, potentially, agency (as the two selves are doing different things).

Metaphorical constructions indicating a 'split self' are not particularly unusual. Indeed, Lakoff notes that an individual has 'not one form of consciousness but many' (Lakoff 1996: 101). This can result in the conceptualization of certain aspects of our inner life (e.g. indecision) as entities in conflict. Emmott (2002) proposes that a potential neurological reason for this may be the fact that people have two brain halves that control different parts of the body (left hemisphere controls the right hand and vice versa). As noted above, these expressions are not always strictly metaphorical, though they can be understood as metonymies.

A more explicitly metaphorical manifestation of this type of reference is *mask* as in Example 30 above. The expression suggests an inner and outer self, comparable to a distinction between public and private personae. Further linguistic manifestations include expressions such as *running away from yourself* and *being alone with your mind*. What makes the initial examples more interesting is that the self parts are constructed as having cognitive capacities (*hated*, *revolted*, *conceive*) of their own, adding a further layer of metaphoricity. The bold expressions in Example 31 and Example 32 are similar, but the different parts of the self are actually involved in independent actions. There are sixteen instances of this type of personified split self in eighteen entries, and the highlighted expressions in Example 31, Example 32 and Example 33 demonstrate some of these.

Example 31

> Some **devilish split** part in my personality had been **whispering** to me all week subconsciously: "Why go back? (Entry 128)

Example 32

> But the cold reasoning mass of gray entrail in my cranium which **parrots** 'I think, therefore I am', **whispers** that there is always the turning, the upgrade, the new slant. And so I wait. (Entry 36)

In the introductory examples, *hated* and *revolted* suggest conflict or disagreement between the parts of the self: a part of the self is doing something that the other one is not. In Ramachandran's terms, these examples can be interpreted as a split in unity and a split agency, respectively. As such, these examples can be subsumed under *AFFECTIVE STATE AS MULTIPLE SELVES*.

Some of the metaphors in this subsection can be compared to Barnden's (n.d.) MIND PARTS AS PERSONS OR OTHER ANIMATE BEINGS metaphor, which is common in mundane discourse such as 'conversations, popular magazines articles, popular novels, news articles, popular science texts, and other factual texts for consumption by the general public' (Barnden and Lee 2001: 3). In such metaphors, a part of a person or their mind is presented as an independent entity in itself – a sort of sub-person – often in communication with the rest of the self. The ATT-Meta Databank includes examples such as *Perhaps a part of my mother's mind she did not know about was making sure she got pregnant then*. However, most of the examples here seem to be at the more creative end of Barnden's examples. In addition to being metaphor clusters, Example 31 combines an *INNER SEPARATION* vehicle (*split*) with the personification in *whispering*. It is, in fact, this combination that gives rise to the *AFFECTIVE STATE AS MULTIPLE SELVES* metaphor. *Devilish* further endows the split part with an attitude, thereby enhancing the personification and sense of individuality. In Example 32, *parrots* and *whispers* similarly combine with the multiple metonymies that are used in reference to the brain/mind. On a textual level, *whispering*, *parrots* and *whispers* are examples of repetition, as all refer to verbal processes.

Example 33 below is similar to Example 32, as the mind is being constructed as a self in its own right once again.

Example 33

> to feel his mind soaring, reaching, and mine caged, **crying impotent, self-reviling** an **imposter** (Entry 154)

Plath's mind acts (*crying*) or does not act (*impotent*) and has attitudes (*self-reviling*) independently from the rest of the self and is further characterized as an *imposter*. A sense of conflict is created by *crying* and is enhanced by *self-reviling*. There is also a sense of stagnation, evoked by *impotent*. Creativity is apparent, in that CONFINEMENT (*caged*) and personifying vehicle terms combine to create a cluster of metaphors and in the reference to part of the self as *imposter*, which is novel at the word level, with connotations of subversion and intentional deceit. These elements extend on MIND PARTS AS PERSONS OR OTHER ANIMATE BEINGS.

Interestingly, within the same journal entry, obstacles in life are personified in a very similar way to Plath's mind: *The list mounted, obstacle after fiendish obstacle, they jarred, they leered, they fell apart in chaos* (Entry 154). Obstacles are personified as taunting adversaries and as fragmented opponents. The positioning of these parallel metaphors in close proximity strengthens the sense of discord between Plath and her mind (which is now associated with *obstacle*). The sense of conflict evoked by all inner division metaphors is not incidental. As Emmott notes, split selves 'commonly occur at times of personal crises' (Emmott 2002: 153).

As I discussed in Demjén (2011a), these metaphors seem to convey a sense of inner conflict as part of the experience of Plath's negative affective state. At various points, more than one self seems to exist, and they sometimes have opposing attitudes. They also act independently from each other.

I now turn to some metaphors that make up a smaller proportion of all metaphors identified in the manual intensive analysis. Although they are less salient in terms of frequency, they nevertheless convey aspects of Plath's experience in a creative way.

6.3.3.3 Affective state as physical pain

Approximately 8 per cent of metaphorical expressions relating to affective states in the eighteen entries selected for manual analysis fall into the following groups:

- Expressions such as *sick*, *sores*, *warts*, *disease*, *gangrenous* etc. suggest a physical illness or a painful physical manifestation thereof.

- Expressions such as *eats away*, *biting away*, *corrosive* etc. suggest some sort of physical aggression that also causes pain. Within context, it becomes clear that the physical aggression is internal.

These groups give rise to the systematic metaphors of *AFFECTIVE STATE AS PHYSICAL ILLNESS* and *AFFECTIVE STATE AS INTERNAL AGGRESSION* and can be seen as subtypes of the broader category *AFFECTIVE STATE AS PHYSICAL PAIN*. Schoeneman et al. (2004) linked metaphors of pain and illness with depression and the examples discussed here also relate to the conventional EMOTIONAL HARM IS PHYSICAL DAMAGE metaphor (Kövecses 2000).

6.3.3.3.1 Physical illness metaphors

There are a number of expressions in the Smith Journal that refer to negative affective states as physical illness. These include *ache*, *disease*, *hurt*, *pain*, *fester*, *cancer*, *malignant*, *lame*, *crippled*, *groggy*, *pestilence*, *agony*, *sores*, *warts*, but the most frequent manifestation (40 per cent) is the lemma *sick**. Example 34 includes three contextualized expressions from this group.

Example 34

> afraid that the **disease** which eats away the pith of my body with merciless impersonality will break forth in obvious **sores** and **warts** screaming 'Traitor, sinner, imposter' (Entry 154)

Some linguistic expressions of *AFFECTIVE STATE AS PHYSICAL ILLNESS* can be regarded as highly conventional. Uses of *sick* as in *Sick with envy* (Entry 154), or *cure* as in *no one has the power to cure you, but yourself* (Entry July 6), are recorded in the *OED* as standard uses of the terms. However, Example 34 elaborates on the conventional EMOTIONAL HARM IS PHYSICAL DAMAGE by specifying the manifestation of the physical illness as *sores* and *warts*. These suggest an additional element of pain and imply a visible form. There is also a certain amount of combination in Example 34. *Disease* in the main clause is animated and constructed as an aggressor in the relative clause by *eats away*. Later on, the *disease* is endowed with the human qualities of mercilessness and impersonality, which act as a form of personification. It is further personified in the reference to its abusive human-like scream: *'Traitor, sinner, imposter'*. The use of direct speech presentation heightens the sense of individuality possessed by the affective state. Finally, *disease* is also conceptualized as contained within the body from which it threatens to *break forth*.

Affective states are elusive, intangible phenomena, and conceptualizing them as if they were physical is not unusual. It is also not unusual to find negative affective states conceptualized as physical illnesses. However, the way in which these conventional conceptual metaphors are exploited in Plath's journal is unusual. They suggest struggle and intensity, perhaps alluding to the severity of the experienced state.

6.3.3.3.2 Internal aggressor metaphors

Example 34 in the previous subsection includes another group of expressions that deserve attention. Expressions such as *eats away*, but also *corrosive* and *biting away* as in Example 35, suggest a form of destruction, and in context it becomes clear that the destruction takes places from within. These expressions, some of which were discussed in the context of the preliminary examples, can be grouped under *AFFECTIVE STATE AS AN INTERNAL AGGRESSOR*.

Example 35

> fear, envy, hate: all the **corrosive** emotions of insecurity **biting away** at my sensitive guts. (Entry 154)

Biting away, in Example 35, constructs the emotion as an attacker/aggressor of an animal nature, while *corrosive* (attracted into the scenario) also adds to the element of aggression, although it is not an example of animation. A corpus search for *eating away*, its synonyms and *corrosion* revealed that this meaning is repeated six times in the Smith Journal. In addition, *corrosion* recurs in reference to lust. The aggression involved in these examples suggests an intense and painful experience once again.

Although emotions can be conventionally conceptualized as a struggle, usually only physical illnesses such as cancer are conceptualized as attacks (Deignan 2008) or as internal aggressors (Sontag 1979). In this sense, these metaphors can be regarded as elaborations on a conventional conceptualization: they make the mental disturbance more concrete, by using the source domains to refer to a slightly different target domain.

6.3.3.4 Further metaphors of note

So far, I have accounted for metaphorical patterns that were most frequent in the eighteen sample entries. Here, I discuss metaphorical patterns that are either less frequent or more conventional, but nevertheless salient in some way, not least because they cluster with the groups of metaphors discussed above:

- Expressions such as *numb, numbness, womb* can be linked in that they can all refer to some sort of absence or dampening of sensations.
- Expressions such as *break through, spew forth, burst, leak, hollow, cavern* all imply some form of container – some empty, some full. These can be seen as linguistic manifestations of the conventional BODY IS A CONTAINER OF EMOTIONS metaphor.
- Expressions such as *died, dead, decay, rot, foul* relate to death and decomposition.

6.3.3.4.1 Affective state as absence of sensations

Expressions grouped under *ABSENCE OF SENSATIONS* account for only 3 per cent of metaphorical expressions referring to affective states in the sample data, and there are only ten instances of *numb* and five instances of *womb* across the Smith Journal. However, these expressions are related to other, more frequent patterns already discussed.

Example 36

> I feel behind my eyes a **numb**, **paralyzed** cavern (Entry 154)

Example 37

> perhaps something good has been sprouting in the small **numb** darkness all this while. (Entry 104)

In its basic meaning, *numbness* denotes the inability to perceive physical contact such as a touch. The contextual metaphorical use, referring to an inability to feel in the sense of perceptions (as in Example 36 and Example 37), is recorded in the *OED* and can therefore be considered conventional. In both examples above, the mind or perceptions is/are numbed. The mind is indicated by the localization of the numbness as *behind my eyes* and in the reference to the interior of the skull (*small, dark*). In addition, as discussed in the preliminary section, *paralyzed* is attracted into the lack of sensations scenario, although it also retains its other meanings (illness, immobility).

While *womb* is not a synonym of the examples above, arguably sensations are subdued there as well. Foetuses in the womb are insulated from the outside world (including sounds and physical sensations) by the amniotic fluid around them. Example 38 makes this connection more explicit.

Example 38

> so I retreat, in a **numb womb** of purposeless business with no integration whatsoever. (Entry 155)

In Example 38, the state of numbness is unconventionally presented as something to aim for, in the sense that it is retreated into. It is explicitly combined with *MOVEMENT AWAY* vehicles (*withdraw*, *retreat*). In the following three examples, *womb* is also a destination of retreat. It appears to provide protection from the conflict or unpleasantness that necessitates retreat (in this case, life in general and perceptions thereof). Therefore, the *womb* must be a place where these perceptions do not exist.

Example 39

> I want to kill myself, to escape from responsibility, to crawl back abjectly into the **womb.** (Entry 154)

Example 40

> [you are] scared to get going, eager to crawl back to the **womb** (Entry July 6)

Example 41

> But this state of mind is born of a renunciation of complexities. It is a negation of sorts. A return to the **womb**, Freud might have it. (Entry 117)

These examples can be considered creative in various ways: the contextual meaning of *womb* does not appear in the *OED*, so there is novelty at the word level. In addition, *womb* is combined with the *MOVEMENT AWAY* vehicles. In fact, womb only occurs in this combination across the Smith Journal. Finally, the reference to Freud in Example 41 also functions as an intertextual metaphor, originating from a culturally salient text, or school of knowledge (Zinken 2003). For Freud, the womb was a type of home, familiar and comfort bringing. But it also symbolized the beginning and end of life; it is a safe and protected but also deathly and frightening place (Thurschwell 2000). In Example 41, *womb* is linked to a place without *complexities* – an adult life without complexities could be seen as no life at all, perhaps implying the latter Freudian sense of the term. The phrase *I want to kill myself* at the beginning of Example 39 additionally makes explicit reference to this.

There is a sense of dejection in these examples, as if it is clear to Plath that numbness is not a positive goal, but there also seems to be no alternative. A decrease in sensations and perceptive powers is often associated with the phenomenology of depression (Kiehl 2005). In this sense, and insofar as this can be considered a physiological process, *AFFECTIVE STATE AS LACK OF SENSATION* metaphors can also be considered metonymically motivated. In addition, the creativity of the language could signify the intensity of the affective state (Ortony and Fainsilber 1987) and suggest that the use of *womb* implies a more intense affective state than simpler and more conventional references to *numbness.*

6.3.3.4.2 Container metaphors

I now move on to expressions such as *break through, spew forth, leak, hollow, cavern, vacuum.* These expressions account for about 8 per cent of metaphors in the eighteen entries selected for manual intensive analysis. They can be subdivided into references to containers that cannot keep their contents in, and to empty containers.

Example 42

> I go plodding on, afraid that the blank hell in back of my eyes will **break through, spewing forth** like a dark pestilence (Entry 154)

Example 43

> And so on this day, you feel you will burst, break, if you cannot **let** the great reservoir **seething** in you **loose**, surging through some **leak** in the dike. (Entry 104)

Expressions in bold in Example 42 and Example 43 refer to containers releasing their contents in some way and involve an element of pressure, as the release tends to be violent. *Leak* is an exception to this, but as it occurs in the context of a *dike*, one can presume an element of pressure (dikes are normally designed to keep large bodies of water contained by withstanding pressure). These expressions can therefore be seen as manifestations of the conventional EMOTIONS ARE LIQUIDS IN A CONTAINER UNDER PRESSURE (Kövecses 2000). These types of metaphors are, at their root, highly conventional – emotions are often expressed as being contained within the body, and intense emotions are often presented as liquid in a pressure cooker (Kövecses 2000). The latter also carries all the associations of temperature, explosivity and the possibility of a violent release. This element can be linked to the control aspect in the emotion script, in particular the attempt at controlling affective states followed by a loss of that control.

These expressions often come in clusters, as in Example 42 and Example 43. In these cases, the repetition in such close proximity may suggest that the affective state is experienced more intensely. In addition, in Example 43 the CONTAINER UNDER PRESSURE conceptual metaphor is combined with the general CONTAINER concept (*dike, reservoir*). That, in turn, is metonymically referred to via the boundary of *dike*. This can be seen as a novel realization of the concept, again suggesting increased intensity.

As in its conventional realizations, the CONTAINER UNDER PRESSURE metaphor here could be indicative of a particular phase of a negative affective state (potentially depression or anxiety) – namely that of reaching a limit. There is definitely a form of agitation involved (*seething* and *spewing* suggest violence), but the limit in particular seems to be the point at which Plath is no longer able to conceal what is going on inside her and so needs to let various elements *spill out, spew forth, break through* etc. In this sense, these expressions represent the point where control is relinquished or lost.

Another group of expressions (as in Example 44) related to the general CONTAINER metaphor suggest an *AFFECTIVE STATE AS EMPTY CONTAINER* systematic metaphor. Linguistic expressions of the *EMPTY CONTAINER* vehicle group in reference to affective states are repeated eighteen times in the Smith Journal. These metaphors are used, first, to describe Plath's fears that she does not have enough ideas, thoughts, creativity to be a successful writer. Secondly, she also has more general feelings of worthlessness.

Example 44

> I am not **solid**, but **hollow**. I feel behind my eyes a numb, paralyzed **cavern**, a **pit** of hell, a mimicking nothingness. (Entry 154)

Cavern and *pit* refer to objects that have boundaries or sides and can therefore be thought of as containers. Although, strictly speaking, *hollow* and *solid* are only opposites in one sense of *solid*, they have been included as examples of emptiness (*not solid* is included here), because of the use of the contrastive *but*, which sets up an opposition allowing for such an interpretation. Hollowness presupposes boundaries, which implies a container. There seems to be no agency in these examples: the emptiness is not a result of anything in particular. In addition, some instances are introduced by relational processes of intensive attribution (Halliday and Matthiessen 2004), implying that the characteristic is relatively permanent. These types of expressions are less conventionally associated with emotions/affective states; however, Reeves et al. (2004) note some examples in the context of suicidal ideation.

6.3.3.4.3 Death and decay

Expressions such as *died, decay, rot, wither* relate to the process of death and decomposition. Together, such expressions account for approximately 6 per cent of metaphors in the sample data. Despite their relatively low frequency, these metaphors are significant in light of Plath's attempted suicide at the end of the Smith Journal. They can be subsumed under *AFFECTIVE STATE AS DEATH AND DECAY*.

Example 45

> You are twenty. You are not dead, although you **were dead**. The girl who **died** and was resurrected. (Entry 155)

Example 46

> Feeling myself fall apart, **decay**, **rot**, and the laurels **wither**, and fall away, and my past sins and omissions strike me with full punishment and import. All this, all this **foul gangrenous** sludge ate away at my insides. (Entry 155)

A corpus exploration of the USAS category 'Dead' (L1–) across the Smith Journal revealed 127 concordance lines, of which only fifteen referred to affective states metaphorically. Eleven were references to negative states, while two were examples of death negated, referring to positive states, and two others were in reference to lust. Additionally, there are four literal references to suicide in the Journal.

The expressions highlighted in these examples imply a previous negative affective state (as in Example 45) or refer to a current state (Example 46). The latter set refers indirectly to death through expressions of decomposition. Example 46 is also another complex cluster of metaphors. *DEATH AND DECAY* references are combined, initially, with a *COMING APART* vehicle (*fall apart* and potentially *fall away*), increasing the negativity that they project. In the second half of the example, however, they are used to characterize the *INTERNAL AGGRESSOR* vehicle (*ate away*). Aside from being another example of combination, these linguistic realizations (*foul*, *gangrenous*) of *DEATH AND DECAY* are also complex in themselves. Both of these could be interpreted as nested metaphors, as they belong to the domain of *PHYSICAL PAIN* as well.

What is most interesting here is that, while decomposition normally takes place after death, these examples convey current affective states. In this sense, decomposition leads to death rather than the other way round. To some extent, this can be related to the *COMING APART* group – after all, decomposition involves the breaking down of something – and explain the meaning of *laurels wither and fall away*: achievements are broken down and are no longer as meaningful. However, these musings are themselves conceptualized as being *foul* and *gangrenous*, making it seem like the thoughts themselves are responsible for the decomposition. This is almost iconic of a vicious cycle and may imply that the affective state is experienced in such a cyclical way.

6.3.3.5 Further investigations with USAS

In the previous two sections on positive and negative affective states, I focused on metaphorical patterns in the Smith Journal based on a qualitative analysis of a sample of eighteen entries. While I drew on corpus evidence to support these discussions, towards the end of Chapter 4, I suggested that the USAS categories in Table 6.1 below may also contain metaphorical references to affective states. I now report on an exploration of these USAS tags.

USAS categories in italics in Table 6.1 relate to various systematic metaphors in the previous two sections so have already been discussed. The unmarked USAS categories in Table 6.1 have little metaphorical content overall; any metaphors are highly conventional (in the case of DARKNESS) and/or are not

Table 6.1 USAS categories that may carry metaphorical references to affective states

USAS tag	Description
B1	Anatomy and physiology
S3.2	Relationship: Intimacy and sex
W4	*Weather*
W2	Light
O4.5	Texture
O4.4	Shape
L1+	Alive
W3	*Geographical terms*
N3.2+	Size: big
X2.1	Thought, belief
O1.2	Substances and materials: liquids
X3.4–	Unseen
N3.7–	Short and narrow
X7+	Wanted
W2–	Darkness
O4.6–	Temperature: cold
A1.7–	*No constraint*
B4	Cleaning and personal care
S5–	Not part of a group
N5.1+	Entire; maximum
X1	Psychological actions, states and processes
O4.6+	Temperature: hot/on fire

relevant to affective states. A number of these unmarked categories also consist mainly of literal/direct expressions. The 'Anatomy and Physiology' category, for example, almost exclusively only contains literal expressions referring to body parts.

Only four (highlighted) categories in Table 6.1 yielded significant metaphorical references to affective states. The categories referring to temperature (hot and cold) contained the highly conventional metaphoric/metonymic references typically associated with emotions (see Kövecses 2000). However, the two most productive categories, in a somewhat unexpected way, were 'psychological actions, states and processes' (X1) and 'thought/belief' (X2.1). Though the lexical items in these categories were mainly literal – the former contained mainly the expression *mind*, while the latter contained references to thinking and feeling – the immediate co-text of these expressions frequently contained metaphorical references to affective states. For example, 'psychological actions, states and processes' includes *mind soared/tried every trick*; *unimaginative state of mind*; *broken*; *weary*; *lethargic-spirited mind*; *state of mind is born*; *lashing a vagrant mind into*. Under 'thought/belief', the lemma *feel** carried the largest number of metaphoric references to affective states in its co-text, but some were also linked to *thinking* and *wondering*. Examples include *I felt sick/the weight of/cold reasoning mass/reality, cold/icy/I think inward/you wonder with quick fear/feeling of belonging to him curl up inside*. Most of these metaphorical expressions do not reveal anything new and, in fact, can be subsumed under the systematic metaphors identified in the manual analysis sections. Some of them are new lexical manifestations of these patterns, but a number of them are repetitions of those already discussed. It is nevertheless interesting that the X1 and X2.1 USAS categories can be potential starting points for investigating metaphors of affective states.

Stefanowitsch (2006) also recommends exploring target domain items quantitatively for metaphorical expressions. I therefore also explored USAS categories referring literally to affective states: 'emotional actions, states and processes' (E1); 'calm' (E3+); 'violent/angry' (E3–); 'fear/shock' (E5–); 'worry' (E6–); 'mental actions', 'states and processes' (X2); 'personality traits' (S1.2); 'success' (X9.2+) and 'failure' (X9.2–), 'happy' (E4.1+), 'sad' (E4.1–). Categories that included direct references to emotions often also included metonymic references to the relevant emotions (e.g. *smiling* under 'happy'), but these always accounted for less than 10 per cent of the concordance lines.

Surprisingly, 'affective states, actions and processes' did not include metaphoric references to affective states, as understood here: the expressions *mental/ly*, *intellectual/ly* and *subconscious/ly* constituted 70 per cent of the concordance lines. Similarly uninteresting from the current perspective were the other explored categories.

I also suggested in Chapter 4 that references to the self (as in *I am* or *you are* for second-person entries) need to be investigated for their relevance to metaphors of affective states. There are 331 concordance lines for the CLAWS tag VBM (am/'m) in the Smith Journal, and there are seventy-six concordance lines for VBR (are/'re) in second-person sub-corpus of the Smith Journal. Of these, approximately 297/331 for VBM and 44/76 for VBR refer to Sylvia Plath. Under VBM ('m/am), about 9 per cent of the relevant concordance lines refer metaphorically to Plath's self, and 90 per cent of those are references to negative affective states. The main examples are: I am *lost, bereft, sick, weak, not strong enough*; *at low ebb, a victim, torn, hypnotized, but one more drop in the sea, spinning in a temporary vacuum, horribly limited, submerged in circling ego, not solid, drowning in negativism, wallowing, not deep, a fool.* Under the CLAWS tag VBR (are), 31 per cent of the relevant concordance lines are metaphoric references to Plath's self, with 97 per cent of those implying negative affective states. This lends further support to the idea that negative affective states are expressed metaphorically with higher frequency than positive affective states.

This section, combined with the results of the qualitative metaphor analysis, seems to suggest two things. On the one hand, automated corpus-based methods still have some way to go before they can cope with the demands of metaphor analysis, especially where only particular metaphors are of interest. They can certainly make it easier to investigate predetermined lexical items, provide supporting evidence for patterns identified, and, with the help of semantic tagging, they can also assist in identifying new lexical manifestations of a particular systematic metaphor (cf. Stefanowitsch 2006 and Koller et al. 2008). Corpus methods cannot, however, identify metaphorical expressions independently. At the same time, corpus methods can make metaphor analysis more efficient for those interested in specific topics or targets. Target domain searches, aided by semantic taggers and the identification of related grammatical categories, seem to be effective ways of identifying significant metaphorical items that can inform the investigation of patterns. In the case of affective states, such key categories are 'psychological actions, states and processes'; 'thought/belief'; and VBM (*to be* in first-person singular).

6.3.4 Summary and conclusions

In this chapter, I explored the implications of metaphorical patterns in the Smith Journal for Plath's experience of her affective states: what they felt like, whether they were constructed as being within Plath's control, whether there were potential indications of change or intensity etc. Throughout, I linked the patterns and entailments of Plath's metaphor use with those commonly associated with depression and related disorders such as suicidality. As a diagnosed depressive, Plath's experience of her affective states is, to some extent, also her experience of depression. Therefore, what her language reveals about her experience may also be relevant for the experience of depression more broadly.

The analysis of figurative language in this chapter shows that positive affective states tend to be conveyed by two main groups of metaphorical expressions in the Smith Journal – *WHOLENESS* and *COMING INTO EXISTENCE* – while negative affective states are associated with a much wider range and higher frequency of metaphorical expressions. This appears to be consistent with the tendency of metaphor to 'attract the negative' (Cameron 2013) but also has bearings for Plath's experience. Table 6.2 summarizes the proportions of the main metaphorical patterns in these sample entries.

The three most frequent metaphorical patterns used to convey the experience of negative affective states in the Smith Journal are various types of *MOTION* metaphors (*CONFINEMENT*, *IMMOBILITY*, *UNCONTROLLABLE KINETIC FORCE*, *MOVEMENT AWAY*); *FRAGMENTATION* metaphors (*COMING APART*, *INNER DIVISION*, *MULTIPLE SELVES*); and physical pain metaphors (*PHYSICAL ILLNESS*, *INTERNAL AGGRESSOR*). Motion metaphors generally describe either a lack of movement or movement in an undesirable direction in the sense of the conventional LIFE IS A JOURNEY metaphor. Some of these (*IMMOBILITY* and *CONFINEMENT* metaphors) have been linked to suicide risk (Reeves et al. 2004). There was often an element of uncontrollability or inevitability in these expressions. An absence of control was the main component of the *AFFECTIVE STATE AS UNCONTROLLABLE KINETIC FORCE* metaphors, but it also featured in metaphors where there was no movement (e.g. *paralyzed*). Whether externally or internally imposed, the inability to move suggests that Plath was not able to overcome her affective state. Similarly, there was an element of inevitability in the *AFFECTIVE STATE AS MOVEMENT AWAY* metaphors: the metaphors construct Plath on the losing side of a potential struggle, where the only way to prevent annihilation is through retreat.

FRAGMENTATION metaphors suggested that Plath's inner world or various aspects of her self are separated or in conflict, or both. Particularly, *AFFECTIVE*

Table 6.2 Summary of the proportions of the main metaphorical patterns

Metaphor type	Proportion of metaphors discussed
Metaphors of Positive Affective states	6%
Metaphors of Negative Affective states	
MOTION	28%
CONFINEMENT	
IMMOBILITY	
UNCONTROLLABLE KINETIC FORCE	
MOVEMENT AWAY	
FRAGMENTATION OF ENVIRONMENT AND THE SELF	12%
COMING APART	
SPLIT SELF	
PERSONIFICATION	
PHYSICAL PAIN	8%
PHYSICAL ILLNESS	
INTERNAL AGGRESSOR	
Other Patterns	24%
ABSENCE OF SENSATIONS	
CONTAINER METAPHORS	
DEATH AND DECAY	
METONYMY	
Not discussed in detail in this analysis[5]	22%
ANIMALS	
BURDEN	
TIGHTNESS	
RELIGION	
PLANTS	
TEMPERATURE	
RUBBISH	
MASK	

STATE AS INNER DIVISION and *AFFECTIVE STATE AS MULTIPLE SELVES* metaphors entail a sense of conflict in that various parts of the self seem to have opposing attitudes and wills. Some of these can be seen as counterparts to the *AFFECTIVE STATE AS WHOLENESS* metaphors of positive affective states, suggesting a stable conceptual scenario.

AFFECTIVE STATE AS PHYSICAL PAIN metaphors construct Plath's negative affective states as involving physical pain, while in *AFFECTIVE STATE AS INTERNAL AGGRESSOR* metaphors, the affective state is constructed as an active entity in itself: the aggressor. Figure 6.1 below summarizes the main metaphorical

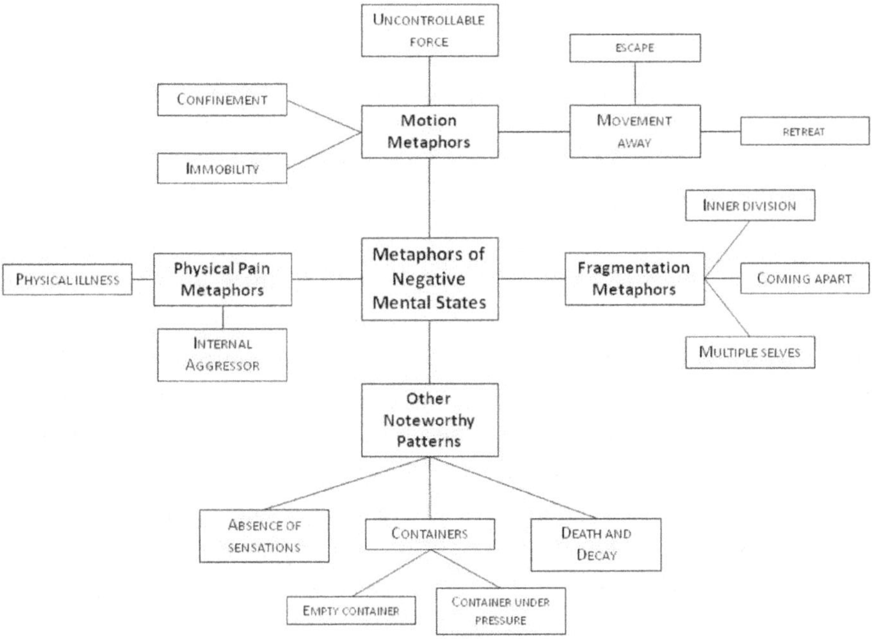

Figure 6.1 Summary of metaphorical patterns.

patterns associated with negative affective states. The categories in bold are the broad groupings of systematic metaphors, while the outer categories represent the respective subtypes.

Additional metaphors that convey negative affective states are expressions such as *numbness* and *womb*, various CONTAINER metaphors and metaphors of DEATH AND DECAY.

These metaphorical patterns suggest a number of insights regarding Plath's lived experience. For example, vehicles of *CONFINEMENT* and *IMMOBILITY* and expressions implying circular motion such as *wallowing* and *whirlpool* imply that Plath finds these negative affective states unpleasant and difficult to get out of. The difficulty and effort involved in attaining positive affective states as conveyed though *AFFECTIVE STATE AS COMING INTO EXISTENCE* metaphors lends further support to this interpretation.

The unpleasantness of negative affective states is also conveyed through unusual realizations of the LIFE IS A JOURNEY conventional metaphor. Specifically, *MOVEMENT AWAY* metaphors and some *AFFECTIVE STATE AS ABSENCE/LACK OF SENSATIONS* metaphors (those that express a desire for the absence of sensation) imply that there is something unpleasant that needs to be avoided. Numbness, after all, is another way of avoiding or alleviating the experience of unpleasantness. In some cases, however, the yearning for a lack of sensations could be interpreted as suicidal ideation.

Various patterns described above suggest that inevitability or helplessness are part of the experience of these negative states for Plath. *AFFECTIVE STATE AS UNCONTROLLABLE KINETIC FORCE* metaphors, in particular, but *CONFINEMENT* and *IMMOBILITY* vehicles as well, convey this sense. Uncontrollability is additionally conveyed through *AFFECTIVE STATE AS INTERNAL AGGRESSOR* and *CONTAINER UNDER PRESSURE* metaphors. Helplessness, in the form of passivity or lack of agency, is additionally conveyed by some *EMPTY CONTAINER* metaphors, in the sense that the experiencer lacks 'the substance' to progress. Instances where agency is lacking are highly significant. In fact, Ramachandran and Blakeslee (2005: 249) suggest that 'a "self" that sees itself as completely passive, as a helpless spectator, is no self at all'.

Plath's metaphors of negative affective states not only convey a sense of general unpleasantness; some also suggest that struggle, conflict and pain are part of her experience. Such a sense of struggle is conveyed through vehicles of *INNER DIVISION*, *MULTIPLE (disagreeing) SELF* and *AFFECTIVE STATE AS INTERNAL AGGRESSOR* metaphors. The sense of division can sometimes also be created by metonymic references to the self or the mind – in particular, when the metonymies involve a difference in status (e.g. using *flesh* to refer to the self). However, a struggle is potentially also implied in RETREAT metaphors – it is to be retreated from. A sense of the physical discomfort and pain is conveyed through *AFFECTIVE STATE AS PHYSICAL ILLNESS*, but also *INTERNAL AGGRESSOR* metaphors.

Finally, a sense of intensity is suggested by textual patterning as well as by conceptual elaboration. Charteris-Black and Musolff (2003) also note that intensity can be expressed through repetition and recurrence of metaphors, but also through combining source domains with similar entailments (as in Example 13). In Plath's case, textual patterning and conceptual elaboration seem to be more frequently used to signal intensity than specific types of metaphors might be (e.g. EMOTION IS A LIQUID IN A CONTAINER UNDER PRESSURE). In addition, according to the vividness hypothesis put forward by Ortony (1975) (cited in Gibbs et al. 2002), the more intense an emotion, the more likely it is to be described metaphorically. As such, the difference in frequency of metaphors for positive and negative affective states may also be indicative of intensity: Plath experiences negative affective states as more intense.

However, the difference between metaphors for negative and positive states is not just a question of frequency. When positive affective states are referred to metaphorically, the expressions/scenarios are often less complex/elaborate and/or novel than those referring to negative affective states. Striking and complex metaphors can also indicate intensity: Ortony and Fainsilber (1987: 183) found that 'the ratio of novel to frozen metaphors was greater for intense emotions (12%) than for mild ones (8%)'. This, again, suggests that for Plath, negative affective states are more intense than positive ones – that is, intensity can also be conveyed through metaphor complexity.

As Plath was diagnosed with depression, her lived experience potentially bears relevance for the experience of depression more broadly. Some of these findings correspond with findings in the literature on emotions (Kövecses 2000) and negative affective states such as depression (McMullen and Conway 2002, Semino 2008) and anxiety (e.g. Pennebaker and King 1999). Reeves et al. (2004) even link metaphors of stagnation (or being stuck) to suicidal ideation. However, *AFFECTIVE STATE AS FRAGMENTATION* and different types of MOTION metaphors, in particular, are described here in greater detail than in other studies. In addition, and contrary to expectations set by the literature, simple down metaphors are not very common. Instead, an element of downward motion is sometimes entailed in more prominent and complex metaphorical source domains.

7

You and Plath

On various occasions in the preceding chapters, I referred to the fact that Sylvia Plath narrated some of the entries in her journal in the second person while still remaining the protagonist of the events she discussed; she wrote about herself as *you*. It is this peculiarity of the Smith Journal that I focus on in this chapter. I begin with an overview of some of the literature on personal pronoun use, zooming in on second-person narration as a form of self-reference, in particular. This is followed by a discussion of potentially different types of second-person narration as they occur in the Journal. I propose a typology of second-person narration based on the co-occurrence of particular types of tense, aspect, mood, deixis and lexical features with *you*, called temporal orientation.

7.1 Personal pronouns in interaction and narration

Pronouns are some of the most basic grammatical words in any language. All languages have person pronoun morphemes, and in some languages the systems of morphemes are more elaborate than in English (Margolin 1990); Hungarian, for example, has three levels of formality. Personal pronouns in English (*I*, *you*, *he*/*she*/*it*, *we*, *they*, *you*) are function words that often refer to people and things. They are usually grouped together with the corresponding possessive determiners, possessive pronouns and reflexive pronouns (Biber et al. 1999).

At the most basic level, personal pronouns are those words that 'refer to the speaker (*I*), the addressee (*you*) or other entities (*it*): ***I must tell*** **you** ***about*** **it**' (Biber et al. 1999: 70). Traditionally, they have been understood as those words that are used to replace nouns. However, Quirk et al. argue that 'it is best to see pronouns as comprising a varied class of closed-class words with nominal function. By "nominal" here we mean "noun-like" or, more frequently, "like a noun phrase"' (Quirk et al. 1985: 335). This means that personal pronouns take on the grammatical/syntactic function of nouns, but can represent all the information included in a noun phrase (*The* <u>*blonde girl in the red dress*</u> *went to see* **her favourite grandmother**. <u>*She*</u> *made* **her** *very happy*). Personal pronouns are also seen as situational (referring to things/people in the speech situation) and anaphoric or cataphoric – referring to something said/written previously or subsequently (Quirk et al. 1985).

While these examples make it seem as if personal pronouns refer to something concrete, Wales notes that reality is somewhat more complicated. 'The referents [for personal pronouns], unlike those for proper names, are not fixed or stable but "shift" according to the situation' (Wales 1996: 3). In a conversation, for example, usually both/all participants take turns at speaking and listening, thereby alternating in their roles as *I* and *you*. In addition, the same form, *you*, can refer to one specific person, a particular group of people and even 'people in general' like the other plural pronouns *we* and *they* (Quirk et al. 1985). This latter 'generic' *you* is usually understood as an informal version of *one*, but it also keeps some of its original second-person meaning. According to Quirk et al., 'It can suggest that the speaker is appealing to the hearer's experience of life in general, or else of some specific situation, … [and] sometimes, the reference is to the speaker's rather than the hearer's life, or experiences' (Quirk et al. 1985: 354). As examples, the authors provide the following: *This wine makes you feel drowsy doesn't it?* – Here, *it* refers to the wine that is present and being drunk in the specific speech situation. If the question went *Wine makes you feel drowsy, doesn't it?* then *it* would refer to the hearer's general experience. On the other hand, the statement *It wasn't a bad life. You got up at seven, had breakfast, went for a walk …* draws on the speaker's rather than the hearer's life. This polysemy means that it can sometimes be difficult to determine whether the referent of *you* is definite or not: 'A speaker's observations on life will invariably be coloured by their own subjective attitudes and experience; conversely, they may feel that their own experiences are of interest or significance to the community at large' (Wales 1996: 79).

7.1.1 Second-person pronouns and narration

In a prototypical conversation or reading situation, the potential ambiguity of personal pronouns may seem rather irrelevant, since the referents of pronouns are not usually confused. Nevertheless, most acknowledge that comprehension is not necessarily straightforward (e.g. Biber et al. 1999). At a basic level, the first-person singular pronouns *I*, *me*, *my*, *mine*, *myself*, refer to the speaker/writer of a message, while the second-person singular pronouns *you*, *your*, *yours*, *yourself* refer to the addressee, but exclude the speaker/writer (Quirk et al. 1985). The main problem with this definition is that it excludes non-prototypical uses of the pronouns such as self-address in the second person or the generic *you*. *You* can additionally be used metaphorically when 'no actual addressee could be literally included in the reference class of a particular token *you*' (Margolin 1990: 428). For example, in *In ancient Rome, you could witness displays of great strength in the form of Gladiator fights*, the *you* is invited to imagine him/herself in a different place and time. It is impossible for the *you* being addressed in the contemporary time, to witness such a fight under any 'real' circumstances. These idiosyncratic characteristics of the second-person pronoun are largely responsible for the effects of what is known as second-person narration.

7.1.1.1 Defining second-person narration

Second-person narration tends to be discussed mostly within the discipline of narratology. Although it might appear simple at first, the phenomenon of second-person narration (SPN) is not straightforward to define (for a summary see Reitan 2011). The following Nuruddin Farah passage is an example of what Fludernik (1994a) calls, 'proper' second-person narration.

> You wondered if the man had made sense to the others since you didn't understand him. You were looking at the other faces for clues when Misra's image came right before you, placing itself between you and the men you were staring at. You would remember the same image when, years later, at school and in Mogadiscio, you were shown the pictures of Egyptian mummies by one of Salaado's relations, namely Cusmaan. The image which insisted on imposing itself on your brain was that of a Misra, already dead, but preserved; a Misra whose body, when you touched it, was cold as ice, as though it had spent a night or two in the mortuary. (Farah 1986: 123)

A number of scholars such as Fludernik (1994a) argue that second-person narratives have not been treated in necessary detail due to the lack of an exact definition of what constitutes a 'second-person text'. She also points out that an overly restrictive definition would be counterproductive, as it would possibly disregard interesting or historical applications, or both, of second-person narration. However, the need for at least clear categories and ways of distinguishing between various types of second-person narration is important in order to avoid diluting 'the specificity and originality of the phenomenon' (Fludernik 1994a: 284).

Underlying the discussions of what does or does not constitute 'proper' second-person narrative is the issue of narrativity itself, that is, what constitutes a narrative? Note that *narrative* in this chapter is understood at a broader level as a genre, rather than a discourse type as in Sections 2.1.1 and 4.3.3.

Traditional notions assume that in order for narrative to exist, there needs to be a chain of events and an acting agent (Fludernik 1994b). The actions themselves should be in the past (relative to narrative time), factive and completed (Herman et al. 2005). This definition seems too restrictive and does not reflect the rich variety of narrative types available. It disregards the fact, for example, that even traditional narratives contain non-factual (in the story-world) events (Margolin 1999). Fludernik (1996) approaches the subject from a cognitive perspective and proposes a redefinition of narrativity that is based on experience (and the presence of an experiencer). Fludernik (1996) understands this 'experientiality' to describe the emotional involvement with and cognitive evaluation of situations that occur in 'real-life'. Therefore, the existence of an experiencer (i.e. a human being to whom something happens), 'sufficiently grounded in active consciousness, observation, perception, and reflective speculation' (Fludernik 1994b: 454), is enough to constitute narrativity.

Aside from the issue of narrativity, Margolin (1990), Fludernik, (1994a, 1994b, 1995), Herman (1994 and 2004), DelConte (2003) and Richardson (2006), among others, have gone to great lengths to define and categorize the different textual manifestations of second-person narration. Definitions have attempted to capture the essential characteristics of the phenomenon. For Richardson (2006), for example, the essential characteristic of second-person narration is the designation of its protagonist by *you*, provided that the text concerned is not an apostrophe (i.e. a direct address of the reader, absent character, unreal being etc. outside of the narration). Richardson also makes explicit that his definition and characterization of SPN should be considered not as categorical but rather as a matter of degree or tendency, since second-person narration's 'very essence is to eschew a fixed essence' (Richardson 2006: 19). Fludernik similarly sees the essential characteristic of second-person narration as the designation of its protagonist by *you* and notes that 'second-person texts frequently also have a communicative level on which a narrator (speaker) tells the story of the *you* to (sometimes) the *you* protagonist's present-day absent or dead, wiser, self' (Fludernik 1994a: 288).

DelConte (2003) sees the definitions above as inadequate, because they assume the existence of a definable narratee-protagonist and so disregard the possibility of hypothetical or conditional second-person narration. He suggests a modification of Fludernik's definition that can account for narratives with hypothetical actants and scenarios, while still maintaining that second-person narratives are those where the narratee is the same as the protagonist:

> second-person narration is a narrative mode in which the narrator tells a story to a (sometimes undefined, shifting, and/or hypothetical) narratee – delineated by *you* – who is also the (sometimes undefined, shifting, and/or hypothetical) principal actant in that story. (DelConte 2003: 207–8)

Allowing for these hypothetical actants and scenarios becomes important when looking at texts such as journals, where most things 'happen' in the narrator's head and could therefore be interpreted as hypothetical.

7.1.1.2 Approaches to second-person narration

Aside from nuanced differences in the definition of second-person narration, various scholars have also classified the different types of *you* that can count as second-person narration differently. In this section, I consider various classifications by some of the main theorists on second-person narration.

7.1.1.2.1 Margolin

Margolin's (1990) account of second-person narration is firmly based on the functions of the second-person pronoun. He appreciates the 'ontological havoc caused when such communication proceeds against the grain, as, for example, when real authors talk to invented characters or when narrative agents talk back to their narrators' (Margolin 1990: 429). Although he does not necessarily see it as 'authentic' second-person narration, his transferred (or displaced) *you* (e.g. Beckett's *Trilogy* and *How It Is*) is the most relevant type of SPN for the upcoming analysis.

Margolin (1990) includes two slightly different types of *you* under the term *transferred*. One is what I would call second-person self-address, that is, speaking to oneself in the second person, in the form of an internal dialogue. Here 'the I-cum-you will normally involve a version of the speaker as a participant in some real or imagined narrated events, and the utilization of the *you* form may be indicative of an inner split, self-alienation, or the like' (Margolin 1990: 428). The other type of displaced *you* is exemplified by what Herman (1994) has called *apostrophe* (Margolin uses Bühler's term *deixis am phantasma*) – directly addressing someone who is not physically present in the communicative situation but only evoked in the mind of the speaker.

I want to focus on the former type of displacement, which, I argue, can be seen as authentic second-person narration with Fludernik's (1996) redefinition of narrative. Margolin subdivides instances of 'internal dialogue' further. In the first case, there are two explicit speakers – an *I-NOW* and a *you-NOW* – of equal weight in a dialogic situation, but 'the *you* role is restricted to the communicative activity' (Margolin 1990: 436). In the second case, there is just one speaker – an I-NOW – and the *you* (through co-referential with the *I*) is a narrated individual in a different temporal location. This means that the *you* personality does not exist outside of the dialogue and does not speak within the dialogue (or in this case, monologue). The narrated *you* and the narrator (though the same person) are not on the same diegetic plane, to use Genette's (1980) terminology. The speaker I-NOW is at a superior discourse level to the *you*, and so there is no talk back. Margolin (1990) does not specify whether the presence of the first-person pronoun is a requirement for this type of displacement. However, the *I* can be implied by the presence of a *you*, as noted before.

In these special cases, Margolin (1990) suggests that it is useful to identify which spatio-temporal version of the speaker is referred to with which pronoun. However, what is most interesting, according to Margolin, is the search for a functional explanation of the transfer and its cognitive interpretation. He suggests two possibilities:

> the speaker may speak to and of part of him/herself as of another, implying an inner duality, distancing or alienation. Or the speaker may be adopting the point of view of a specific or generalized other toward him/herself. In this second case we may also say that the speaker has internalized the voice of others as they speak/spoke of him or her. (Margolin 1990: 436)

Margolin (1990), helpfully, also looks at the effect of tense on the status and functions of second-person narratives, or rather, how it helps in classifying them. According to him, second-person narratives in the past tense resemble court prosecutions or eulogies. Here, the narrated and the addressed *you* will be the same person but in different spatio-temporal locations. Second-person narratives written in the future tense [sic] resemble predictions, warnings and promises and are just another example of modality. Present-tense second-person narration resembles sports reporting where an ongoing activity is being reported. The narrated *you* and the addressed *you* share the same spatio-temporal location in these instances. Questions and instructions of the narrator can only be seen as carrying their full illocutionary force if the second-person narration is in the present tense, as the locutions can then feed back into the narrated system and affect its future course.

7.1.1.2.2 Herman

Herman (1994) sets out to examine the discourse functions of the second-person pronoun *you* in narrative contexts by applying linguistic theories of person deixis to *A Pagan Place* (O'Brien 1984). He suggests that 'narrative *you* produces an ontological hesitation between the virtual and the actual by constantly repositioning readers to a fundamentally indeterminate degree' (Herman 1994: 379). In order to account for this phenomenon, he looks at two discourse models: one model accounts for the referential, the other for the address function of the second-person pronoun. The referential model 'prompts us to assume that the entity evoked by *you* exists in the world of the narrative as the fictional protagonist who addresses to herself [sic] a narrative of which she [sic] is in turn the (intradiegetic) narratee' (Herman 1994: 380). This prevents identification with the narrating entity because the reader perceives him or her as distant from the reader's own world, that is, virtual. Within the address function, the 'textual *you* evokes an entity – that is, a reader – actual or at least actualizable in our world and eo ipso more or less virtual in the world of the narrative' (Herman 1994: 380). This model focuses on the address function of the pronoun and allows the readers to identify with the narrative/addressee more easily.

Herman (1994 and 2004) then proposes his own model, consisting of five types of *you* in narratives. The first two types of you originate from the referential function of the pronoun, while the second two originate from its address function. The final type, Herman argues, stems from a combination of the two functions:

1. Generalized *you*
2. Fictional reference
3. Fictionalized address
4. Apostrophic address
5. Doubly deictic *you*

Herman argues that Types 2, 3 and 5 are examples of real second-person narration. Fictional reference, according to Herman (1994), can be observed in *You had to pass your own gates to go to your aunt's* (O'Brien 1984: 189). Here, the specific part of the story-world that is evoked by the description ensures that the reference cannot be misunderstood as generic. Herman exemplifies Type 3 with an instance of direct address in *A Pagan Place*: a mother addressing her daughter as *you* (*… not you, darling*).

The most interesting, however, is Type 5. The doubly deictic *you* 'ambiguates virtualized and actualized discourse referents or rather superimposes the deictic roles of nonparticipants and participants in the discourse' (Herman 1994: 392). This means that the audience will feel somewhat addressed by, perhaps even conflated with, the textual *you* (Herman 2004). As an example of this type, Herman uses the following passage from O'Brien: *you heard panting from the next room, the amateur actor's room. It was like something you had heard before, distantly, a footprint on your mind, you did not know from where* (O'Brien 1984: 169–70). This phenomenon was also noticed by Phelan (1994), and Herman himself uses Phelan's words to simplify his own meaning: 'When the second-person address to a narratee-protagonist both overlaps and differentiates itself from an address to actual readers, those readers will simultaneously occupy the positions of addressee and observer' (Phelan 1994: 351).

7.1.1.2.3 Fludernik

Fludernik (1994b) looks at a variety of different types of texts, relying on her own classification based on the models of Austrian narratologist Stanzel and French narratologist Genette. Her revised *communicative* and *non-communicative* modes are based on Stanzel's (1984) teller and reflector mode, respectively. The reflector mode (non-communicative narration) is when the story is presented through the eyes of a *reflector* character (or internal focalizer). This narrator narrates in a similarly distanced manner to an authorial narrator (and is also in the third person) but tends to avoid description and excessive detail regarding the environment and focuses more on displaying a character's mind (Herman et al. 2005). In these narratives, the protagonist is the deictic centre, and all deictic expressions relate to him/her, and the first and third person can alternate without disruption to the ontological frame (Fludernik 1994b). Examples of such narratives are 'slice-of-life' and stream-of-consciousness stories (Herman et al. 2005: 365).

Stanzel's (1984) other models fall under Fludernik's communicative model, as these narratives establish a more direct line of communication between any addresser and addressee (author/reader, narrator/narratee or character/character etc.). The communicative mode, however, also expands on Genette's (1980) terminology in that it differentiates between those (homo-) communicative texts where the narrators/narratees function as protagonists (and therefore exist in the story-world) and those (hetero-) communicative texts where the narrators/narratees are separate from the fictional world (Fludernik 1994b). Fludernik argues, however, that these are not distinct categories but should, rather, be understood as two ends of a cline.

In terms of this new model, Fludernik situates second-person narratives in between homo- and heterocommunicative texts, arguing that they can fall into either category, because the narrator and narratee can, but need not, share a 'realm of existence'. In homocommunicative second-person narratives, the narrator and narratee are on the same levels of discourse and story. As an example of homocommunicative second-person fiction, Fludernik offers Calvino's *Un re in ascolto*, where the king (protagonist and narratee) is given instructions by an initially unidentified *I* on how to act. Butor's *La modification* is given as an example of heterocommunicative second-person fiction – the narration is heterodiegetic, and there is no address in the sense that the *you* is not being spoken to but spoken about. Fludernik, however, also notes some problematic cases such as Stout's *How Like a God*. In this example, the *you* address is used to retrospectively represent the protagonist's actions (to himself) making it similar to an internal monologue. Fludernik argues that internal monologues should not be included under 'proper' second-person narration, due to the lack of 'narrative', however:

> To the extent that a dramatic monologue shifts its emphasis from the situation of talking or self-expression to the telling of a story with the current addressee as its prime protagonist, that text moves towards second-person fiction. [...] the distinction between interior monologue and second-person fiction can prove to be entirely arbitrary. (Fludernik 1994a: 289)

The problem of including or excluding certain types of texts in second-person narration, of course, also applies to (and is exacerbated in) non-communicative texts – especially since their main manifestations are interior monologues. However, the redefinition of narrativity in terms of experientiality (Fludernik 1996) does alleviate some of these issues.

7.1.1.2.4 DelConte

DelConte (2003) demonstrates the problems with dominant models of narration in accounting for and categorizing the variety of narratives available. He suggests that traditional definitions are inadequate because second-person narration, rather than being defined by the narrator as first- and third-person narrative are, is defined by the one listening, that is, the narratee (DelConte

2003). He therefore proposes a new approach, based on the idea of defining texts not according to voice (i.e. narrating person) but according to the relationships between narrator, narratee and protagonist. These three 'actants' are understood as corresponding to the elements of speaker, text and audience. DelConte's model includes five categories of narrative (second- as well as first- and third-person narratives) based on these relationships, as Figure 7.1 (DelConte 2003: 211) demonstrates.

Type 1 (Non-coincident narration) is when narrator, protagonist and narratee are all distinct or exist on different diegetic planes. In Type 2 (Completely coincident narration), the narrator, protagonist and narratee are all the same and exist on the same diegetic plane. This is where a narrator speaks to themselves about themselves. Type 3 is partially coincident narration (narrator/protagonist), where narrator and protagonist are the same and exist on the same diegetic plane. Here a narrator speaks about themselves to someone else. Type 4 is also partially coincident narration (narrator/narratee), but here a narrator speaks to themselves about someone else. Finally, in Type 5 (another partially coincident narration – protagonist/narratee), the protagonist and narratee are the same and exist on the same diegetic plane. Here the narrator

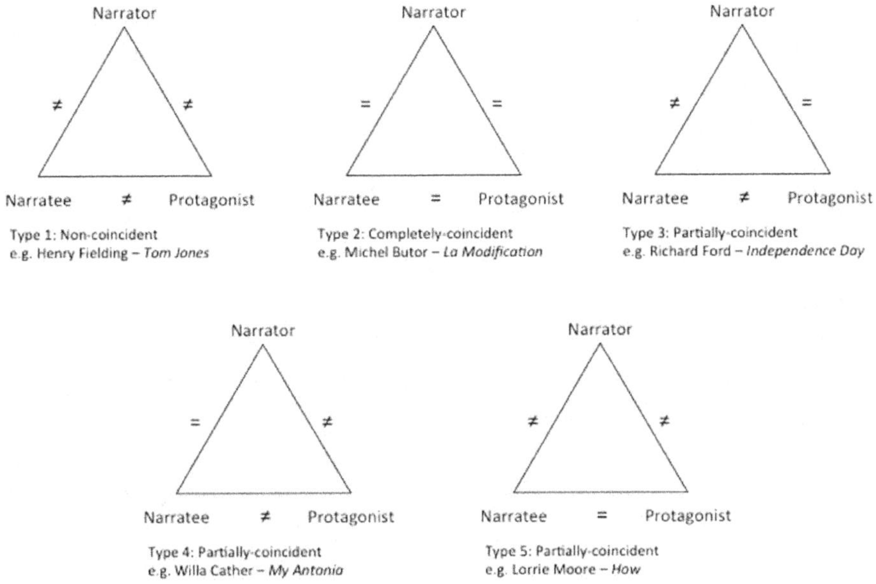

Figure 7.1 Adapted from DelConte (2003).

speaks to an external narratee who is also the protagonist, for example, a mother telling her son about something he does. Here the reader occupies the position of narrative audience but not narratee, the reader just 'overhears' the narrative. Just like Herman (1994), DelConte uses Phelan's (1994) notion of the reader oscillating between feeling addressed to highlight the effects of this type.

7.1.1.3 Functions of second-person narration

Second-person narration can have a variety of functions, and most of these depend on the type of narration and the properties of the second-person pronoun as described in more detail in the previous section. Second-person narration in the form of self-address is common in Latin American writing. It is usually framed within a primarily first- or third-person narrative and thereby functions as a representation of interior monologues (Fludernik 1994a and 1994b). But, SPN also had other non-genre-specific effects. Bruce Morrissette, for example, notes that second-person narration carried a number of 'curiously varied psychological resonances' (Morrissette 1965: 2), thereby producing effects in fictional texts that other forms of narrative were not capable of. One of the main psychological resonances of second-person narration seems to be the sense of tension or conflict that it creates:

> second-person narrative can, and frequently does, correlate with great emotional depth since the dialogic relationship it puts at its very centre allows for an in-depth treatment of human relationships, especially of relationships fraught with intense emotional rifts and tensions. (Fludernik 1994b: 466)

In other instances, the use of *you* can suggest that the speaker is viewing themselves as 'other', from a virtual distance (Margolin 1990). This kind of 'othering' perspective can potentially suggest a striving for objectivity and alternative interpretations of events.

Second-person narration can further achieve not only a tension in the narrative but also a tension with the reader, because of its inherently ambiguous referent and potential to evoke empathy (Fludernik 1994b). Ambiguity partly stems from the facts that the pronoun's precise referent depends on context and is not necessarily specific. Empathy is evoked by the direct address function of *you*, which puts the reader in the position of natural addressee (Herman 2004, Phelan 1994). Although this is not always the primary function of the pronoun in context (and *you* is not the only pronoun with multiple functions), it is the most resistant to disambiguation or neutralization within texts: *you* 'always relies on the submerged deictic significance of the original address function of this pronoun' (Fludernik 1994b: 468).

A very specific effect of second-person narration can be seen in instances of self-address, that is where the narratee is the protagonist and also the narrator. This effect is the sense of 'split' as outlined by Margolin (1990). Fludernik (1994b: 450) suggests that in passages of self-address the sense of split arises because *you* can only denote both narrator and addressee if 'an *I* splits into two voices that interact dialogically'. Margolin additionally notes that in some of these *transferred* second-person narratives, the speaker *you* is superior to the spoken to *you* in terms of 'knowledge and/or understanding and/or judgment as regards the actions or the psychological nature of the [self]' (Margolin 1990: 444). A possible explanation for this may lie in the unusualness of using a pronoun other than *I* to refer to the self. As Katie Wales puts it, 'When non-first-person singular forms are used for [+ego], the "distancing" that results is a social one of "power", confirming the speaker's authority' (Wales 1996: 70).

Overall, then, SPN may be a distancing device, it may signal points of emotional upheaval in a text, it may indicate a sense of inner split/duality and it may evoke readers' empathy by drawing them in to the narrative. In fact, all these effects of second-person narration (though they may be contradictory to some extent) are discernible in instances of self-address in the Smith Journal, albeit at different points.

7.1.1.4 Synthesis and concluding remarks

The various approaches introduced above seem to agree on a need for a redefinition of the basic concepts and for describing the various ways that a second-person pronoun can appear in texts, and they have all tried to do this in various ways. One of the issues that scholars seem to come up against is restrictiveness: what counts and what doesn't. For example, Margolin (1990) insists on the presence of 'a singular global narrator on the highest level of textual embedding, such that the whole (fictional) discourse originates with him or her' (Margolin 1990: 430). While this may be a useful notion, I see no reason why the narrator needs to be explicitly present, nor why there should only be one. DelConte's redefinition of second-person narration already rectifies this, but Fludernik's (1996) redefinition of narrativity also reduces the need for an explicit and identifiable narrator.

At the same time, Fludernik's model also seems to be somewhat exclusive, despite her recognition of the need for a less restrictive approach. The problem of including or excluding certain types of texts under the term second-person narration is exacerbated in less prototypically communicative narratives. Fludernik's model seems to completely exclude those examples of reflector mode narrative from 'proper' second-person narrative that belong to DelConte's completely coincident narration category. There is not necessarily a traditional 'narrative' in these texts, due to the self-address aspect. One need not tell oneself a story, there may just be a rendering of thoughts, perceptions, emotion etc. in the form of an interior monologue. Fludernik does acknowledge that the distinction between narratives and non-narratives is harder to draw when interior monologues are addressed to the self. She concedes that as long as there are no extensive descriptions of the surroundings, such texts may be included under second-person narration, but this is more of an afterthought and not completely accounted for in her framework.

In Herman's and DelConte's frameworks, there are issues with some of the terminology. In Types 2 and 3 of Herman's *you* typology, the use of *fiction* seems problematic. *Fictional reference* is the term given to the use of *you* where it could be replaced by *I* or *s/he* without altering the rhetorical effect of the narrative, while 'fictionalized address' is used to describe the use of *you* in direct address between characters at the story level. In the former, I do not really see the significance of using the term *fictional* at all – the same phenomenon can occur even if the text is non-fictional, making it purely a case of text-internal reference. But, to the best of my knowledge, there are no extensive studies of second-person narration in non-fictional texts (and especially not in journals). Fictionalized address, on the other hand, may be better discussed in terms of *diegesis*. Type 2 SPN could be described as intradiegetic reference, Type 3 could be intradiegetic address and Type 4 could become extradiegetic address. The model would then be more applicable to the scrutiny of non-fictional texts.

In DelConte's model, I find the idea of diegetic planes somewhat difficult to operationalize. DelConte does not adequately specify what exactly he means by 'the same diegetic plane' and how this can be identified in a text. In the case of completely coincident narration, for example, is it enough to be talking to oneself about one's actions later that same day? Or is it necessarily just when internal states are narrated to the self 'on-line'? Indeed, DelConte seems to mean the latter. However, the question of how diegetic planes can be determined still remains unanswered. I imagine that diegesis is not so much made up of distinct planes, but is more of a cline, where two spatio-temporal positions can be closer together or further apart. Where then, is the cut-off point? Perhaps verb tenses can be used as an indicator for (intended) diegetic planes. In this vein, *you* + present tense may be seen as providing a stronger sense of simultaneity and so be counted as 'the same diegetic plane'.

Despite these potential issues, a better understanding of the potential functions of the second-person pronoun as well as second-person narration is a useful starting point for this study. I adopt DelConte's relatively open definition of second-person narration, as it seems to allow for the largest variety of texts to be included in it. In terms of the different types of *you*, Herman's doubly deictic *you* as well as Margolin's *transferred you* are very relevant. They are interesting not only as typologies but also as ways of describing and understanding the functions of second-person narration.

7.2 The role of *You* in the Smith Journal

Having discussed second-person narration in general, I now turn to the use of *you* in Plath's Smith Journal. The second-person pronoun is not just unusual when it comes to personal journals; it is also statistically significantly overused in the Smith Journal in comparison with SWTPAuto. As such, investigating its relevance for Plath's experience of her affective states is essential.

I first look at a selection of entries written in the second person qualitatively and in detail. I describe the different types of *you* present in the Smith Journal before turning to the patterning of second-person entries and suggesting links to events in Plath's life. This is followed by a detailed analysis of second-person narration in different entries, considering the possible effects of the phenomenon in each case. *Effects* in this sense are understood as synonymous with *what is likely to be conveyed* (i.e. what affective state a lay reader or a professional may attribute to the writer/character). Finally, I propose a way of distinguishing between different types of second-person narration on the basis of what I call temporal orientation. The manual intensive analysis in this chapter is supported and expanded by a second corpus analysis in Chapter 8, comparing the linguistic composition of second- and first-person entries in the Smith Journal.

Before discussing individual SPN entries in the journal, I want to consider the applicability of narratological concepts as outlined in the previous section to this specific data set. I have already alluded to the fact that these frameworks were developed and have mostly been applied to works of fiction. The Smith Journal of Sylvia Plath is, of course, different: it is non-fictional and (arguably) a private journal. This creates some problems when trying to classify and describe it in terms of the traditional narrative models developed to describe fiction. In the majority of entries, Plath describes what happens to herself, and in these entries, therefore, the narrator is the protagonist. Arguably, one can also assume that the entries were not written for anyone other than Plath herself, or at least with no specific external audience in mind. Therefore, she can also be seen as the most immediate intended narratee. This creates a situation where the narrator is the protagonist and also the narratee, at least in terms of physical entity. Despite this physical coincidence of the three narrative participants, putting the journal entries into any one of DelConte's (2003) types is not immediately straightforward.

First of all, the narratee is a problematic concept in journals. One can assume, as I have done so far, that the narratee of the journal is the same as the writer. A person writes a journal for their own benefit and rereading. However, this is a contested assumption and difficult to prove. Linguistically, the narratee is only present in private journals when explicitly mentioned – by the second-person pronoun *you*, for example. Otherwise, the narratee can be seen as a kind of 'parasite' of the narrator – one tends to assume that s/he exists because an addresser implies an addressee. However, one could also assume that there is no narratee at all in journals. Journals do not necessarily have a communicative purpose. Their function is only partially that of record-keeping for the future reference of the writer. The other function of journals is simply that of an outlet (Schiwy 1994), without any dialogic relationship.

Secondly, Plath uses different tenses and times in her journals: sometimes she narrates in the past and present tense and sometimes using the future/conditional times. This potentially has implications for the diegetic planes that the narrative participants occupy. When narration is in the past tense, one can assume that the narrator is at a different temporal location to, minimally, the protagonist and perhaps also the narratee. When the narration is in the present tense, the situation is somewhat more complex. Plath sometimes employs the so-called historic present tense[1] in her narrations. On these occasions, the narrator is still at a different temporal location from the narratee and protagonist, despite the tense. The third complication arises because all of the above can actually occur in a single entry.

All these complications raise the issue of the unit of analysis at which DelConte's models (and all other narratological frameworks) are meant to operate. If his models are meant as a way of describing a text overall, then most of the issues raised are irrelevant. The journals could then fall into the category of completely coincident narration (assuming that journals are characterized by simultaneity, that is, protagonist and narrator are on the same diegetic plane). However, such an overgeneralization would ignore the interesting shifts that occur between the individual entries. Applying the model to smaller units of analysis (such as entries or even paragraphs) gives a more accurate picture of the narrative structure of a text, but there is the danger of overcomplication. After all, narrative shifts can occur from one sentence to another, but the distinctions may become nonsensical at some point. DelConte's (2003) model is a useful way of describing the Journal in general and illustrating how it is different from other types of texts; it is not practical for smaller units of analysis.

7.2.1 Different types of *You*

I begin by demonstrating the various ways that *you* appears in the Smith Journal. Here, I am not yet focusing on second-person narration, but merely on the presence of the second-person pronoun. Entry 45 is particularly rich in different types of *you* and is therefore an ideal starting point. In the following demonstration, different typefaces are used to differentiate various types of *you* in the examples:

You – Bold represents instances of the narrative *you*, that is, where *you* refers to the protagonist of the narrative.

<u>***You***</u> – Bold italics underlined represents instances of the generic *you* (Herman's Type 1).

You – Italics represents character level direct address (fictionalized address (Type 3) in Herman's terms). This type is only highlighted in the first few examples to illustrate the various types of *you*; I do not analyse it in detail.

Example 47 is an excerpt from Entry 45, which deals with a date with 'Bill'. It begins with a description of how he picks Plath up and is followed by a description of their initial 'small talk'. There is a scene in a fraternity house where they have a 'real' conversation. Bill then takes Sylvia for a walk in the dark woods. He tries to sleep with her and to have her masturbate him, against her will. She expresses feeling impotent against his strength and wishes to be a man.

Example 47

> **You** meet Bill in the car. It's his convertible. **You** get a side glance as he drives: not bad – hair receding on temples, but manly. Good blue eyes and a neat mouth. Neat features.
>
> Conversation is bad from the beginning.
>
> 'Do *you* like football?' (This is like highschool: find out her interests.) **You** don't, but **you** can't squelch him quite so soon. **You** parry: 'Do *you*?' (The old double-switch.)
>
> 'Yes. Where do *you* come from?'
>
> 'Wellesley, Mass.' **You** run off glibly.
>
> 'Don't give me a hard time.'
>
> 'What?' **You** don't get it.
>
> (Entry 45; underlining in the original, my bold and italics)

This first example begins with second-person narration. The **you** (in bold) refers to Plath, the protagonist and potentially the addressee. However, within this stretch of second-person narration, there is also direct speech presentation where the first and third *you* (in italics) refers to Plath, whereas the second refers to Bill. This is Herman's (1994) fictionalized address. Between the first and the second instance of *you* there are two more examples of narrative **you**, as well as two after the third direct speech *you*. The fact that both of these discourse levels use the present tense makes the distinction between them unclear, thereby achieving vividness in storytelling.

A little later in the entry, there is an example of the generic ***you***.

Example 48

> **You** notice briefly that **you** can get lost in his eyes. An encouraging sign. They aren't lazy, they blaze at **you**. Heartened, **you** go on:
>
> '*You* know, it's too bad ***you*** don't get to know people in a crowd, like this. So often ***you*** never do more than find out where ***your*** date lives.'
>
> He agrees. (Entry 45; my underlining, bold and italics)

Similar to Example 47, **you** here denotes the protagonist and addressee of the narrator and *you* denotes examples of fictionalized address. The referent in this case is Bill, as Plath (the protagonist) is speaking. In addition to these, however, there are three examples of the second-person pronoun marked in bold, italics and underline. I suggest that these are examples of the generic *you*. The generic you can include more than just the direct addressee of the speech – it can even include those who are only over-hearing (or 'over-reading'), suggesting that the reader could feel like they are also addressed by the pronoun. This draws readers into the heart of the narrative (cf. Phelan 1994).

Another, slightly different, example of the generic ***<u>you</u>*** occurs later on in the entry, when Bill is asked to describe what it is like to be a soldier.

Example 49

> 'What's it like to fight? to kill someone?' (**Your** curiosity is aflame. Granted **you** can't be a man, but he can tell **you** how it was.)
>
> He is nonchalant. '***<u>You</u>*** go from one island to another, practicing. Then one day ***<u>you</u>*** start out again. "This one isn't taken," they say. ***<u>You</u>*** get out. ***<u>You</u>*** eat, sleep, joke.'
>
> (Entry 45; my bold, italics and underlining)

Bill's speech is framed in Plath's narrated **you**, but when he speaks, ***<u>you</u>*** actually only refers to a limited generic group. This is a generic ***<u>you</u>*** as it could easily be substituted with *one*, however, the context ensures that it refers only to a specific group: those who have been at war. To a certain degree, of course, every generic use of pronouns only refers to a limited group, as it will be more meaningful for, or inclusive of, those people who have experienced the topic being spoken about. The difference, however, is that in this case it is a contextually very clearly delineated group that is included under ***<u>you</u>***. Therefore, it is possible to differentiate it from the 'purely' generic use in Example 48.[2]

These short examples, taken from one entry, demonstrate that the second-person pronoun has at least five different functions/referents on different levels of narrative embedding in the Smith Journal. On the character-character level, *you* can refer to either of the participants in a dialogue, as well as to an undefined generic group of people. The narrative *you*, at a higher level of narrator-narratee, can refer to both the topic of a narrative (protagonist) and the apparent narratee of the narrative. Due to the nature of second-person narration in private journals, both these referents are Plath. In the third example, another type of generic *you* occurs – a more specified one. The consistent use of the present tense in Entry 45 blurs the boundaries between these referents. Highlighting various types of *you* in this way ensures that these multiple functions do not get conflated in the subsequent analysis.

7.2.2 Second-person narration in the Smith Journal

Almost 75 per cent of entries in the Journals of Sylvia Plath are written in the first person. Example 50 is typical of this type of narration. In such entries, Plath often writes about relatively insignificant events (e.g. a fire drill) in an introspective manner and in great detail.

Example 50

> Last night we had our first fire drill. [...] My nerves pained keenly. My fever made me restless, uneasy. So this is what we have to learn to be part of a community: to respond blindly, unconsciously to electric sirens shrilling in the middle of night. I hate it. (from Entry 30)

My concern here, however, is with those entries that are written in the second person (but perhaps framed in first person, as in Example 52). In the Smith Journal, sixteen out of 182 entries are written in this way. That represents approximately 8,330 out of roughly 77,900 words (about 11 per cent)[3]. A short prototypical example of SPN is Example 51.

Example 51

> ... There_EX comes_VVZ a_AT1 time_NNT1 when_RRQ you_PPY walk_VV0 downstairs_RL to_TO pick_VVI up_RP a_AT1 letter_NN1 you_PPY forgot_VVD, and_CC the_AT low_JJ confidential_JJ voices_NN2 of_IO the_AT little_JJ group_NN1 of_IO girls_NN2 in_II the_AT living_NN1 room_NN1 suddenly_RR ravels_VVZ into_II an_AT1 incoherent_JJ mumble_NN1 and_CC their_APPGE eyes_NN2 slide_VV0 slimily_RR through_II you_PPY, around_II you_PPY, away_II21 from_II22 you_PPY in_II a_AT1 snaky_JJ effort_NN1 not_XX to_TO meet_VVI the_AT tentative_JJ half-fear_NN1 quivering_VVG in_II your_APPGE own_DA eyes_NN2. And_CC you_PPY remember_VV0 a_AT1 lot_NN1 of_IO nasty_JJ little_JJ tag_NN1 ends_NN2 of_IO conversation_NN1 directed_VVN at_II you_PPY and_CC around_II you_PPY, meant_VVD for_IF you_PPY, to_TO strangle_VVI you_PPY on_II the_AT invisible_JJ noose_NN1 of_IO insinuation_NN1. (beginning of Entry 41, POS-tagged)

In Example 51, 'the narrator tells a story to a (sometimes undefined, shifting, and/or hypothetical) narratee – delineated by *you* – who is also the (sometimes undefined, shifting, and/or hypothetical) principle actant in that story' (DelConte 2003: 207–8). The principle actant in the story is Plath, and she can also be assumed to be at least the hypothetical narratee. As Example 51 demonstrates, second-person entries are not necessarily different in terms of subject matter from first-person entries. Seemingly insignificant events are discussed in detail in Entry 41 as well. Although the actions seem to have happened in the recent past, *there comes a time when* suggests that the incident might be the beginning of a series or one in a number of similar instances.

Sylvia Plath herself is always the narrator in her journals. Therefore, prototypical examples of second-person narration in the Smith Journal are those that are characterized by the predominant presence of the second-person pronoun, mainly used to designate the protagonist. I use *predominant* here to allow for the fact that, occasionally, second-person entries are framed in the first person or by the use of a 'generic' pronoun, or both. An example of this 'framing' (Example 52) can be found at the beginning of Entry 81, where there is shift from first-person *I*, to a generic *one* and then to second-person *you*:

Example 52

> I am caught in musing – how life is a swift motion, a continuous flowing, changing, and how one is always saying goodbye and going places, seeing people, doing things. Only in the rain, sometimes, only when the rain comes, closing in your pitifully small radius of activity, only when you sit and listen by the window, as the cold wet air blows thinly by the back of your neck – only then do you think and feel sick. (Entry 81)

The rest of the entry proceeds in second-person narration, where the protagonist is only referred to with the second-person pronoun *you*. Table 7.1 below lists the entries that can be considered examples of second-person narration in the Smith Journal, giving a brief overview of what each of these entries is about.

Focusing on the topics alone, there seems to be a negative undertone in a slight majority of these entries. Margolin (1990) suggests that any significant clustering in instances of second-person narration is worth noting. Already, from Table 7.1, it can be observed that second-person entries seem to occur in loose clusters. There is a cluster of '40s entries', '80s entries', a couple of entries in the early 100s and a final cluster consisting of the last two entries in the Smith Journal. There are also a few isolated examples. Figure 7.2 below aims to visually represent the aforementioned clusters. The 80s and 100s clusters are considered together due to their temporal proximity. In Figure 7.2, the clusters are also presented on a time line with significant life events.

Table 7.1 Entries written in the second person

Entry	Topic
41	Reflections on isolation from housemates.
42	Description of a girl, focusing especially on her breasts.
43	Description of Linda and a comparative (unflattering) reflection on Plath's self.
44	Description of a conversation with a hated housemate about men.
45	Description of a blind date with Bill, who attempts to sleep with Plath against her will.
56	Elaborate description of the experience of a bike ride.
81	Musings on the passage of time and the purpose of life.
82	Description of an outing to the Cape with friends and allusions to first sexual encounter.
85	Description of being in a car with mother and grandmother. Reflections on belonging.
86	Description of putting Mayo kids to bed – maternal instincts awakened.
104	Interior monologue on feeling blocked, trapped.
105	Description of feeling wise and ageless.
138	A summary of own achievements.
156	Expressions of an inability to make decisions and take chances.
July 6	Descriptions of fear, paralysis and a desire to escape.
July 14	Descriptions of paralysis and lack of courage.

As Figure 7.2 shows, there seems to be a concentration of second-person entries in the first half of 1951: twelve out of a total of sixteen occur in this period. At this point in her life, Plath has left home to go to university and is approaching the end of her first year. She returns home for her first summer vacation and takes on her first full-time job as an au pair in the Mayo household. At university she experiences tensions with her housemates and a non-consensual sexual encounter (Entry 45). Plath's first consensual sexual experience also takes place later that year. In this sense, 1951 could be described as an 'era of firsts'.

The final group of entries (including 138 and 156) were written in 1952 and the summer of 1953. This corresponds to Plath's second year at college and the summer thereafter. In 1952, she becomes editor of the *Smith Review* – the college

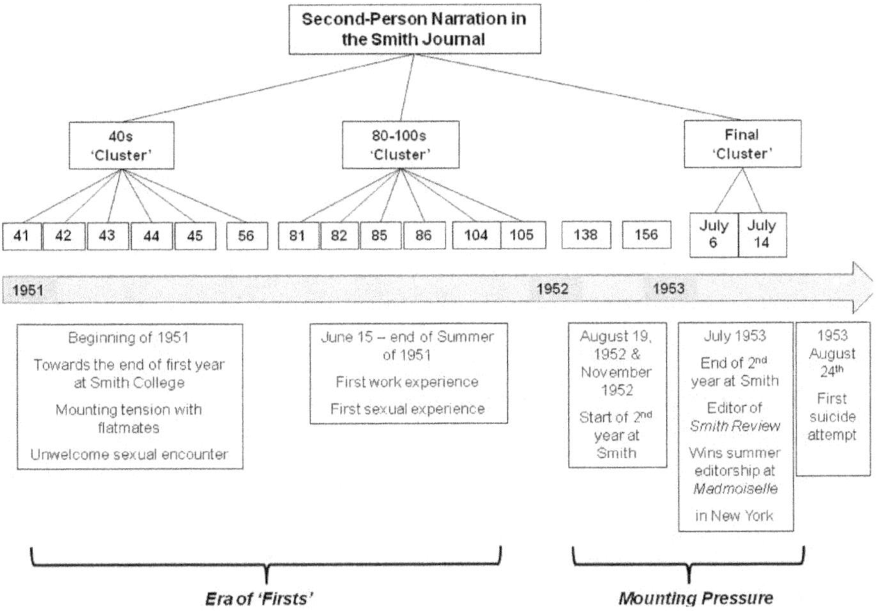

Figure 7.2 Distribution of second-person narration in the Smith Journal.

newspaper. Later that academic year, Plath additionally wins a guest editorship at a women's magazine in New York *(Mademoiselle)*. These positions are professional recognition but also involve additional work and responsibilities. Both 138 and 156 are relatively short entries, and 138, in particular, can be linked to the final cluster by topic. In it, Plath explicitly describes a professional angst. Entry 156 seems to describe a more general frustration with herself, more specifically, her general indecision. This period could be described as a time of mounting tensions as Plath begins to make her mark professionally. The way Plath agonizes over her successes in the final two entries seems to support this interpretation: *the one time in your life you'll have a chance to prove your own discipline* (Entry July 6); *Fear, big & ugly & sniveling. Fear of not succeeding intellectually and academically* (Entry July 14); *Fear of failing to live up to the fast & furious prize-winning pace of these last years – and any kind of creative life* (Entry July 14).

Overall, then, the general coincidence of second-person narration with significant events in Plath's life broadly indicates that second-person narration in the Smith Journal relates to situations of emotional depth and tension (cf. Morrissette 1965, Fludernik 1994b).

From the clusters in Figure 7.2, I now investigate five entries in more detail. Entries 45, 82, 104 and July 6, 1953 and July 14 represent examples from each of the main clusters described above and provide a representative chronological range. I discuss the entries in the final cluster together due to their mutual temporal proximity and their proximity to Plath's suicide attempt.

7.2.2.1 Typology of second-person narration in the Smith Journal

Margolin (1990) proposes the following six questions to consider in any description of second-person narration. Questions in **bold** are answered for each entry individually:

1. Is it an authentic second-person narration?
2. **What is the spatio-temporal position of the narrated individual (protagonist) with respect to the narrator's NOW?**
3. How much access does the narrator have to the inner life of the narrated *you* (protagonist)?
4. **What proportion of the discourse consists of *you* as the topic of narration and what proportion of the *you* as addressee?**
5. **What type of activity is the narrated *you* engaged in?**
6. What is the ontological status of the narrated ***you*** within the actual text-world? (Does the *you* exist independently of the narrator, or is s/he the creation of the narrator?)

Questions 1, 3 and 6 can be answered together for all journal entries written in the second person in the Smith Journal. All highlighted instances of *you* in the subsequent examples are authentic second-person narration, since the *you* in these cases refers to the protagonist of the story and is not an example of an apostrophe or direct speech presentation. In each case, the narrator has complete access to the inner world of the protagonist. This can be assumed, since they are the same entity, but it is also indicated linguistically, by the direct presentation of the protagonist *you*'s thoughts.

The question of ontology is problematic to answer for a non-fictional personal journal, where the story-world is arguably the 'real' world. In the Smith Journal, the narrator is physically the same entity as the protagonist, and the protagonist is therefore neither independent of the narrator nor her creation – they are one and the same. On the other hand, the narrated *you* is, at times, in a different spatio-temporal location to the narrator. Where appropriate, this will be considered for individual entries as well.

In the following discussion of the five selected entries, the narrative uses of the second-person pronoun are in **bold**.

Entry 45

Entry 45 was used to illustrate the different types of *you* at the beginning of this section, but some of the excerpts are reproduced here for ease of reference. The entry tells the story of a blind date Plath has with Bill and was written some time at the beginning of her second semester at Smith in 1951. The whole entry is written in the present tense, but after the events described.

Example 53

> **You**_PPY meet_VV0 Bill_NN1 in_II the_AT car_NN1. It's_PPH1/VBZ his_APPGE convertible_NN1. **You**_PPY get_VV0 a_AT1 side_NN1 glance_NN1 as_CSA he_PPHS1 drives_VVZ: not_XX bad_JJ hair_NN1 receding_VVG on_II temples_NN2, but_CCB manly_JJ. Good_JJ blue_JJ eyes_NN2 and_CC a_AT1 neat_JJ mouth_NN1. Neat_JJ features_NN2.
>
> Conversation_NN1 is_VBZ bad_JJ from_II the_AT beginning_NN1.
>
> 'Do_VD0 you_PPY like_VVI football_NN1?' (This_DD1 is_VBZ like_JJ highschool_NN1: find_VV0 out_RP her_APPGE interests_NN2.)
>
> **You**_PPY don't_VD0/XX, but_CCB **you**_PPY can't_VM/XX squelch_VV0 him_PPHO1 quite_RG so_RG soon_RR.
>
> **You**_PPY parry_VV0: 'Do_VD0 you_PPY?' (The_AT old_JJ double-switch_NN1.)
>
> 'Yes_UH. Where_RRQ do_VD0 you_PPY come_VVI from_II?'
>
> 'Wellesley_NN1, Mass_NP1.' **You**_PPY run_VV0 off_RP glibly_RR.
>
> 'Don't_VD0/XX give_VVI me_PPIO1 a_AT1 hard_JJ time_NNT1.'
>
> 'What_DDQ?' **You**_PPY don't_VD0/XX get_VVI it_PPH1. (Beginning of Entry 45, POS-tagged, underlining in the original, my bold)

In Example 53, the narrated you is spatio-temporally separate from the narrator. The protagonist of the story is at an earlier temporal point and a spatially removed location from the narrator's NOW, although it is unclear what the temporal distance is between the narrated events and the narration. The protagonist *you* is engaged in the activities of a date, including making small talk and a car journey. Later on in the entry, Plath describes a walk in the woods and an unwanted sexual advance by Bill. Due to this distinction between narrator and protagonist, these are examples of one type of transferred *you* (Margolin 1990). In these instances there is just one speaker – an 'I-NOW' – and the *you* (though co-referential with the *I*) does not exist outside of the situation: the *you* is mainly the topic of narration.

The following example contains similar instances of *you* and comes from later on in the same entry.

Example 54

> What's it like to fight? to kill someone?" (**Your** curiosity is aflame. Granted **you** can't be a man, but he can tell **you** how it was.)
>
> He is nonchalant. 'You go from one island to another, practicing. Then one day you start out again …
>
> (Entry 45; my bold)

However, in Example 54, Plath also provides narration in parentheses, in the second person. The same phenomenon occurs in Example 53, but there she actually refers to herself with the third-person *her*, effectively adopting the deictic position of her date. These can be seen as various types of thought presentation. The presented thoughts give a strong sense of the narrator's direct access to the mind of the protagonist (Short 1996: 315), thereby allowing the reader to glimpse Plath's thought processes at the time of the narrated events. These instances of second-person narration can largely be described in the same way as the previous examples. However, the type of activity that the narrated *you* is involved in is different. While, in the previous example, the narrated you was also engaged in a conversation and the events of a date, in Example 54 the protagonist is involved in mental activities.

One effect of second-person narration that seems to be apparent here is a sense if emotional upheaval (Fludernik 1994). Undoubtedly, this has to do with what is revealed in the course of the entry (Bill tries to force Sylvia to touch his penis), but this combines with the foregrounded shift from first- to second-person narration. This gives the reader a heightened sense that the story being told is of emotional significance. The sense of emotional upheaval is also a result of the reader potentially being pulled into the narrative, by virtue of the ambiguities of the second-person pronoun. The present tense of the narration contributes to these effects by obscuring the temporal distance between narrative and narration and allows for a more vivid description of past events. The implicitness or backgrounding of the temporal distance between the story and narration allows the emotional intensity to be perceived stronger. At the same time, the protagonist's mental actions are separated orthographically by parentheses. This actually recreates the distance between the story and the narration to some extent, slightly reducing the emotional intensity.

Another effect of second-person narration potentially at play in Entry 45 is the sense of inner split. This is to be understood in Fludernik's (1994b) terms as instances where 'an *I* splits into two voices that interact dialogically' (Fludernik, 450). Second-person narration in a journal (because it is a form of self-address) always implies a slight sense of inner split. The orthographic separation of the reported thoughts from the reported speech suggests the presence of two voices but also a certain distance between them. A sense of split is potentially created by this duality, mostly in combination with the fact that, in reality, both voices belong to the same real person. However, in these examples, there is no direct dialogue between the various splinters of Plath's *I*.

Entry 82

Entry 82 was written in the summer of 1951. At this point, Plath has finished her first year at university and is working as a mother's helper in the Mayo family. She describes occasional 'sadness' due to stress and fatigue (she takes care of three small children). The entry is a description of and reflection on a trip Plath takes to Cape Cod with five of her friends. They spend the day taking part in various activities, and she becomes close with one of the men. In the evening, he asks her up to his room and Plath, presumably, has her first sexual experience.

Example 55

> and_CC then_RT **you**_PPY felt_VVD the_AT lovely_JJ placating_JJ touch_NN1 of_IO hands_NN2 on_II hair_NN1 in_II a_AT1 long_JJ light_JJ caress_NN1 that_CST could_VM have_VHI been_VBN termed_VVN possessive_JJ. **You**_PPY felt_VVD very_RG gay_JJ, very_RG foolish_JJ, very_RG cold_JJ and_CC wet_JJ in_II the_AT big_JJ chilly_JJ room_NN1 with_IW all_DB the_AT boys_NN2 and_CC girls_NN2. [...] Almost_RR surprised_JJ **you**_PPY let_VV0 **yourself**_PPX1 be_VBI enfolded_VVN in_II strong_JJ arms_NN2, in_II a_AT1 last_MD futile_JJ attempt_NN1 to_TO conserve_VVI and_CC gather_VVI the_AT lovely_JJ warmth_NN1 and_CC life_NN1 pulse_NN1 spilling_VVG from_II the_AT fibers_NN2 of_IO the_AT other_JJ. **You**_PPY saw_VVD blue_JJ eyes_NN2, light_JJ blue_JJ and_CC keen_JJ, suddenly_RR intent_JJ and_CC was_VBDZ it_PPH1, was_VBDZ it_PPH1 misting_VVG? Downstairs_RL then_RT, and_CC good-bye_UH, good-bye_UH my_APPGE love_NN1, goodbye_UH. **You**_PPY felt_VVD no_AT reality_NN1, no_AT knife_NN1 of_IO sorrow_NN1 cut_VVD **your**_APPGE intestines_NN2 to_II bits_NN2. (Entry 82, POS-tagged, my emphasis)

The protagonist in Example 55 is in an earlier temporal and different spatial location to the narrator's NOW as indicated by the use of the past tense. The past tense explicitly signals a distance between story time and narrative time. The discourse consists mainly of *you* as the topic. One can assume that there is a narratee due to the nature of journals and the functions of the pronoun (as discussed previously), or one can assume that the protagonist is identical with the narratee and is therefore present everywhere that the protagonist is. The narrated *you* is engaged in the activities of the day (together with others) but also in mental processes such as thinking, remembering and feeling.

Several of the potential effects of second-person narration discussed in the literature review are applicable to this entry as well. First, a sense of emotional significance is again evoked by the mere presence of second-person narration. This effect was already mentioned in conjunction with Entry 45, and, indeed, even the topic of this entry is similar. Additionally, due to the presence of the second-person pronoun, there is a potential for the reader to be pulled into the narrative. However, both these effects are probably less pronounced in this particular example. The entry is narrated in the past tense, and that also makes an explicit distinction between the story and the reader's NOW, potentially making it harder for him or her to be drawn in to the narrative. This effect also depends on the level of detail in the narrative, of course. The more detailed the characterization, the less likely it is that the reader will identify with *you*, as the character is more individuated (Phelan 1994).

The narrator in Example 55 can be assumed to be superior to the protagonist and addressee in terms of knowledge, again due to the past tense. As a result of the temporal distance between the protagonist and the narrator, the narrator will presumably have the advantage of hindsight, at least. However, the sense of 'inner split' that can sometimes be evoked by narrator superiority (cf. Margolin 1990) is not very strong in this example. There is no explicit display of superiority, and there seems to be no dialogic interaction between two splinters of a self. This is despite the fact that addressing oneself using the second person always brings with it a potential sense of split. What this example conveys most strongly is a sense of calm retrospection from a certain distance. This is probably a result of the explicit distance between the narrator and protagonist created by the past tense. DelConte (2003) suggests that in some cases, this may imply a level of objectivity.

Entry 104

Entry 104 was also written in the summer of 1951, while Plath was working at the Mayo house. It is a relatively short entry, so the majority of it is reproduced here in Example 56. In this entry, Plath describes feeling paralysed and uncomfortable in general. The children are not at home, so she goes downstairs to try and find relief in playing the piano, but she ends up disturbing the owners of the house.

Example 56

> *There*_EX *comes*_VVZ *a*_AT1 *time*_NNT1 *when*_RRQ all_DB **your**_APPGE outlets_NN2 are_VBR blocked_VVN, as_CSA with_IW wax_NN1. **You**_PPY sit_VV0 in_II **your**_APPGE room_NN1, feeling_VVG the_AT prickling_NN1 ache_VVI in_II **your**_APPGE body_NN1 which_DDQ constricts_VVZ **your**_APPGE throat_NN1, tightens_VVZ dangerously_RR in_II little_JJ tear_NN1 pockets_NN2 behind_II **your**_APPGE eyes_NN2. One_MC1 word_NN1, one_MC1 gesture_NN1, and_CC all_DB that_DD1 is_VBZ pent_JJ up_RP in_II **you**_PPY festered_VVD resentments_NN2, gangrenous_JJ jealousies_NN2, superfluous_JJ desires_NN2 – unfulfilled_JJ – all_DB that_DD1 will_VM burst_VVI out_II21 of_II22 **you**_PPY in_II angry_JJ impotent_JJ tears_NN2 in_II embarrassed_JJ sobbing_NN1 and_CC blubbering_VVG to_II no_one_PN1 in_II particular_JJ. No_AT arms_NN2 will_VM enfold_VVI **you**_PPY, no_AT voice_NN1 will_VM say_VVI, 'There_RL, There_RL. Sleep_VV0 and_CC forget_VV0.' No_UH, in_II **your**_APPGE new_JJ and_CC horrible_JJ independence_NN1 **you**_PPY feel_VV0 the_AT dangerous_JJ premonitory_JJ ache_NN1, arising_VVG from_II little_JJ sleep_NN1 and_CC taut_JJ strung_JJ nerves_NN2, and_CC a_AT1 feeling_NN1 that_CST the_AT cards_NN2 have_VH0 been_VBN stacked_VVN high_JJ against_II **you**_PPY this_DD1 once_RR, and_CC that_CST they_PPHS2 are_VBR still_RR being_VBG heaped_VVN up_RP. (Entry 104, POS-tagged, my emphases)

In Entry 104, the spatio-temporal location of the protagonist with respect to the narrator's NOW is more difficult to determine than in some other cases. The phrase in italics at the beginning of Example 56 suggests that the events here are not necessarily bound temporally or spatially but are potentially habitual. This means that the protagonist seems to exist in the same spatio-temporal location as the narrator but, at the same time, also on other planes. There is a distance between story and narrative time, but it is difficult to specify. *You* as the topic of narration makes up the majority of the discourse, and there is no linguistic sign of the addressed *you* aside from the pronoun itself. The narrated *you* is engaged mainly in mental activity; she feels, rather than acts. This is the main difference between Entry 104 and others that have been discussed so far.

One might be tempted to say that, in Example 56, the instances of *you* in bold are not really second-person narration but are examples of the generic *you*. This impression comes from the relatively indeterminate spatio-temporal location of the actions described. However, even if one were to argue that the above is written using the generic *you* (and is therefore not really second-person narration), one would have to argue that it is narrated in the 'specified' or limited generic *you*. Only people with very similar experiences to those that Plath is describing will be included in the group that is referred to by *you*.

The instances of *you* in bold in Example 56 could also be interpreted as examples of Herman's (2004) *doubly deictic you*. Phelan (1994) (and Fludernik 1994a) noted that as a result of the various possible meanings of *you*, actual readers will feel both addressed by second-person narratives (and therefore identify with the protagonist addressed by *you*) and separate from them. The more fully defined the *you* character is, the larger the distance/difference will be between the actual reader and the protagonist (and so the more likely that readers will see themselves in the observer role). However, due to the nature of the second-person pronoun, they may not be able to remain fully distanced from the character. What remains is a heightened awareness of the differences between the character *you* and the actual reader *you*. This effect has been mentioned before, but it is particularly relevant to Entry 104 due to the aforementioned ambiguities. They reduce the distance between the reader and the protagonist and create a stronger sense of dynamic tension.

A sense of emotional depth and tension is present in Entry 104, as in all others. The effects seem to be very much the same as for Entry 45, with one main difference. Since the spatio-temporal location of the protagonist cannot be determined, the distancing effect seems diminished. Therefore, despite perhaps not necessarily being able to relate to the strong emotions expressed in Entry 104, the reader may empathize with Plath.

7.2.2.1.1 The final two entries

In the entries for July 6 and 14, 1953, Plath does not describe events the majority of the time. Rather, she is summing up her own personality and giving orders to herself, trying to find the motivation to write. I consider both entries together due to their similarity in terms of style and topic, as well as due to their temporal proximity. At this particular point in her life, Plath has had a number of professional achievements; however, shortly after the July 14 entry (on 24 August) she attempts suicide and is hospitalized for psychiatric treatment.

Example 57

> don't_VD0/XX panic_VVI. Begin_VV0 writing_NN1, even_CS21 if_CS22 it_PPH1 is_VBZ only_RR rough_JJ & ununified_JJ. First_MD, pick_VV0 **your**_APPGE market_NN1: Journal_NN1

or_CC Discovery_NN1? Seventeen_MC or_CC Mlle_NNB? Then_RT pick_VV0 a_AT1 topic_NN1. Then_RT think_VV0. If_CS **you**_PPY can't_VM/XX think_VV0 outside_II **yourself**_PPX1, **you**_PPY can't_ VM/XX write_VV0. [...] **You**_PPY fool_VV0 – **you**_PPY are_VBR afraid_JJ of_IO being_VBG alone_JJ with_IW **your**_APPGE own_DA mind_NN1. **You**_PPY just_RR better_RRR learn_VVI to_TO know_VVI **yourself**_PPX1, to_TO make_VVI sure_JJ decisions_NN2 before_CS it_PPH1 is_VBZ too_RG late_JJ. 3_MC months_NNT2, **you**_PPY think_VV0, scared_VVD to_II death_NN1. **You**_PPY want_VV0 to_TO call_VVI that_DD1 man_NN1 – **You**_PPY earned_VVD enough_DD money_NN1 to_TO go_VVI. Why_RRQ don't_VB0/XX **you**_PPY go_VVI? Stop_VV0 thinking_VVG selfishly_RR of_IO razors_NN2 & self-wounds_NN2 & going_VVG out_RP and_CC ending_VVG it_PPH1 all_DB. (Entry July 6, 1953, POS-tagged, my emphasis)

Example 58

Fear_NN1 of_IO failing_VVG to_TO live_VVI up_II21 to_II22 the_AT fast_JJ & furious_JJ prize-winning_JJ pace_NN1 of_IO these_DD2 last_MD years_NNT2 – and_CC any_DD kind_NN1 of_IO creative_JJ life_NN1. Perverse_JJ desire_NN1 to_TO retreat_VVI into_II not_XX caring_VVG. I_PPIS1 am_VBM incapable_JJ of_IO loving_JJ or_CC feeling_VVG now_RT: self-induced_NN1.

Out_II21 of_II22 it_PPH1, kid_NN1. **You**_PPY are_VBR making_VVG monumental_JJ obstacles_NN2 of_IO what_DDQ should_VM be_VBI taken_VVN for_IF granted_VVN – living_VVG on_II a_AT1 past_JJ reputation_NN1 – [...]

Read_VV0 a_AT1 story_NN1: Think_VV0. **You**_PPY can_VM. **You**_PPY must_VM, moreover_RR, not_XX continually_RR run_VVN away_RL while_CS asleep_JJ – forget_VV0 details_NN2 – ignore_VV0 problems_NN2 – shut_VV0 walls_NN2 up_RP between_II **you**_PPY & the_AT world_NN1 & all_DB the_AT gay_JJ bright_JJ girls_NN2 – please_RR, think_VV0 – snap_VV0 out_II21 of_II22 this_DD1. (End of Entry July 14, POS-tagged, my emphasis)

These final entries are written mainly in the present tense, and contain vocatives (e.g. *fool, kid*) and imperatives. Example 58, in particular, also contains highly elliptical sentences and relatively few finite verbs. These create a fragmentary structure that is highlighted by the use of dashes.

In these examples, the protagonist seems to be in the same spatio-temporal location as the narrator – that is, there seems to be little or no distance between story and narrative time. The immediacy of the imperatives contributes to this impression. The narrated *you* is not involved in any 'active' activities – she is mainly described in terms of her momentary emotions and perceptions. In this way, these entries are only narrative in Fludernik's redefined sense of narrativity, where mental events are sufficient.

As opposed to previous examples where the presence of the addressed *you* was ambiguous, here she is very much present. In fact, one could say that vocatives and imperatives put the narratee into the text explicitly by presupposing an addressee. Vocatives and imperatives are, by default, interactive linguistic features. Since all three participants are, in fact, the same entity, they are narrated and addressed simultaneously. All three entities (narrator, narratee and protagonist), therefore, are on the same diegetic plane, in what DelConte (2003) would call completely coincident narration. As a result, it is difficult to determine whether the discourse consists mainly of the narrated *you* or the addressed *you*.

Some of the same effects of second-person narration can be seen in these examples as in previous ones. There is a sense of emotional depth, created by the presence of second-person narration. Phelan's (1994) dynamic relationship between reader and text (where the reader is simultaneously pulled into and kept at a distance from the text) seems to apply here as well and may be stronger in these examples. Vocatives and imperatives highlight the address function of the pronoun, making the protagonist less well defined (as less space is devoted to narrative description). Phelan (1994) suggests that the dynamic effect of second-person narration is strongest in such cases.

What is most interesting about these entries, in terms of effect, is the strong sense of split and the superiority of the speaker *you*. This is despite the fact that, as opposed to entries discussed in previous sections, there is little spatio-temporal distancing in Example 57 and Example 58. The narratee, narrator and protagonist are on the same diegetic plane. In this situation of immediacy, Plath's direct self-address – effectively talking to herself – evokes the sense of inner split. Such self-address has been described as a 'variant of the canonical speech situation, of an *I* speaking to a *you* … the self as both speaker and addressee' (Wales 1996: 72). There is sometimes an element of self-criticism in an address of the self as another, as in: *You idiot!* (Wales 1996), and it can also be used as a form of self-analysis. The sense of split is intensified by the presence of *I* towards the middle of Example 58. The *I*'s statement of its capabilities is directly followed by an order that is produced by a different voice. This is a very unusual example, where both the voice of the *you* and the voice of *I* coincide in the text. In addition, in Example 57, conflict in the dialogue between the two selves becomes explicit through self-threatening (*You just better learn …*). The lack of response to self-questioning (*why don't you go?*) could also suggest a bigger divide between the two selves in terms of agency, as one part of the self does not seem to have the answer.

These are clear examples of Margolin's self-address transferred *you*, where there are two explicit speakers – an 'I-NOW' and a 'you-NOW'. The speaker 'I-NOW' is superior to the addressee, and this stems from a difference in authority. This authority is a given and not something gained through reflection and hindsight, since there is no temporal distance between narrative and narration. The narrator is able to give commands and therefore has the authority/power to influence the addressee's future actions. The present tense is necessary for this effect, but it is only felt so directly due to the imperatives and vocatives. This contrasts with the difference in authority noted in Entry 45, where the superiority stemmed from hindsight.

7.2.2.1.2 Preliminary summary

In this discussion of five second-person entries, I have dealt with examples that demonstrate each of the effects of second-person narration as described in the literature. I have used slightly different terminology from the previous chapter on metaphor as a result of a difference in disciplinary orientation underpinning the two approaches to Plath's journal. In this chapter I refer to effects on readers, while in Chapter 6 I discussed what the metaphors imply about Plath's experience of her affective states. In practice, the two are effectively the same in the current context, where explanations of effect and implication are both grounded in the language. When I describe an effect on readers, I do not mean that they are made to feel a particular way. The effects I describe are to do with what affective states readers might attribute to the narrator and protagonist of these second-person narratives as a result of the language of narration. The link between these attributed affective states and narrators' real experiences of affective states can be assumed on the basis of research in narrative psychology (cf. Pólya et al. 2005 and 2007).

All entries narrated in the second person and discussed here seem to imply emotional depth and intensity. In addition to the topic of some of the entries combined with the shift from first- to second-person narration, this is because of a dynamic tension created by the semantic ambiguity of *you*. However, this effect applies to various extents in the different examples, and the same is true for other effects such as the sense of inner split or distancing. This highlights a need for a systematic way of differentiating between the examples presented here. How particular effects come about appears to be linked to the interaction of the second-person pronoun with other linguistic features. Some of the frameworks outlined in the literature review can be useful for differentiation – Herman's doubly deictic *you* will reasonably have different effects from Margolin's dialogic *you*. However, I indicated throughout that tense seems to be significant in determining which effects predominate in the individual examples (cf. Margolin 1990), and other linguistic features, such as imperatives and vocatives, are also potentially responsible for certain effects. In the next section, I propose a possible typology based on a variety of linguistic characteristics.

7.2.2.2 Second-person narration and temporal orientation

The linguistic framework I propose here is designed to account for differences in the perceived effects of the various second-person entries discussed above. Although I only discuss second-person narration here, the typology itself may apply to other types of narration as well. An earlier version of this framework was published in Demjén (2011b).

The importance of verb tenses in differentiating between various types of second-person narration is relatively well established (e.g. Margolin 1990, Herman 1994, Richardson 2006), and my approach is encouraged by these types analyses. However, I also draw on narrative psychological research, in particular on the framework proposed by Pólya et al. (2007). Pólya et al. (2007) look at the health benefits of recalling life stories in various narrative perspectives, making an explicit connection between narration and affective state. *Narrative perspective* refers to the point of view (in a non-technical sense) from which a story is recounted. The authors distinguish between three different types of perspectives: the retrospective, experiencing and metanarrative. These are based on the relative spatio-temporal locations of the narrated event and the narration itself:

> In the case of a *retrospective form*, the narrative content is located in the narrated events while the position [of the narrator] is located in the narration. In the case of an *experiencing form*, both the narrative content and the position are located in the narrated events. Finally, in the case of a *metanarrative form*, both the narrative content and the position are located in the narration. (Pólya et al. 2007: 51)

Pólya et al. (2007) specify a number of linguistic indicators that can be used to differentiate between the narrative perspectives – these are summarized in Table 7.2. The unit of analysis for narrative perspective is the clause. This means that the overall narrative perspective of a text can be seen as a matter of degree, rather than a discrete categorization.

Table 7.2 Narrative perspectives by Polya et al. (2007)

Linguistic markers	Retrospective Form	Experiencing Form	Metanarrative Form
Temporal deixis **Tense** **Temporal adverbs**	Past *e.g. Then*	Present *e.g. Now*	Present *e.g. Now*
Spatial deixis **Spatial adverbs** **Demonstrative pronouns**	*There* *That*	*Here* *This*	*Here* *This*
Specific terms	Date and space terms *e.g. Yesterday, January, Budapest, at the beach*	Interjections *e.g. Oops, well, so*	Mental process verbs and modal adjectives *e.g. I remember, probably*
Sentence types	Only statements	No constraint	No constraint

From a linguistic perspective, these categorizations make sense. The past tense and distal deixis, for example, are both used to situate events at a spatial and temporal distance and to suggest that an action is completed (and potentially no longer relevant) (Biber et al. 1999). Similarly, Biber (1988) categorizes interjections and questions as markers of involvement and online production, and the present tense can be used to recount stories in a more vivid manner – as if it was being experienced in the moment. However, there are some issues with the operationalization of narrative perspectives. First, the clause-based analysis can be cumbersome and potentially inaccurate. Even with such a small unit of analysis, one may run into problems when a clause includes indicators of more than one perspective (e.g. the past tense in a question which is not part of direct speech). A more serious concern is that texts often include linguistic features that are not part of any of the named perspectives. In Example 57 and Example 58, for instance, highly elliptical clauses, progressive aspect and imperatives were noted as significant. Pólya et al. (2007) do not explicitly discuss any of these.

Despite these issues, Pólya et al.'s narrative perspectives can be applied to the entries in the Smith Journal. Focusing on second-person entries, Entry 82 has the linguistic characteristics of the retrospective perspective, while Entries

45 and 104 mainly contain features of the experiencing perspective. Based on narratological principles, I suggested that the distancing effect is strongest in Entry 82, while the sense of emotional depth and tension with the reader are stronger in Entries 45 and 104. These effects correspond to what was found by Pólya et al. (2005 and 2007). A combination of their findings (Pólya et al. 2005 and 2007) suggests that readers' perception of narrators based on the effects of narration correlates with the actual affective states experienced by the narrators in question, in this case Plath. The retrospective narrative perspective suggests emotional balance, while the experiencing perspective 'reflects the instability of emotion regulation' (Pólya et al. 2007: 60). *Emotion regulation* refers to the ability to influence or control the types of emotions one has, how these are expressed and how one reacts to them (Gross 2008).

At the same time, a wholesale application of the narrative perspectives to the second-person entries of the Smith Journal is problematic. First, Pólya et al. (2007) acknowledge that the metanarrative perspective is statistically unreliable based on its linguistic features. Secondly, and more importantly, Pólya et al.'s (2007) narrative perspectives do not account for all significant linguistic features in the entries I discuss above. Linguistic features in Example 57 and Example 58 such as imperatives, progressive aspect and direct self-address orient towards the future as much as towards the present. Imperatives, for example, require a future in order to realize their perlocutionary effect – to be acted upon. Similarly, the progressive aspect indicates that an activity is in progress and extends into the (near) future (Quirk et al. 1985).

The fragmentary elliptical structure of Example 58 and the absence of finite verbs are also not accounted for in the narrative perspectives. Although these do not orient towards the future, they are reminiscent of stream-of-consciousness writing in the Jamesean sense of 'flow of thought or impressions' (Wales 2001: 367). Such writing relies on unstated association and cohesive links and results in readers 'scrutinizing the impulse-driven flow of a character's mental activity' (Toolan 2001: 122). In this way, stream-of-consciousness writing suggests the coexistence of narrator, protagonist and narratee in DelConte's (2003) terms and contributes to a sense of immediacy.

In order to at least deal with the issue of linguistic features unaccounted for, I propose a slightly different set of three categories. The first two are based on Pólya et al.'s (2007) narrative perspectives, and the distinction between them will, hopefully, be relatively uncontroversial. The third category, on the other hand, is designed to go beyond the experiencing mode and takes into account immediacy and the potential for a future. I acknowledge that the distinction between this category and the previous one is not straightforward.

Rather than narrative perspective, I propose the term 'temporal orientation' for two reasons. First, it makes a clear distinction between Pólya et al.'s (2007) narrative perspectives and my own categories. Second, the term highlights the most important differentiator between the categories: time. The three categories I propose are: past temporal orientation (based on the retrospective perspective), present temporal orientation (based on the characteristics of the experiencing and metanarrative perspectives) and present-future temporal orientation. Table 7.3 summarizes the linguistic markers of these temporal orientations.

Despite its problems, I also propose a clause-by-clause analysis for temporal orientation. Each clause needs to be marked for temporal orientation based on what linguistic features it includes, and the overall orientation of a text is determined by which type of clause constitutes the majority.

Features of both the experiencing and the metanarrative perspective (e.g. mental process types and modalizations) are included in the present temporal orientation because these features all contribute to the emotional involvement of the reader, and such involvement may then also be attributed to the narrator/character. Toolan (2008) notes that, in particular, mental process verbs of evaluation and volitive modality (e.g. gladly, want, hope), but also hedging (e.g. probably, perhaps) contribute to reader empathy, which in turn results in emotional involvement. Note that hedging can involve modal adjectives and adverbs, while volitive modality includes mental process verbs of volition – these are the linguistic features named in Table 7.3. These features contribute to a stronger sense of involvement in the present orientation than in the past. However, the same features also suggest introspection and evaluation, in particular in self-narratives, which suggest less of a sense of immediacy than the present-future orientation.

Both the present and the present-future orientation use the present tense, chiefly due to the multiple functions of the present tense in English (Biber et al. 1999). It can describe states that exist in the present ('state present', Quirk et al. 1985), habitual actions ('habitual present', Quirk et al. 1985) and also instantaneous actions ('instantaneous present', Quirk et al. 1985), as in sports commentaries. However, the present tense can also refer to past and future time. Where it is contextually possible to determine the type of present tense in the narration, it will lead to different categorizations of temporal orientation. For example, the use of the present tense to denote habitual events or states would fall into middle

Table 7.3 Linguistic characteristics of the different temporal orientations

Linguistic markers	Past	Present	Present-Future
Deixis	Past tense Distal spatial and temporal deixis *e.g. there, then, that*	Present tense Proximal spatial deixis *e.g. here, now, this*	Present tense progressive aspect, and future time Proximal spatial deixis *e.g. here, now, this*
Specific terms	Date and space terms *e.g. yesterday, January, Budapest, at the beach*	Interjections *e.g. oops, well, so* Mental and relational process verbs *e.g. remember* Modal adjectives and adverbs *e.g. probably*	Interjections *e.g. oops, well, so* Vocatives and direct address *e.g. you fool!*
Sentence types	Only Declaratives	Declaratives, interrogatives, exclamatives	Declaratives, interrogatives, exclamatives, imperatives, highly elliptical phrases (lack of finite verbs)
Other	Includes description and action narration *e.g. I slowly walked to the crowded newsstand in the pouring rain*	Can include description and action narration Direct speech reporting[4]	Absence of description and action narration

group, as habitual events are not firmly anchored at any point in time (Toolan 2001). Instances of present tense included in the present-future category, on the other hand, are more firmly anchored in the immediate present and may imply the future. In practice, however, these different uses of the present tense are difficult to disentangle (Biber et al. 1999). As such, the main differentiating linguistic markers of each category are underlined in Table 7.3. These can be used to more definitively place a clause within a temporal orientation, as they are unique to their own category. This means that if a clause only includes characteristics of the present orientation, then it will be classed as such. It can only be classed present-future if it additionally includes an underlined feature of that category (e.g. imperatives).

There is also an explicit link between highly elliptical clauses and a lack of finite verbs and temporal orientation. As outlined above, such clauses (see for instance the beginning of Example 59 below) resemble traditional stream-of-consciousness writing and thereby have a sense of the progressive – something that is happening online (cf. Toolan 2001). In Example 59, the progressive aspect of some verbs further enhances this sense of immediacy. As such, they represent the same temporal orientation as progressive aspect, that is, present-future.

Example 59 is a reproduction of Example 58 above. Rather than highlighting the relevant instances of *you*, the tags for temporal orientation are included. This example demonstrates how the temporal orientation framework above can be applied. The classification of each clause is represented by a tag in square brackets: [p] for past, [e] for present and [f] for present-future temporal orientation.

Example 59

> Fear of failing to live up to the fast & furious prize-winning pace of these last years – **[f]** and any kind of creative life **[f]**. Perverse desire to retreat into not caring **[f]**. I am incapable of loving or feeling now **[e]**: self-induced **[f]**.
>
> Out of it, kid **[f]**. You are making monumental obstacles of what should be taken for granted – **[f]** living on a past reputation – **[f]** [...]
>
> Read a story **[f]**: Think **[f]**. You can **[f]**. You must, moreover, not continually run away while asleep **[f]** – forget details – **[f]** ignore problems – **[f]** shut walls up between you & the world & all the gay bright girls **[f]** – please, think – **[f]** snap out of this **[f]**. (End of Entry July 14)

As the tags show, this example can be classified as present-future oriented overall. The vast majority of clauses are either imperative or without finite verbs and therefore belong to this category. There is only one clause that is not present-future oriented. It is a declarative in terms of sentence type, but it only includes a present-tense verb. It does not include any of the defining features of the present-future orientation and so has to be classed as present oriented. This is the type of analysis that was conducted for all sixteen second-person entries in the Smith Journal. Table 7.4 summarizes results of the clause-by-clause analysis. The final label is arrived at based on the relative percentages of the clause types. Of course, as can be seen with Entries 56 and 86, in some cases the differences between the percentages are very small. This illustrates what was pointed out earlier: the categories represent tendencies more than clear-cut distinctions.

Returning now to the five entries discussed in detail in this analysis, the table shows that Entries 45 and 104 and July 6 are present oriented, Entry 82 has a

Table 7.4 Results of temporal orientation analysis

	Percentage of Clauses			
Entry	**Past (%)**	**Present (%)**	**Present-future (%)**	**Classification**
41	13	83	3	Present
42	4	96	0	Present
43	48	39	12	Past
44	18	81	1	Present
45	4	92	5	Present
56	44	47	9	Present
81	28	68	4	Present
82	70	30	0	Past
85	73	18	9	Past
86	50	48	2	Past
104	0	79	21	Present
105	0	100	0	Present
138	9	32	59	Present-Future
156	5	95	0	Present
July 6	8	54	37	Present
July 14	16	20	65	Present-Future

past temporal orientation, while the final entry in the Journal is present-future oriented. Entries 45 and 104 (I will discuss July 6 separately) are mainly written in the present tense and include some direct quotations. Entry 45 in particular consists, to a large extent, of a dialogue. This feature is therefore mainly responsible for its classification. Entry 104, as was pointed out in the context of Example 56, is not particularly time anchored and is somewhat similar to what could be called 'eternal truths'. The present tense in English has a 'state' present type, which 'is used without reference to specific time: that is, there is no inherent limitation on the extension of the state into the past and future' (Quirk et al. 1985: 179). So-called 'eternal truths' fall into this category, for example, 'it is better to be safe than sorry'. This type of present tense exhibits no time restriction. In Entry 104, the sense of universal applicability is signified by the absence of time anchoring terms. It does not have any past oriented clauses, which could include such terms (e.g. *on Saturday*). This can, potentially, account for the stronger sense of general reference in the pronoun *you*, which leads to Phelan's (1994) dynamic tension with the reader.

Example 56 also demonstrates that, in addition to categorizing a text overall, it is useful to know its make-up in terms of temporal orientation. The specific effects of any type of temporal orientation can be influenced by the presence or absence of clauses belonging to other orientations in the co-text. The key linguistic feature that places Entry 82 in the past temporal orientation group is its use of the past tense. The most common function of the past tense is to refer to past time. In this role, it suggests two things about the action: it took place in the past, and the temporality of the action is definite (Quirk et al. 1985). This implies a temporal gap between the NOW (narration) and the action (story). Building on Pólya et al. (2007), this creates a sense of distance between the events and the narration. Other indicators of the past temporal orientation, such as distal deixis, time and place terms, emphasize this distance. This, in turn, could explain the stronger distancing effect of second-person narration in this particular entry, and why it implies a calmer affective state on the part of Plath.

Given that Entry July 6 was discussed as similar to Entry July 14, it is surprising to find that they have different temporal orientations. Indeed, such a difference could be challenged on the basis of a comparison between just Example 57 and Example 58. However, Example 57 is only an excerpt from Entry July 6. In the second half of the entry (where the example comes from), roughly 50 per cent of clauses are present-future oriented, 45 per cent are present oriented and 5 per cent are past oriented. This part of the entry can, indeed, be classed as present-future oriented. The beginning of the entry, on the other hand, contains fewer present-future-oriented clauses. This highlights two things. First, as was outlined towards the beginning of this analysis, the unit of analysis is crucial, as the analysis of small excerpts can be misleading. Second, manual analyses are best augmented by more quantitative methods such as the one outlined here. That way, the degree to which a text fits any one category can also be specified.

The effects outlined in the discussion of Example 57[5] and Example 58 can, potentially, be accounted for by the linguistic make-up of the present-future orientation displayed in the specific excerpts. The effects of the progressive aspect and the fragmentary structure have already been discussed, so here I focus on imperatives and vocatives. In the Smith Journal, the narrator, protagonist and narratee (if it can be said that one exists) tend to be the same entity. Therefore, it could easily be said that when the protagonist is designated by *you*, it is always self-address, suggesting a 'dialogue' between two selves. However, I would like to argue that vocatives and imperatives greatly increase the sense of split most pronounced in these examples. Vocatives are normally used in conversation to maintain social relationships (Biber et al. 1999). They can signal familiarity and intimacy or social distance; but they are also used to obtain the attention of the person one wishes to address (Quirk et al. 1985). What all of these descriptions have in common is the dialogic element: vocatives presuppose at least two interlocutors. Using a vocative in reference to oneself therefore implies the presence of two entities within that self. Similarly, imperatives are speech acts with intended perlocutionary effects (Austin 1962): they are uttered in the hope of achieving a reaction. This also implies the existence of two interlocutors. In fact, imperatives are normally used when the intended addressee is obvious and familiar (Biber et al. 1999). In this way, imperatives and vocatives emphasize the direct address function of *you* through setting up this explicit dialogic situation. This accounts for the strong sense of split in these examples.

Of course, one cannot completely disregard the topic and lexical choices in various entries. Some of the entries include allusions to suicide and metaphorical references to negative affective states of varying degrees (these are discussed in detail in Chapter 5 and Chapter 6). It is inevitable that these will influence the effects of the text (cf. Fludernik 1995). However, the framework presented above provides a more objective way of identifying and explaining the effects of second-person narrative entries. Temporal orientation is not dependent on the topic of a narrative but focuses on its style.

7.2.3 Conclusions

This chapter has so far focused on different types of second-person narration in Sylvia Plath's Smith Journal. I explored the implications for Plath's experience of her affective states by proxy of the effects associated with this narrative mode. An assumption that the effects of narrative mode can represent the narrator's (Plath's) real experiences of affective states underlies this endeavour, supported by the correlation of second-person narration with significant life events. Second-person entries mainly occur at times of 'firsts' (e.g. first time away from home, first job, first sexual experiences) and mounting professional tensions.

The detailed analysis of excerpts of second-person narration revealed that it could convey both a sense of distance from the narrated events and a sense of emotional involvement, in addition to a sense of inner split. Some of these effects appeared to be present in all instances of second-person narration, while others are more apparent in some examples than others. The need to account better for this type of difference resulted in a linguistic typology of second-person narration. I suggested that the crucial difference between the effects of the various second-person entries, and therefore the different affective states they imply, is their temporal orientation. The concept of temporal orientation is partly based on the narrative perspectives of Pólya et al. (2007) and consists of the following types:

1. Past temporal orientation, characterized by the past tense, names of locations, time references and distal deictic expressions. It can only consist of declaratives and can include substantial amounts of description and action narration.
2. Present temporal orientation, characterized by the present tense, the presence of interrogatives, exclamations, interjections and the proximal deictic expressions. It can include some description and action narration and also some evaluative/interpretative elements. These are signalled by mental process verbs, modal adverbs. It can also include relational process types.
3. Present-future temporal orientation, also characterized by the present tense, interrogatives, exclamations, interjections and proximal deixis. Additionally, it includes imperatives, vocatives, progressive aspect but no action narration or description. It can sometimes resemble stream-of-consciousness writing in its potentially fragmented structure.

The grammatical and semantic functions of the linguistic components of these categories account for the different effects noted in the initial analysis of the five sample entries. They also explain how the different effects might emerge. A sense of distance and calm is projected by second-person narration in combination with the past temporal orientation, while a sense of crisis and split is conveyed in combination with linguistic characteristics of the present-future orientation. The present orientation conveys a sense of emotional intensity, but it can also suggest some sense of reflection.

Much of what is discussed here does not necessarily apply to second-person texts exclusively. Just as Pólya et al.'s (2007) concept of narrative perspectives is applicable to all types of narratives, so is temporal orientation. Effects such as (psychological) distancing are relevant to all types of narration. Temporal orientation mainly helps to explain why they are more apparent in some examples of second-person narration than in others. However, effects such as a sense of inner split are unique to second-person narration. They come about through an interaction between the inherent properties of the second-person pronoun and the temporal orientation of the text.

It is interesting to note a connection between present-future-oriented second-person entries and some FRAGMENTATION metaphors outlined in the previous chapter. Both of these convey a sense of inner conflict and potential inner split. The emergence of this pattern in two different types of analyses suggests that this was a highly significant aspect of Plath's lived experience. Given Plath's diagnosis, it might be interesting to investigate whether such a sense is present in experiences of depression more broadly.

8

Investigating Second-person Entries Further – Corpus Analysis II

In this chapter, I build on the quantitative analysis of Chapter 4 and the qualitative analysis of second-person narration in Chapter 7 and focus on the statistically significant linguistic differences between first- and second-person narration in the Smith Journal. Having established the connection between second-person narration and Plath's affective states, this comparison allows me to explore further what her use of this narrative mode suggests about her lived experience.

After a brief description of relevant aspects of corpus methodology (in addition to what was outlined in Chapter 4), I move on to an automated corpus comparison between SPN and first-person narration (FPN) and Shift entries (FPN + Shifts), where the narration alternates between first and second person. This allows me to identify linguistic features that are characteristic of second-person narration in the Journal, but not of first-person narration. A POS analysis of second-person entries versus first-person and Shift entries is followed by a discussion of the results of a semantic comparison. Where appropriate, results are discussed in the context of Chapter 4.

8.1 Methodology

The general corpus methodology in Chapter 4 applies here as well. The software and techniques are the same as in Part I of the book: I use Wmatrix (Rayson 2009) for the comparison, and the texts are compared not only in terms of word, but also in terms of POS and USAS tag frequencies. However, as the comparisons are intra-textual (between subsections of one text) (Adolphs 2006) and there are fewer results at higher levels of significance, the LL critical value is lowered to 3.84. At the same time, the minimum frequency is adjusted up, in accordance with the recommendations of Rayson et al. (2004a), to 13. This ensures the reliability of results, even at a lower level of LL.

The Smith Journal overall comprises approximately 77,900 words. Of that, entries written in the second person total approximately 8,330 words, and entries written in the first person total approximately 58,900 words. The remaining entries shift between first-person and second-person narration and comprise around 10,700 words. I combine Shift and first-person entries in this comparison because of their similarity in terms of composition. As demonstrated by Table 8.1 and Table 8.2, the significant differences between SPN and Shift entries are mostly the same ones as those between SPN and just FPN. There is only one POS that is significant in Table 8.2., but not present in Table 8.1: the singular article AT1. In addition, as Shift entries include elements of SPN, there are fewer differences between SPN and Shift entries than between SPN and FPN entries. Combining FPN and Shift entries therefore has the advantage of size and inclusivity and also

Table 8.1 POS comparison SPN versus FPN

POS tag	Freq. 1	% 1	Freq. 2	% 2	LL	Category
PPY	488	6.09	381	0.68	939.22	second-person personal pronoun (you)
VBR	76	0.95	200	0.36	44.56	are
VV0	267	3.33	1271	2.27	30.01	base form of lexical verb (e.g. give, work)
VBDR	22	0.27	78	0.14	6.93	were
VD0	41	0.51	185	0.33	5.86	do, base form (finite)
APPGE	208	2.6	1212	2.16	5.67	possessive pronoun, pre-nominal (e.g. my, your, our)
PPHS1	117	1.46	641	1.14	5.58	third-person sing. subjective personal pronoun (he, she)
IF	64	0.8	320	0.57	5.57	for (as preposition)
XX	96	1.2	525	0.94	4.64	not, n't
PPX1	30	0.37	137	0.24	4.08	singular reflexive personal pronoun (e.g. yourself, itself)
VBZ	122	1.52	703	1.25	3.73	is

Table 8.2 POS comparison SPN versus shifts

POS tag	Freq. 1	% 1	Freq. 2	% 2	LL	Category
PPY	488	6.09	211	2.06	191.85	second-person personal pronoun (you)
PPHS1	117	1.46	77	0.75	21.13	third-person sing. subjective personal pronoun (he, she)
APPGE	208	2.6	182	1.78	14.08	possessive pronoun, pre-nominal (e.g. my, your, our)
VD0	41	0.51	20	0.2	13.49	do, base form (finite)
VBR	76	0.95	56	0.55	9.99	are
VV0	267	3.33	281	2.74	5.23	base form of lexical verb (e.g. give, work)
AT1	231	2.88	245	2.39	4.19	singular article (e.g. a, an, every)
PPX1	30	0.37	22	0.21	4	singular reflexive personal pronoun (e.g. yourself, itself)

ensures that only the most significant differences will be revealed. Given that the LL cut-off point is at a relatively low 3.63 ($p \leq 0.05$), this is particularly useful.

In the following analysis, where concordances are presented, the titles of the concordances include the POS/USAS tags that they show examples of, as well the total frequency of the occurrences in the data. While only sample concordances are presented, the statements and interpretations are based on a detailed examination of complete concordances.

8.2 Comparing different types of entries

I outlined in Chapter 7 that around 75 per cent of the Smith Journal is written in first-person narration, as would be expected for a journal, while around 11 per cent of entries are written using the less expected second-person pronoun. Second-person entries refer to the protagonist of the story, who is also the narratee, with the second-person pronoun *you*. First-person entries, on the other hand, are those where the first-person singular pronoun is used to write about the protagonist. Figure 7.2 in Chapter 7 shows how SPN entries are distributed in the Smith Journal. In addition, there are entries where the narration shifts between different pronouns – that is, both *you* and *I* are used (repeatedly) to refer to the protagonist. These types of entries make up just under 15 per cent of the Smith Journal. Entry 61 below is a good example, (the relevant self-references are in italics):

> *I*_PPIS1 don't_VD0/XX care_VVI any_DD more_DAR about_II the_AT handsome_JJ wealthy_JJ boys_NN2 who_PNQS come_VV0 gingerly_RR into_II the_AT living_NN1 room_NN1 to_TO take_VVI out_RP the_AT girl_NN1 they_PPHS2 thought_VVD would_VM look_VVI nice_JJ in_II an_AT1 evening_NNT1 cocktail_NN1 dress_NN1 ... *I*_PPIS1 said_VVD *I*_PPIS1 wanted_VVD to_TO go_VVI out_RP with_IW them_PPHO2 to_TO meet_VVI new_JJ people_NN. *I*_PPIS1 ask_VV0 *you*_PPY, what_DDQ logic_NN1 is_VBZ there_RL in_II that_DD1? [...] Face_VV0 it_PPH1, kid_NN1: unless_CS *you*_PPY can_VM be_VBI *yourself*_PPX1, *you*_PPY wont_JJ stay_NN1 with_IW anyone_PN1 for_RR21 long_RR22. *You*'ve_PPY/VH0 got_VVD to_TO be_VBI able_JK to_TO talk_VVI. That's_CST/VBZ tough_JJ. But_CCB spend_VV0 *your*_APPGE nights_NNT2 learning_VVG, so_RR *you*'ll_PPY/VM have_VH0 something_PN1 to_TO say_VVI. Something_PN1 the_AT attractive_JJ intelligent_JJ man_NN1 will_VM want_VVI to_TO listen_VVI to_II. All_DB this_DD1 preamble_NN1 (above_RL), and_CC what_DDQ *I*_PPIS1 really_RR wanted_VVN to_TO get_VVI down_RP before_CS *I*_PPIS1 head_VV0 off_RP to_II New_NP1 York_NP1 was_VBDZ more_RRR like_II this_DD1 (Entry 61, POS-tagged, my emphasis)

The example above begins and ends with first-person references to the protagonist, with second-person references in between. This pattern results in a 3:5 split between second- and first-person references. In longer entries, such a pattern of shifting might be repeated. In the following comparisons, such Shift entries are combined with FPN entries and used to investigate the key linguistic characteristics of second-person narration.

8.2.1 Parts-of-speech results

Given that both subcorpora (SPN and FPN + Shifts) come from the same overall text, one would not necessarily expect there to be many significant differences in their linguistic make-up. However, there are a few interesting patterns. Table 8.3 shows the overused items in second-person narrative entries. The first column shows the POS tags. The second and third columns show the absolute and relative frequencies of the items in SPN, while the fourth and fifth columns show these for FPN + Shifts. The sixth column shows the respective LL values.

Table 8.3 Key parts-of-speech in second-person entries versus FPN + shifts

POS	F1	% 1	F2	% 2	LL	Category	Examples
PPY	488	6.09	592	0.89	821.73	second-person personal pronoun	*you*
VBR	76	0.95	256	0.39	39.75	are	*are*
VV0	267	3.33	1552	2.34	26.13	base form of lexical verb	*remember, dance, see*
PPHS1	117	1.46	718	1.08	8.36	third-person sing. subjective personal pronoun	*she, he*
VBDR	22	0.27	89	0.13	7.78	were	*were*
VD0	41	0.51	205	0.31	7.74	do, base form (finite)	*do*
APPGE	208	2.6	1394	2.1	7.63	possessive pronoun, pre-nominal	*your, her, their, his*
IF	64	0.8	380	0.57	5.57	for (as preposition)	*for*
XX	96	1.2	619	0.93	4.86	not, n't	*not, n't*
PPX1	30	0.37	159	0.24	4.52	singular reflexive personal pronoun	*yourself*

The penultimate column lists what the POS tags stand for, while the final column provides a few examples from the SPN sub-corpus.

The keyness of the majority of these POS (the first six items and PPX1) can, to a large extent, be explained by the simple fact that second-person narration is being compared to first-person narration. The keyness of *you*, for example, is a straightforward result of this, with about 87 per cent of the occurrences being due to narration (and about 7 per cent to direct speech presentation). Similarly, about 62 per cent of *are*, approximately 70 per cent of 'base form of lexical verbs' (others are due to imperatives), 55 per cent of *were*, 61 per cent of *do*, 55 per cent of the possessive pronouns and about 90 per cent of reflexive pronouns are directly linked to the narrative person. The rest of the occurrences of *are*, *were* and 'base form of lexical verbs' are mainly due to references to plurals (people and things). Although 55 per cent for the possessive pronoun seems like only a small majority, the other 45 per cent are split between different tokens – mainly *his* and *her*.

At the same time, although the majority of instances of 'base form of lexical verbs' and of *do* are linked to the narrative person (as described above), such base forms are equally used in conjunction with the first-person singular pronoun (and all personal pronouns except the third-person singular for that matter). This means that the keyness of these verbs is interesting beyond their connection with the narrative person. Instances of *do* are interesting, as about 58 per cent are actually negated – that is, they are examples of *don't*. This is important, given that the negated form is a dispreferred, especially in writing (cf. Biber et al. 1999). In addition, *n't* and *not* are themselves key in this comparison. Concordance 15 shows some examples of *do* in the second-person narrated entry.

:tend you do n't know , you	do	n't really mean , you do n't und
›u do n't really mean , you	do	n't understand . Sometimes you c
:e some modern creature (I	do	n't know much about dancing .)
ıda is the sort of girl you	do	n't remember when you meet her f
:d brat , " you say . " You	do	n't know how it is , " he says .
inside . " (O.K. , so you	do	n't .) At last he forgives you
›ack of your neck only then	do you think	and feel sick . You feel the day
ı begin to get scared . You	do	n't believe in God , or a life-a
' and myriad choices , what	do	you pick for yourself out of the
ıatever tangible things you	do	have , they can not be held , bu
you care , and somehow you	do	n't want to live just one life ,
ıerable , because you still	do	n't have faith in yourself , you
: grandparents , now . What	do	you know about them ? Sure , the

Concordance 15 VDO/41.

In addition to being part of negation, *do* is also used as an auxiliary verb in questions. Approximately 21 per cent of the instances of *do* are examples of questions. This could lead one to assume that there are also significantly more questions in SPN entries than in FPN + Shifts; this, however, is not the case. A concordance of question marks in the SPN and FPN + Shifts corpora and an LL calculation revealed that the difference in the number of questions between the two corpora is not statistically significant (LL is only at 1.04).

Concordance 15 also shows examples of the processes types linked to the auxiliary *do*. All processes have Plath in acting function, and of fourteen processes (in line 7 both *think* and *feel* are linked to *do*), eleven are mental-affective process types, with the majority (9/11) denoting cognition. Interestingly, 70 per cent of these mental-affective processes are in the negated form. This is representative of the overall concordance (for those instances where *do* refers to Plath and is not part of direct speech presentation): mental-affective process types where Plath is the active actor[1] constitute 64 per cent of the total; of those, approximately 80 per cent denote cognition; and about 70 per cent are again negated.

Concordance 16 shows a representative sample of the verbs included in the VB0 ('base form of verbs') category. This sample does not include any of the verbs that are presented in conjunction with *do* or *don't* in Concordance 15. Based on the overall concordance, in 70 per cent of cases, Plath is acting in mental-affective or behavioural processes. Neither of these has an effect on or involves third parties. The remaining 30 per cent are split relatively evenly between material and verbal process types. The mental-affective process types are mainly of the cognitive (55 per cent) and emotional (27 per cent) nature. Examples of these from Concordance 16 include *think, believe, know* (e.g. lines 1, 6 and 11) for the former and *hate, feel* (e.g. lines 12 and 19) for the latter.

1	too late . 3 months , you	think	, scared to death . You w
	k , scared to death . You	want	to call that man You earr
	an introvert for 3 months	stop	thinking of noise , names
	. Neurotic women . Fie .	Get	a job . Learn shorthand a
5	women . Fie . Get a job .	Learn	shorthand at night . NOTE
	g that is against all you	believe	in . Impasse : male relat
	to escape , retreat , not	talk	to anybody . Thesis panic
	u to masturbate him . You	pull away	, disgusted , yet not dis
	It 's only . . . but you	say	" No no no no no no no .
10	, only eighteen . So you	go	back to the fraternity hc
	he fraternity house . You	know	that you wo n't go out wi
	s and aloneness . And you	hate	him because he is a boy .
	arrow of your bones . You	spin	across a bridge , and the
	more vibrant note as you	ride	on the grill-work , with
15	destination one . So you	hoist	the bike over a fence , a
	e bike over a fence , and	walk	it up the rutted mud path
	activity , only when you	sit	and listen by the window
	y , only when you sit and	listen	by the window , as the cc
	think and feel sick . You	feel	the days slipping by , el
20	gh your fingers , and you	wonder	what you have for your ei
	eighteen years , and you	think	about how , with difficul
	for you ; so do they who	stab	you . But the game is for
	d you and your antagonist	rival	each other with brave smi
	es while the poison darts	quiver	, maliciously , in your m
25	fight back , because you	know	the fear and the inadequa
	out in your words as they	crackle	falsely on the air . So y
	lsely on the air . So you	hear	her say to you " We 'd re
	f you grit your teeth and	try	hard enough .) " Oooh ,
	with last weekend . " You	toss	off a thumbnail sketch of
30	, noticing that when you	say	he 's good-looking she sh
	stand to hear that . You	go	on about Bob from Renssal
	a damn about him , so you	pretend	. She 's really deaf now
	he just wants to have you	make	her feel good the way you
	ants to have you make her	feel	good the way you used to

Concordance 16 VB0/267.

In addition to the features that are directly related to the narrative person in some way, the keyness of third-person singular pronouns and the keyness of negation are also noteworthy. The third-person singular pronouns are relatively evenly split between *he* and *she*, with the latter at 60 per cent. This is not surprising, given that Plath, at this point in her life, lives in an all-female college and therefore has contact with women more than men.

The keyness of negation is interesting, as various psychological studies of language use (as outlined in Chapter 3) emphasize its importance for affective states. Negation seems to be used differently across the second-person entries. About 48 per cent of negation occurs in Entries 41–5. There are no instances of negation in Entry 56. Only 28 per cent of negation occurs in Entries 81–156. However, 24 per cent occurs in the final two entries that are only 1,179 words long combined. An LL comparison between these frequencies shows that the difference between the first group of entries and the last group of entries is statistically insignificant (LL = 0.12). However, the difference between the last group of entries and the middle group, as well as the first group and the middle group, is significant. Negation is statistically overused in the final group when compared with the middle group (LL = 14.2) and in the first group when compared with the middle group (LL = 18.58). This means that negation occurs significantly more in Entries 41–5 and the final two entries than in the other SPN entries.

When comparing texts or corpora that are very similar (e.g. being subcorpora of a larger corpus), it is important to look at what is underused as well as what is overused. To this end, Table 8.4 shows those POS that are key in FPN + Shifts.

Table 8.4 Key parts-of-speech in FPN + shift entries versus SPN entries

POS	F1	% 1	F2	% 2	LL	Category
PPIS1	2375	3.58	35	0.44	332.1	first-person sing. subjective personal pronoun (I)
AT	3596	5.43	345	4.31	17.88	article (e.g. the, no)
NN1	9001	13.58	974	12.16	11.05	singular common noun (e.g. book, girl)
PPH1	640	0.97	53	0.66	7.79	third-person sing. neuter personal pronoun (it)
JJ	6305	9.51	695	8.68	5.43	general adjective
NP1	867	1.31	83	1.04	4.39	singular proper noun (e.g. London, Jane, Frederick)
IW	578	0.87	53	0.66	4	with, without (as prepositions)

Similar to the discussion of Table 8.3 above, the keyness of the first item in this reverse comparison can also be explained by the fact that the two corpora are narrated in a different person. Any references to first-person singular pronouns are due to a difference in narrative person.

The keyness of items such as 'articles', 'singular common nouns', 'singular proper nouns', 'general adjectives' and the pronoun *it* in this comparison can be linked to Plath's tendency to describe her environment and physical aspects of scenes in minute detail, as previously outlined. These results seem to suggest that FPN + Shifts contain more of this type of description than SPN. This is confirmed by the manual intensive analysis of some of the second-person entries. In the next section, I discuss the implications of these findings.

8.2.1.1 POS discussion

In Chapter 5 on self-descriptions and direct references to affective states, I showed that, in SPN, *you are* is almost exclusively followed by negative characteristics, while similar self-descriptions (VBM – *am*, *'m*) in FPN and Shift entries are more balanced. This suggests that when Plath writes about herself in the second person, her affective state is more negative than when she writes about herself using *I*. Since Plath had diagnosed depression, and one of the key indicators of depression is increased references to the self, at this point it is necessary to explore whether there are more references to the self in SPN than in FPN + Shifts. This, however, is not a straightforward comparison, as the tokens used for self-reference (pronouns and verbs) are different in the two subcorpora – they take

Table 8.5 Changes made during manipulation

Original pronoun/verb relating to that pronoun	Changed to ...
You (second-person singular subject)	I
You (second-person singular object)	Me
You (second-person plural subject) when contextually the I was included	We
You (second-person plural object) when contextually the I was included	Us
Your/yourself (second-person singular possessive/reflexive)	My/myself
Yours (second-person singular possessive demonstrative)	Mine
Are/'re/aren't (where it referred to the 'you' subject)	Am/'m/am not
Were/weren't (where it referred to the 'you' subject and it was not hypothetical)	Was/wasn't

Table 8.6 Results for self-references in second-person narration

			SPN manipulated versus FPN + Shifts			
POS	**F1**	**% 1**	**F2**	**% 2**	**LL**	**Category**
PPIS1	379	4.74	2375	3.58	23.77	first-person sing. subjective personal pronoun (I)
PPIO1	81	1.01	400	0.6	16.04	first-person sing. objective personal pronoun (me)

the form of first-person pronouns in one and second-person pronouns in the other sub-corpus. I therefore compared a manipulated version of the SPN sub-corpus to the FPN + Shifts sub-corpus. This manipulation consisted of changing all second-person references (including the corresponding verbs) to Plath as narratee and protagonist, to first-person references. The instances of *you* as part of speech presentation, or in reference to others, were not altered. The precise changes made can be seen in Table 8.5.

Table 8.6 shows that there are more references to the self in terms of pronouns (both subjective and objective) in SPN than in the rest of the Smith Journal. This means that not only are there more references to the self in the Smith Journal than in the reference corpus (SWTPAuto) as discussed in Chapter 4, but self-references are even more frequent in entries written in the second person. As I outlined previously, increased references to the self, which can be interpreted as increased self-focus, are associated with depression (e.g. Rude et al. 2004, Hargitai et al. 2007), anxiety (e.g. Pennebaker et al. 2003) and potentially suicidality (e.g. Fekete 2002).

As outlined above, the lexical items associated with personal pronouns also suggest increased self-focus in SPN. In instances of auxiliary *do* and the base form of lexical verbs where Plath is actor, 49 per cent of process types are mental-affective, 22 per cent are behavioural, 12 per cent are material, 11 per cent are verbal and 6 per cent are relational in SPN. By definition (Thompson 1996), both mental-affective and behavioural process types have no direct affected entity (except the activated actor themselves). As with self-references, the percentages for mental-affective and behavioural process types are also higher in SPN than in the Smith Journal overall (which does, of course, include SPN entries). While in the Smith Journal overall, approximately 55 per cent of processes have no effect on third parties or external things, the percentage is around 70 per cent in SPN.

This kind of increased self-focus tends to be associated with depression (e.g. Rude et al. 2004, Hargitai et al. 2007), anxiety (e.g. Pennebaker et al.

2003) and potentially suicidality (e.g. Fekete 2002). At the same time, Hargitai et al. (2007) point out that increased self-reference can occur in narratives of achievement as well, with a different significance. The authors explain it thus: 'The narratives of achievement are similar to the narratives of fear in relation to self-reference, since in the background of our successes there is the delight of "acting individually", which is coupled with autonomy' (Hargitai et al. 2007: 33–4). On the other hand, in narratives of fear or anxiety, self-reference can be explained by the need to 'overcome the emerging difficulties alone. Solitude, separation, lack of connections, or frustrated relations become dominant' (Hargitai et al. 2007: 33). This shows that the topic of writing is not irrelevant.

Entries narrated in the second person in the Smith Journal are more similar to narratives of fear than to narratives of achievement. In Chapter 5 on self-descriptions and direct references to affective states, I showed that over 75 per cent of self-descriptions in SPN express something negative or, at least, self-doubting/questioning, and only one of the self-descriptions in these entries suggests anything explicitly positive. This is in contrast with overall percentages in the Smith Journal, where approximately 55 per cent of self-descriptions are negative, but approximately 40 per cent are also positive (the remaining 5 per cent can be considered 'neutral'). In addition, an increase in references to the self in object position (*me*), a key feature of SPN as shown in Table 8.6, has been linked with depression (Fekete 2002). As such, the increased self-focus aspect of Plath's experience of affectives states appears to be linked with depression, anxiety etc. more broadly.

The overuse of negation in second-person narration is also interesting – it is characteristic only of SPN, as it is not a key POS or semantic category for the Smith Journal as a whole. Negation is known to require more cognitive processing than the positive forms and therefore foregrounds a locution (Halliday 1994) and is the dispreferred form in writing (Biber 1988 and Biber et al. 1999). Hasson and Glucksberg (2006) provide evidence that the comprehension of negation can involve the construction of the affirmative scenario first; Sweetser (2006) confirms this from the perspective of mental space theory. This suggests that the comprehension of negation is more complex than that of affirmatives. As such, negation is an interesting linguistic feature in narrative accounts and generally invites questions (Coulthard and Johnson 2007). This is because narratives

> are essentially accounts of what happened and to a lesser extent what was known or perceived by the narrator and thus reports of what did *not* happen or was *not*

> known are rare and special. There is, after all, an infinite number of things that did not happen and thus the teller needs to have some special justification for reporting any of them. (Coulthard and Johnson 2007: 176)

In psychological terms, negation is associated with anger (in combination with rhetorical questions and direct references to others) (Pennebaker et al. 2003), negativism and a potential for self-harm (Hargitai et al. 2007) or suicidality, when in combination with markers of dichotomous thinking, such as polarized language (Fekete 2002). While dichotomous structures are not significantly over- or underused in SPN, they are overused in the Smith Journal overall. This potentially means that polarized language is relatively evenly distributed across the Smith Journal, including in SPN. In SPN, however, these dichotomous structures co-occur with increased negation and self-focus. This combination provides tentative evidence for a suicidal component in Plath's lived experience.

However, as with self-focus, the data need to be examined more closely. Within the SPN sub-corpus, almost 40 per cent of concordance lines of *not/n't* are from Entries 44 and 45 – Concordance 17 shows some examples of this. These entries mainly consist of dialogue, so only about 50 per cent of *not/n't* refer to Plath. In fact, a corpus exploration of quotation marks in SPN and in FPN + Shifts suggests that there is more direct speech in SPN than in the rest of the Smith Journal (LL = 11.11). In these cases, Biber et al.'s (1999) notion that this type of negation is most common in speech can reasonably account for the presence of negation.

't your own security enough ? Maybe	not	. 45 . ... Another blind date . This one
edroom as Pat gets ready . She did	n't	know what she was getting you in for . Yo
ou get a side glance as he drives :	not	bad hair receding on temples , but manly
: find out her interests .) You do	n't	, but you ca n't squelch him quite so soo
erests .) You do n't , but you ca	n't	squelch him quite so soon . You parry : "
Mass . " You run off glibly . " Do	n't	give me a hard time . " " What ? " You do
e a hard time . " " What ? " You do	n't	get it . Traffic occupies his attention .
es . An encouraging sign . They are	n't	lazy , they blaze at you . Heartened , yo
: " You know , it 's too bad you do	n't	get to know people in a crowd , like this
u 'll do the same . Then tonight wo	n't	be a total los . You 'll say : I know a l
he says . " I want to talk . We ca	n't	talk here . " You get your coat . Out the
when he died . I came back and did	n't	talk to anyone . I went out with girls wh
one . I went out with girls who did	n't	give a damn . . . . He used to talk to me
uriosity is aflame . Granted you ca	n't	be a man , but he can tell you how it was
you start out again . 'This one is	n't	taken , ' they say . You get out . You ea
you do to your guys in war . It 's	not	so different . " You want to be worldly .
' " A girl in high school . She was	n't	at all like you . She liked to drink alot
This is one time your innocence wo	n't	help you ; you 're done . But then you 'r
Once a woman has intercourse she is	n't	satisfied . " " You need time and securit
spoiled brat , " you say . " You do	n't	know how it is , " he says . " You ca n't
ow how it is , " he says . " You ca	n't	, when you 're all burning , on fire insi

Concordance 17 XX in entry 45/96.

In the final three SPN entries, however, there is no dialogue. 30 per cent of concordances of XX (not/n't) occur in these three entries (156, July 6 and July14), and over 95 per cent of negations in these entries refer to Plath. The negation appears either in the form of imperatives (*don't do x*), questions (*why don't you do x*) or with modals (*can't*). As these examples are not part of actual dialogues, they can more likely be interpreted as indicators of suicidality as noted by Fekete (2002).

are anybody , which you are no doubt	not	, you should not be bored , but should k
ich you are no doubt not , you should	not	be bored , but should be able to think ,
e able to think , accept , affirm and	not	retreat into a masochistic mental hell w
fear make you want to stop eating do	n't	ignore all the people you could know , s
m : but please yank yourself up &; do	n't	spend years gaping in horror at the one
nalyze , to recreate in your own mind	not	merely to shovel the hole full of other
om here is your life , your mind : do	n't	panic . Begin writing , even if it is or
pick a topic . Then think . If you ca	n't	think outside yourself , you ca n't writ
a n't think outside yourself , you ca	n't	write . And do n't mope about saving $15
out and ending it all . Your room is	not	your prison . You are . And Smith can nc
your prison . You are . And Smith can	not	cure you ; no one has the power to cure
d , sick , lethargic , worst of all ,	not	wanting to cope . You saw visions of you
Colossal desire to escape , retreat ,	not	talk to anybody . Thesis panic lack of c
ink . You can . You must , moreover ,	not	continually run away while asleep forget
n you and love and mankind . You must	not	seek escape like this . You must think .

Concordance 18 XX in the final two entries/96.

References to others are also significantly overused only in SPN. As mentioned above, an increase in references to other people in conjunction with rhetorical questions and negation can be an indication of anger. However, in this case, increased references to third parties are not spread evenly throughout the SPN entries. They are concentrated mainly in five entries where the topic is actually another person or an encounter with another person. Over 80 per cent of concordance lines for PPHS1 ('third person sing. subjective personal pronoun') occur in Entries 41, 42, 43, 44 and 45 (i.e. the 40s cluster, or 30 per cent of the sub-corpus). Similarly, instances of *is* and the abstract concepts they refer to are a reflection of Plath's topic in these entries. As such, this feature is best explained by the subject matter of the entries.

The results from the reverse comparison (comparing FPN + Shifts to SPN) suggest that some key linguistic features in FPN + Shifts (and therefore underused items in SPN) are features that were interpreted as part of Plath's style of description. In Demjén (2007), I indicated that there seemed to be a decline in descriptive language in the final two entries in the Smith Journal, which I suggested was a symptom of the depressive affective state – a sort of reduction of mental faculties. The automated corpus comparison in this analysis seems to suggest this as well. However, a semantic analysis is needed for further exploration of this.

8.2.2 Semantic results and discussion

The semantic comparison highlights key semantic fields in the data when compared to a reference corpus and can reveal something about the content of a text (Hunston 2002). In this case, two subsections of a larger corpus are being compared to each other, so any differences revealed reflect the content differences at various points in the same overall text. Table 8.7 shows the key semantic fields in the second-person sub-corpus. The first column shows the semantic tag assigned by Wmatrix, with the full name of the category in the penultimate column; the second column shows the absolute frequency in SPN; the third column shows the relative frequency. Column F2 shows the absolute frequency in FPN + Shifts; while the fifth column shows the relative frequency. The sixth column shows the respective LL values. The last column includes a few examples from the SPN sub-corpus.

The first thing to note about Table 8.7 is its length. In Chapter 4, the semantic analysis produced fifty-nine key USAS tags. Here, on the other hand, only seven categories are statistically significant despite the lower LL cut-off point (the LL cut-off point in Chapter 4 was 6.63). This is not unusual in two subsections of the same overall text, but it is worth exploring, in light of the idea above that there is potentially less description in SPN than in other parts of the Smith Journal.

The LL cut-off points for the comparison in Chapter 4 and the comparison here are not the same, so the aforementioned two numbers of significant USAS categories are not strictly comparable. However, when SPN is compared with SWTPAuto, there are only twenty-seven key USAS tags at the LL cut-off point of 6.63. When FPN + Shifts are compared to SWTPAuto, there are sixty significant USAS categories. These two numbers are comparable. Since several USAS categories were linked to the presence of description in the Smith Journal, one could argue that fewer key USAS categories imply less description. This supports the interpretation that there is less description in SPN than in the rest of the Smith Journal.

The Pronouns semantic category includes personal and other types of pronouns, so it is not surprising that it sits at the top of Table 8.7. As discussed in detail in the POS comparison, second- and third-person pronouns are all

Table 8.7 Key semantic fields in SPN versus FPN + shift entries

USAS tag	F1	% 1	F2	% 2	LL	Category	Examples
Z8	1191	14.87	8372	12.63	26.62	Pronouns	*you, she, her, them, which, that, yourself*
B1	205	2.56	1232	1.86	16.65	Anatomy and physiology	*eyes, lashes, breasts, shoulder, guts, lungs*
E5–	29	0.36	101	0.15	14.23	Fear/shock	*fear, scared, shocked, panic, afraid*
H2	53	0.66	298	0.45	6.14	Parts of buildings	*downstairs, room, window, door, floor, walls*
A9 +	86	1.07	529	0.8	6.06	Getting and possession	*get, has, take, own, keep, catch*
E6–	16	0.2	69	0.1	4.8	Worry	*nervous/ly, agonize, tension, worries*
T1.1.1	23	0.29	117	0.18	4.07	Time: past	*last week, used to, past, yesterday, already*

overused in the SPN sub-corpus. This is only a characteristic of the SPN corpus, as Z8 ('Pronouns') is not key in the Smith Journal or in the FPN + Shifts corpus when compared to SWTPAuto.

The second item ('Anatomy and physiology') in Table 8.7 is a key feature not only of second-person narration but also of the Journal in general when compared to the reference corpus. However, 'Anatomy and physiology' items seem to be used differently at the beginning (up to Entry 56) and end (from Entry 81 onwards) of the SPN sub-corpus. Concordance 19 shows some examples from the beginning of the corpus, and Example 60 shows a fuller extract from the SPN at this stage, including the last five lines of Concordance 19.

Example 60

> You_Z8 are_A3+ always_N6+++ aware_X2.2+ of_Z5 her_Z8 insolent_S7.2- breasts_B1 which_Z8 pout_B1 at_Z5 you_Z8 very_A13.3 cutely_X9.1+ from_Z5 their_Z8 position_M6 as_Z5 high_N3.7+ and_Z5 close_to_A13.4 her_Z8 shoulders_B1 as_Z5 possible_A7+. They_Z8 are_A3+ versatile_A6.3+ breasts_B1, always_N6+++ clamoring_X3.2 for_Z5 attention_X5.1+. Perhaps_A7 they_Z8 are_A3+ angry_E3- at_Z5 her_Z8 face_B1 which_Z8 does_Z5 not_Z6 notice_X3.4+ them_Z8, but_Z5 smiled_E4.1+ lashily_Z99 and_Z5 innocently_G2.2+ above_Z5 them_Z8. They_Z8 are_A3+ gay_S3.2/B1 breasts_B1, pushing_out_M2 delightfully_O4.2+ plump_O4.4 curves_O4.4 in_Z5 her_Z8 weak-willed_S1.2.5- sweaters_B5. They_Z8 are_A3+ proud_E4.2+/S1.2 breasts_B1 ... (beginning of Entry 42, USAS-tagged)

and Wendy and Snow White . Her	face	is cute . She talks cute wi
ute . She talks cute with white	teeth	under a bright lipsticked m
teeth under a bright lipsticked	mouth	. Her smile is cute , and s
re always aware of her insolent	breasts	which pout at you very cute
e of her insolent breasts which	pout	at you very cutely from the
sition as high and close to her	shoulders	as possible . They are vers
s possible . They are versatile	breasts	, always clamoring for atte

Concordance 19 Anatomy and physiology – beginning/205.

Entry 42 is typical of the way items belonging to the 'Anatomy and physiology' USAS tag are used in the first few SPN entries. The entire entry is a description of a young woman Plath has encountered. Plath focuses on the physical characteristics, in particular, of someone she met in a very detailed and mainly literal way (with the exception of *breasts* above). In the later entries of the sub-corpus, on the other hand, very similar words are used mostly in reference to Plath rather than others. Concordance 20 and Example 61 come from this last section of SPN. The first five lines of Concordance 20 appear in Example 61.

Example 61

> You_Z8 sit_M8 in_Z5 your_Z8 room_H2, feeling_X2.1 the_Z5 prickling_X5.2+ ache_B2- in_Z5 your_Z8 body_B1 which_Z8 constricts_A1.7+ your_Z8 throat_B1, tightens_A1.7+/A2.1 dangerously_A15- in_Z5 little_N3.2- tear_B1 pockets_B5 behind_Z5 your_Z8 eyes_B1. One_N1 word_Q3, one_N1 gesture_Q1.1/B1, and_Z5 all_N5.1+ that_Z8 is_A3+ pent_up_in_A1.7+ you_Z8 festered_M3/O2 resentments_E2-, gangrenous_B2- jealousies_E4.1-/S3.2, superfluous_N5.2+ desires_X7+ unfulfilled_X9.2- all_N5.1+ that_Z8 will_T1.1.3 burst_A1.1.2 out_of_Z5 you_Z8 in_Z5 angry_E3- impotent_S7.1- tears_B1 in_Z5 embarrassed_E4.1- sobbing_E4.1- and_Z5 blubbering_E4.1- to_Z5 no_one_Z8/Z6 in_Z5 particular_A4.2+ . (beginning of Entry 104, USAS-tagged)

Although the body parts mentioned refer to actual body parts and are thereby literal, the co-text often contains metaphorical or metonymic expressions – the second, third and fourth lines in Concordance 20 are examples of this. In addition,

g the prickling ache in your	body	which constricts your throat ,
r body which constricts your	throat	, tightens dangerously in litt
ghtens dangerously in little	tear	pockets behind your eyes . One
tle tear pockets behind your	eyes	. One word , one gesture , and
out of you in angry impotent	tears	in embarrassed sobbing and blu
to no one in particular . No	arms	will enfold you , no voice wil
little sleep and taut strung	nerves	, and a feeling that the cards
of the great weight on your	shoulders	. Quick footsteps up cellar st
tairs . A sharp thin annoyed	face	around the banister . " Sylvia
tairs . " Paralyzed , struck	numb	, branded by his cold voice yo
is gone . And you grit your	teeth	, despising yourself for your

Concordance 20 Anatomy and physiology – towards the end/205.

some of these expressions contain metaphorical references to affective states: concordance lines 7, 8 and 10 all imply negative affective states. For example, *great weight on your shoulders* is a very conventional linguistic manifestation of the negative EMOTIONS ARE BURDENS conceptual metaphor. Similar examples can be seen in Concordance 21, which comes from the final SPN entries. Here again, the items from the 'Anatomy and physiology' USAS tag either refer to Plath or are indicative of affective states.

Metaphorical/metonymic references to affective states (in particular to emotional states) commonly draw on more concrete bodily processes that occur together with them (see Kövecses 2000 and Chapter 6 for a more detailed discussion). In fact, even in the first few SPN entries, the descriptions of somebody's physical appearance are coloured by Plath's negative perception of the person. In this sense these may also indicate Plath's affective states – albeit with more inferencing.

References to affective states of course also make up the vast majority of the semantic category 'fear/shock'. Concordance 22 shows some of these examples. As in the metaphorically implied negative affective states above, these examples refer to Plath.

A similar sentiment is expressed in some expressions from the 'worry' semantic field, where individual tokens include *care*, *agonize*, *worry* and doing something *nervously*. However, this semantic field is more balanced in terms of

want to go home , back to the	womb	. You watch the world bang dc
bang door after door in your	face	, numbly , bitterly . You hav
illated like a nervous seesaw	gulped	, chose blindly and immediate
ch choice would take the most	guts	: and which kind of guts . Me
most guts : and which kind of	guts	. Marcia is working &; taking
psych at BU " if you had the	guts	to commute . You could be tak
, shutting yourself up in a	numb	defensive vacuum : but please
, eager to crawl back to the	womb	. First think : here is your
ou . Pray to yourself for the	guts	to make the summer work . One

Concordance 21 Anatomy and physiology – final entries/205.

just from the hometown : and a	fear	that you have n't done well eno
of your mother . And you were	frightened	when you heard yourself stop ta
you remember the white look of	fear	about his mouth that day they h
and in every desk at school .	Mortified	, yet secretly excited by such
: do n't spend years gaping in	horror	at the one time in your life yo
own . You are frozen mentally	scared	to get going , eager to crawl b
your life , your mind : do n't	panic	. Begin writing , even if it is
&; friends . You fool you are	afraid	of being alone with you own min
late . 3 months , you think ,	scared	to death . You want to call tha
being creative , and you felt	scared	, sick , lethargic , worst of a
ations ; (jealousy &; frantic	fear.	) female relations : ditto . Lo
, not talk to anybody . Thesis	panic	lack of other people to be with
ination for past wrong choices	Fear	, big &; ugly &; sniveling . Fe

Concordance 22 Fear/shock/29.

the agents it takes: third parties as well as Plath are portrayed as experiencers of tension and worries. In general, both the 'fear/shock' and the 'worry' category mainly contain direct references to the respective emotions, albeit in a potentially hyperbolic form (e.g. lines 4 and 5 in Concordance 22). Kövecses (2000) calls these types of references *labels*. Such dramatization of emotions is relatively characteristic of the Smith Journal – the 'fear/shock' category is key when the Smith Journal is compared to SWTPAuto – and seems to reflect Plath's experience of her surroundings and feelings. However, the keyness 'fear/shock' and 'worry' in SPN suggests that this sub-corpus deals even more with worries and fear than the FPN + Shifts sub-corpus. In fact, when FPN + Shifts are compared to SWTPAuto, 'fear/shock' is not key, but the semantic category 'happy' is. On the other hand, when comparing SPN to SWTPAuto, 'fear/shock' comes up as highly significantly overused in SPN (LL = 20.76). This could reflect not only an *ad hoc* difference in topicality but also an underlying preoccupation in SPN entries that would agree with previous indicators that SPN itself correlates with negative affective states.

The semantic field of 'Parts of buildings' seems somewhat out of place in a text that does not deal with buildings as a topic. Nevertheless, the tokens are mainly literal references to parts of buildings such as *room*, *windows*, *stairs* (Concordance 23 has more examples). These items occur with such frequency because Plath describes the physical settings of her narratives in detail.

room is a senior suite on the	first floor	. A fire is going , and the rug
hin glass of the rain blurred	window	you could see the ocean , remote
eat on the canvas beach wagon	roof	. Inside the windows steamed fr
beach wagon roof . Inside the	windows	steamed from breath and heat of
ging through some leak in the	dike	. So you go downstairs and sit
leak in the dike . So you go	downstairs	and sit at the piano . All the
houlders . Quick footsteps up	cellar	stairs . A sharp thin annoyed f

Concordance 23 Parts of buildings/53.

omb . You watch the world bang	door	after door in your face , numbl
atch the world bang door after	door	in your face , numbly , bitterl
b . First think : here is your	room	here is your life , your mind :
have called Marcia , cancelled	room	&; she is relieved . It would h
g out and ending it all . Your	room	is not your prison . You are .
t details ignore problems shut	walls	up between you &; the world &;

Concordance 24 Parts of buildings/53.

'Parts of buildings' is only key in SPN and not in the Smith Journal overall. This means that it is characteristic of the SPN sub-corpus. Approximately 20 per cent of the time, items from this semantic field are used more symbolically. In Concordance 24 above, various parts of buildings represent a feeling of isolation and constraint, where opportunities are taken away (lines 1–2), and life is contained within a space (lines 3, 5–6). In this sense, they can be taken as somewhat metaphorical and, potentially, as manifestations of the CONTAINER conceptual metaphor.

These instances of metaphoricity again have a negative resonance. The symbolic room or wall is an obstacle or a boundary that makes living and progress impossible for Plath. Even in lines 1–2 in Concordance 24, where the door represents 'opportunity', the image is a negative one, as the doors are shut. This key feature of the text, then, adds to the evidence outlined above that potentially indicates a preoccupation with negative emotions or just a generally more 'troubled' affective state in SPN when compared to FPN + Shifts.

The keyness of the semantic category of 'Time: past' reflects types such as *already* and *last night* (see Concordance 25). The expressions generally do not give precise dates etc. but, rather, relate events to the narrator/writer's NOW. In this sense they could be seen as deictic.

Pólya et al. (2007) associate such items with the retrospective narrative perspective and thereby emotional stability. Similarly, I have used these as indicators of the past temporal orientation in Chapter 7. However, in order to indicate the retrospective narrative perspective or the past temporal orientation, this feature would have to co-occur with other features such as the past tense

t seemed so real and genuine a	few months ago	. You could n't even say i
to go out with a Williams man	last week	. " Got a letter from Bill
en : " Who did you go out with	last weekend	. " You toss off a thumbna
make her feel good the way you	used to	before you got sick of her
is speeding into finality now	already	on the wings of mails , mi
r 2hours only of sleep for the	last two nights	, to shut yourself off frc

Concordance 25 Time: past/23.

So this is what it 's like to	have	a boy want you to masturba
f he asks . But you will never	take	a walk . You will never be
bridge , and the whir of tires	takes on	a lower more vibrant note
more , for a little , and I am	caught	in musing - - how life is
gers , and you wonder what you	have	for your eighteen years ,
elf out of the grab-bag ? Cats	have	nine lives , the saying go
lives , the saying goes . You	have	one ; and some-where along
ing to work . Hard , too . You	have	will-power and are getting
. You have will-power and are	getting	to be practical about livi
about living and also you are	getting	published . So you got a g

Concordance 26 Getting and possession/86.

and distal spatio-temporal deixis. As this is not the case, the keyness of these expressions is likely to simply reflect the mixture of temporal orientations that can occur within sentences and entries.

A final key semantic field in Table 8.7 is that of 'Getting and possession'. Items in this category sometimes denote relational processes that can allude to affective states. Relational processes 'define' an entity in terms of what it is and of the characteristics or possessions that it has (or lacks) (Thompson 1996). In this sense, the example in line 7 in Concordance 26 *you wonder what you have for your eighteen years* is an indirect question about the worth of the self rather than a question about material possessions. Lines 10–12 similarly characterize the self in terms of a trait and potential achievements. The fact that this semantic field is key in SPN when compared to FPN could once again indicate a stronger self-focus in SPN.

Although a brief analysis of the key features of FPN + Shifts (compared to SPN) was conducted, that analysis is less useful for finding out something about SPN. The features overused in FPN + Shifts are those that are underused in SPN, and, where this complemented the overused items in SPN, it was commented on. However, it is difficult to comment on the significance of the various semantic fields that are underused in a text, as it entails hypothesizing about the (lack of) content as opposed to the language of a text. The FPN + Shifts sub-corpus is eight times the size of the SPN sub-corpus, which means that there is a lot more room in it to write about a variety of topics. It is for this reason that more space is not devoted to that comparison here.

8.3 Summary and conclusions

In this chapter, I explored the statistically significant linguistic differences between second-person narration and the rest of the Smith Journal. I discussed differences in personal pronoun and verb usage, negation and topicality. Broadly speaking, second-person narration can be associated with negatively valenced emotions/thoughts, increased references to the self, increased negation and increased references to third parties.

The most significant difference between SPN and the rest of the Journal was, unsurprisingly, in pronoun usage, especially in reference to Plath directly. Self-references in the form of pronouns were key in the Smith Journal overall, but they are also key in just SPN, indicating even more self-focus in these entries. Aside from pronouns, the larger proportion of mental-affective and behavioural process types among the VV0 (base form of verbs) and VD0 (do) CLAWS categories in SPN; the relational process types in the USAS category 'Getting and possession' also supported this interpretation. Increased self-focus can therefore be reasonably described as an integral part of Plath's experience of negative affective states. Self-focus has, of course, been associated with depression in a number of studies (Rude et al. 2004, Pennebaker et al. 2003, Fekete 2002), in particular when in the context of negative narratives (Hargitai et al. 2007). Evidence that the narrative is negatively valenced was provided in the form of more negative self-descriptions in SPN and in the keyness of the 'fear/shock' and 'worry' USAS categories. This means that, while there seems to be a general tendency towards self-focus, Plath's focus on herself increases in the narrative mode (SPN) where her view of herself is more negative. Such a difference in self-focus could therefore indicate the intensity or severity of Plath's negative affective state and, potentially, her depression.

Another important finding from the perspective of Plath's lived experience is the co-occurrence of increased self-focus in SPN with negation. Negation is partly a result of numerous instances of direct speech presentation in early SPN entries, but in the later entries written using *you*, there is no direct presentation of speech. In these entries, it is possible to look for psychological implications of an overuse of such negation. It can be evidence of a tendency towards self-harm (Hargitai et al. 2007), and, in combination with increased self-references, dichotomous structures and emotion words it can indicate suicidal ideation (Fekete 2002). There is some tentative evidence that these do, indeed, co-occur with negation in SPN, which points towards suicidality as an aspect of Plath's affective state. This is particularly pertinent in light of Plath's attempted suicide one month after the final SPN entries in her Journal.

9

So What?

Throughout this book, using various linguistic techniques, I explored what the language of Sylvia Plath's Smith Journal reveals about her mental and emotional life. I wanted to investigate how her stylistic, grammatical and lexical choices related to her *affective states* – aspects of her inner world that can be placed on a cline of positive to negative. Plath's Smith Journal was particularly appropriate for this purpose, as most of the text is devoted to Plath's reflections on her inner turmoil. In this final chapter, I summarize the findings of different analysis chapters and elaborate on the overall picture that Plath's language paints of her affective states. In the final section, I zoom out slightly to discuss Plath's affective states in the context of prominent theories of depression and to reflect on the value of analyses such as this. In other words, I try to respond to the question: So what?

Across the two parts of this book, I looked in detail at: what distinguishes the language of the Smith Journal from other first-person texts; how Sylvia Plath describes herself and her affective states explicitly; what metaphors she uses to indicate her affective states; and how and why she uses the second-person pronoun to write about herself in some sections of the Journal. In conjunction with these broader linguistic aspects, I also discussed temporal orientation, polarized language and negation. This was achieved by a combination of traditional qualitative linguistic analyses, manually working through samples of the Smith Journal and quantitative corpus linguistic techniques, statistically comparing the whole Smith Journal to a reference corpus in terms of POS and semantic categories. This mixed-methods approach allowed me to exploit the strengths while offsetting the weaknesses of each individual method. Intensive manual analysis leads to insights that are rich and subtle but difficult to generalize. The results of automated quantitative comparisons, on the other hand, are relatively robust but require interpretation, and any interpretation needs to be based on detailed knowledge of the text. In combination, one arguably obtains a more comprehensive view of what is distinctive about Plath's lived experience.

The chapters in Part I of the book set the theoretical and methodological scene for this study. In Chapter 3, I outlined the theoretical background for the types of analyses I used, drawing on such concepts and tools as mind style and transitivity. I also reviewed literature in social, clinical and narrative psychology that helped to determine which aspects of Plath's language were important in relation to her experience of affective states. In Chapter 4, I discussed the key grammatical and semantic characteristics of the Smith Journal based on a comparison with the autobiography section of the SWTP corpus (Semino and Short 2004) and using Wmatrix (Rayson 2009). The key linguistic features relevant for Plath's experience of affective states that emerged from this chapter were first, personal pronouns – in particular, *I* and *you*, in combination with the verb *to be* in first-person present tense (*am, 'm*). The first-person singular pronoun was used almost exclusively with reference to Plath, and in some journal entries the same was true of the second-person pronoun. A closer examination of such self-references highlighted their relevance for affective states: a large proportion prefaced direct or metaphorical descriptions, or both, of Plath's person and inner world. This corpus comparison also revealed the overuse of polarized language in the Smith Journal, such as references to eternity, maximums and extremes. The link between pronouns, polarized language and affective states was established on the basis of research by Pennebaker and colleagues (e.g. Rude et al. 2004, Fekete 2002 and Hargitai et al. 2007).

The results from the quantitative analysis in Chapter 4 shaped Part II of the book, where I explored qualitatively and in greater depth Sylvia Plath's self-descriptions, metaphors and personal pronoun use. Although Chapters 5, 6 and 7 are mainly qualitative in nature, they draw on quantitative evidence to substantiate the discussions where appropriate. In Chapter 5, I focused on how Sylvia Plath directly, or using 'literal' language, described herself and her affective states. Overall, she described herself negatively more frequently than positively and wrote more about negative than positive affective states. She repeatedly questioned herself and often expressed self-hatred, demonstrating a sense of insecurity and low self-esteem. This pattern applied throughout the Smith Journal, but it was particularly pronounced in entries written in the second person.

In Chapter 6 on metaphorical expressions, I also observed the tendency for Plath to focus on the negative in relation to affective states and herself. Sylvia Plath's writing, in general, is filled with creative and complex figurative language, but she used metaphors more frequently and in more complex ways (conceptually and textually) in the context of negative affective states. I identified and discussed the following frequent systematic metaphors in the Smith Journal:

- *POSITIVE AFFECTIVE STATE IS WHOLENESS*
- *POSITIVE AFFECTIVE STATE IS COMING INTO EXISTENCE*
- *NEGATIVE AFFECTIVE STATE IS CONFINEMENT*
- *NEGATIVE AFFECTIVE STATE IS IMMOBILITY*
- *NEGATIVE AFFECTIVE STATE IS UNCONTROLLABLE KINETIC FORCE*
- *NEGATIVE AFFECTIVE STATE IS MOVEMENT AWAY*
- *NEGATIVE AFFECTIVE STATE IS INNER DIVISION*
- *NEGATIVE AFFECTIVE STATE IS COMING APART*
- *NEGATIVE AFFECTIVE STATE IS MULTIPLE SELVES*
- *NEGATIVE AFFECTIVE STATE IS AN INTERNAL AGGRESSOR*
- *NEGATIVE AFFECTIVE STATE IS PHYSICAL ILLNESS*
- *NEGATIVE AFFECTIVE STATE IS THE ABSENCE OF SENSATIONS*
- *NEGATIVE AFFECTIVE STATE IS AN EMPTY CONTAINER*
- *NEGATIVE AFFECTIVE STATE IS A CONTAINER UNDER PRESSURE*
- *NEGATIVE AFFECTIVE STATE IS DEATH AND DECAY*

This list itself demonstrates how many different types of metaphors Plath used persistently to describe or allude to her negative affective states, in contrast with only two systematic patterns for positive affective states. Overall, only 6 per cent of her metaphorical references to affective states described positive ones. Work by Ortony and Fainsilber (1987) and Gibbs et al. (2002) suggests that this is an indication that Plath experienced negative affective states more intensely than positive ones.

In Chapter 7, I picked up on another thread from the corpus analysis in Chapter 4 and discussed personal pronouns in the Smith Journal, focusing specifically on the role of second-person narration. In the course of a qualitative analysis, I found that Plath wrote about herself in the second person around the times of emotionally charged life events and in ways that at times suggested a distancing from these events but at other times suggested complete immersion and a sense of inner split. To deal with this potential contradiction, I proposed a framework of temporal orientation for differentiating between various types of second-person narration. Temporal orientation, a framework based on Pólya et al.'s (2007) narrative perspectives, distinguishes between texts that orient towards the past, the present or the present-future, based on the linguistic make-up of the clauses they contain. Second-person narration with a past temporal orientation presents a sense of distance and calm, as a result of the predominance of statements in the past tense, distal deictic and temporal references and a substantial amount of description and/or action narration. The present temporal orientation, characterized by the present tense, questions, exclamations, interjections and proximal deictic expressions, suggests more emotional involvement. On the other hand, emotional crises, for want of a better term, were associated with second-person narration with a present-future temporal orientation. This present-future orientation can include linguistic features associated with the present temporal orientation but also includes imperatives, vocatives and progressive aspect and contains no action narration or description. The linguistic differences between these categories were able to account for the seemingly contrasting roles of second-person narration in the Smith Journal.

Finally, in Chapter 8, I returned to Wmatrix and quantitatively compared journal entries written in the second person with the rest of the Smith Journal to further characterize differences between them. This comparison confirmed that second-person narration contained even more references to negatively valenced emotions/thoughts and that Plath referred to herself even more often than in the rest of the Journal. In addition, negation turned out to be more frequent in second-person narration. In combination, these findings suggested that second-person narration itself may indicate increased negativity or more severe depression for Sylvia Plath and that it might tentatively be linked to suicidal ideation in the Smith Journal.

The various methods and analyses outlined in this book allowed me to describe what kinds of affective states Plath experienced and what these subjectively felt like. It is undeniable that Plath's writing is dominated by negative affect. Her literal and metaphorical language indicates a negative self-image, insecurity and self-doubt, both in terms of the frequency with which she writes about these and in terms of the way she does so. While this could be considered part of the common existential angst of a young woman working out her place in life, the complexity, clustering and repetition of metaphors describing these negative affective states suggest an intensity of experience that seems to go beyond what could be considered normal.

This negative bias seems to go together with a strong self-focus and a categorical world view: Plath's use of polarized expressions suggests that she sees things in black and white extremes rather than nuances of grey. Of course, the self is generally the topic of personal journals and autobiographies, but even compared to other first-person narratives, Plath writes about herself from her own point of view more than would be expected. She describes events and actions (often mental ones) that have no effect on the outside world or other people but are only related to her. This type of inward focus, combined with the tendency towards extremes and negative bias, means that Plath interprets external events as personal, as attacks or severe judgements on her specifically. It also means that she is less able to take a step back, to mitigate and re-evaluate her experiences. These are characteristics that are often associated with depression more generally.

ESCAPE and *RETREAT* metaphors indicate another aspect of Plath's experience than seems to deviate from what could be considered 'normal'. Plath seems to be drawn to places and aspects of life that, most people would agree, should be avoided, while wanting to escape from things that most people would consider normal, even positive parts of life. She expresses a desire to retreat into *non-thought, blubbering, numbness, womb, masochistic mental hell, not caring*; and to escape from herself, *routine, responsibility* and *freedom*. This suggests that she feels unable to cope with certain aspects of everyday life.

Self-focus, negative bias and deviation from some social norm are not necessarily problematic in themselves, but Plath's language indicates that she is struggling. A number of metaphors she uses systematically entail the unpleasantness of her affective states. *PHYSICAL ILLNESS* metaphors, furthermore, indicate that intense pain is a persistent aspect of her experience, along with inner conflict and a sense of split. *MULTIPLE SELVES* metaphors suggest that parts of her would like to think, feel and behave differently, but other parts prevent her from doing so. However much she wants to, she does not seem to be able to affect her situation. She feels incapacitated by her circumstances, as indicated by *CONFINEMENT* metaphors, but also by her own self (cf. *IMMOBILITY* metaphors). Bringing about any improvement in her affective states seems to be difficult and exhausting, like giving birth. She does not feel in control of herself, her emotions and her circumstances (cf. *COMING APART* and *UNCONTROLLABLE KINETIC FORCE* metaphors). In some ways, all this implies an experience of contradictions: affective states that are violent and forceful but at the same time also incapacitating and immobilizing.

Some of these aspects of Plath's experience appear to be exacerbated at times, when she writes about herself using *you*. She seems to turn inwards more, to focus on herself even more strongly than in the rest of the journal. In light of her diagnosed depression, this in itself indicates a worsening of her condition (cf. Rude et al. 2004). In addition, her self-image becomes more negative, and, in present and present-future-oriented entries, she seems to be more conflicted and split. In these particular types of second-person entries, increased negation coupled with the aforementioned increase in self-references and an underlying categorical world view suggest a further deterioration – one that points towards suicidal thoughts. Hints towards suicide are embedded in some of Plath's metaphors throughout first-person entries too (especially in instances of *womb*, *ESCAPE* and *EMPTY CONTAINER* metaphors), but the thoughts turn into action shortly after Plath stops writing her journal. One month after writing two entries in present and present-future-oriented second-person narration, she attempts suicide on 24 August 1953.

9.1 Zooming Out

Linguistic choices, whether one considers them to be conscious or not, can provide clues about affective states without having to ask someone directly whether they are happy, sad or depressed. Linguistic style – *how* someone says what they say – and relative frequencies of certain words indicate this, irrespective of the topic and content of texts. In this way, linguistic analysis, by relying on a systematic framework for going beyond the surface of a text, is a productive way of approximating what is called the 'lived experience' or phenomenology of affective states, such as depression. As a diagnosed depressive with suicidal tendencies, Plath's experience of her affective states is, to some extent, also her experience of these disorders. Her lived experience, as embedded in her language, is therefore also relevant for, and crucial to, an understanding of depression more broadly:

> In order to understand and intelligently treat mania or depression it is not enough simply to establish the presence or absence of a clinical syndrome; it is necessary to have a genuine feel for the phenomenology of the symptoms that make up the syndrome, a visceral awareness of the devastating consequences of having depression or mania.... Personal accounts by writers are irreplaceable sources in helping to do this. (Jamison 2006: 197)

The entailments of Sylvia Plath's linguistic patterns discussed in this book are broadly consistent with prominent theories of depression, but they add to the clinical descriptions by highlighting aspects of the experience that might otherwise be backgrounded.

According to the cognitive theory of depression (originally proposed by Beck in 1961), depression sufferers tend to demonstrate a certain 'cognitive triad': repetitive, unintended and not easily controllable thoughts reflecting negative views of the self, the world and the future (Haaga et al. 1991: 215). The degree of negativity is thought to be proportional to the severity of the depression. Plath's negative self-image and questioning of the future and the repetition both in direct and in metaphorical patterns reflect this cognitive triad in the Smith Journal, and the increased frequency of these patterns in second-person narration also indicates a link with severity of the disorder.

The helplessness theory of depression, on the other hand, focuses more on notions of agency, thereby covering an aspect of Plath's experience that is not captured fully by the cognitive theory. In the helplessness theory of depression, *hopelessness* is seen as an integral part of the disorder and refers to two interconnected elements: '(a) negative expectations about the occurrence of highly valued outcomes (a negative outcome expectancy), and (b) expectations of helplessness about changing the likelihood of occurrence of these outcomes' (Abramson et al. 1989: 359). The persistence of metaphors implying a lack of control and agency indicates that this is an important aspect of Plath's affective states. Haaga et al. (1991) further claim that a combination of hopelessness and the cognitive triad positively correlates with suicidal ideation. While this link is somewhat more complicated – people may show signs of suicidal ideation in severe depression, but the risk of them acting on this impulse does not increase until they start to recover (cf. Myers 2010) – it appears to be consistent with parts of Plath's experience.

However, there are aspects of Plath's experience with potential relevance for how depression is understood that are not fully captured by either of these theories. Examining her language permits a more qualified and comprehensive discussion of what increasingly severe depression might feel like and when and how it might tend towards suicidal ideation. Pain, a sense of inner division and struggles to overcome these affective states, as well as a seemingly categorical world view and aversion to 'normal' aspects of everyday life, are all part of Plath's experience of depression. Some of these aspects seem to be consistent with behavioural theories (Ainsworth 2000), while others might be consistent with some (often controversial) evolutionary theories of the disorder (Nettle 2004). However, starting with the lived experience of one individual as embedded in her language allows a more comprehensive insight into a potential disorder than any one theory and may hint at ways of helping them.

In fact, there are potentially significant practical applications for this kind of analysis. 'Since both the experience of illness and clinical encounters occurring in the course of physical and psychological care are mediated and achieved through language, linguistic analysis has the potential to offer valuable insights into many areas of healthcare' (Hunt and Carter 2012: 28, cf. Charteris-Black 2012). And because language both reflects and influences reality, linguistic analysis may even provide new forms of intervention in therapy contexts. For example, knowing that a sense of helplessness is discernible in language could lead to a focus on alleviating such a sense by actively reframing how individuals talk about their experiences. The metaphors people use appear to be a particularly effective means for doing this (Sims 2003) and are helpful in understanding the inherent difficulties in overcoming these states (McMullen and Conway 2002, Meier and Robinson 2006). For example, Tay (2012) notes that metaphors can help reveal and alter people's 'maladjustive conceptualizations' – unproductive ways of talking/thinking – of significant aspects of their lives.

Similarly, while textual analysis alone may not be sufficient as a diagnostic tool, monitoring individuals' use of pronouns, negation and polarized language could potentially function as a kind of early warning system, highlighting individuals who may be moving towards more severe depression or suicidal ideation. This is particularly useful in a context where healthcare professionals are expected to assess suicide risk (Reeves et al. 2004) but where there is no accurate or reliable way of doing so. Linguistic patterns or metaphors indicative of suicidal ideation (e.g. images of being stuck) could help to identify such a risk in patients and allow therapists to take pre-emptive measures.

In Sylvia Plath's case, perhaps it would have been helpful for a therapist to encourage her to construct metaphorical scenarios where she has agency, where she is in control and able to influence her life and experiences. Similarly, it might have helped her if therapy could have focused on reconciling and reintegrating the parts of the self that were split and in conflict. Finally, a therapist could have attempted to steer her towards a more outward looking perspective – a technique that has already proved to be effective in dealing with trauma (e.g. Pennebaker et al. 2003, Pennebaker and King 1999).

My hope is that the study presented in this book will encourage more focus on the very real and complex lived experience of individuals with mental health disorders. This will not only facilitate a deeper understanding of and compassion for the individuals concerned but also potentially improve the general understanding of the specific disorders and expand the range of tools that healthcare professionals can draw on in treating them.

Notes

Chapter 3

1 Psychological Distancing is 'a composite variable based on the LIWC scores for articles and words of more than six letters and inverse scores for first-person singular pronouns, words indicating discrepancy from reality (e.g., would, should, could), and present-tense verbs' (Cohn et al. 2004: 689).

Chapter 4

1 For information, see Leech et al. (1994).
2 For information, see Wilson and Rayson (1993).

Chapter 6

1 While, traditionally, CMT treated metonymy as subordinate to or subsumed under metaphor, it is now generally recognized that metonymy deserves individual consideration (Deignan 2005). Some common metonymic mappings include INSTITUTION FOR PEOPLE, PRODUCER FOR PRODUCT, THE PLACE FOR THE INSTITUTION, THE PLACE FOR THE EVENT, THE PART FOR THE WHOLE, THE OBJECT FOR THE USER.
2 'Basicness' in this case refers to semantic categories, and not 'basicness' as understood by cognitive scientists. Less basic emotions are annoyance and rage (Kövecses 2000).
3 This conceptual metaphor, incidentally, is an example of what one would normally call personification.
4 This is different from Lakoff and Turner's (1989) notion of 'extension', which is defined in terms of novel mappings of elements across domains rather than a textual pattern.
5 These have not been discussed in detail in this analysis but have been mentioned in the context of the main groups of metaphorical expressions.

Chapter 7

1 Using the present tense to describe something that obviously happened in the past.
2 Although the examples of the generic '*you*' here occur in the context of character level speech reporting, similar example can occur at the level of narration.
3 Approximately 15 per cent of journal entries shift between using the first- and the second-person pronoun for narration.
4 Pólya et al. (2007) include direct quotations as a feature of the experiencing perspective, even though they did not include it in their summary table.
5 Although the entire entry is not classed as present-future oriented, the effects discussed do apply to particular excerpts in the example.

Chapter 8

1 I am using the term 'active actor' generically for all process types.

References

Abramson, L. Y., Metalsky, G. I. and Alloy, L. B. (1989), 'Hopelessness Depression: A Theory-Based Subtype of Depression', *Psychological Review*, 96(2): 358–72.

Adolphs, S. (2006), *Introducing Electronic Text Analysis*. London, UK: Routledge.

Ainsworth, P. (2000), *Understanding Depression*. Jacson, MS: University Press of Mississippi.

Allport, G. (1942), *The Use of Personal Documents in Psychological Science*, Prepared for the Committee on Appraisal of Research. Social Science Research Council.

Appignanesi, L. (2008), *Mad, Bad and Sad: A History of Women and the Mind Doctors from 1800*. London: Virago Press.

Archer, D., Wilson, A. and Rayson, P. (2002), Introduction to the USAS Category System. Available online: http://ucrel.lancs.ac.uk/usas/usas%20guide.pdf (accessed: 16 January 2011).

Austin, J. (1962), *How to do Things with Words*. Oxford: Oxford University Press.

Baddeley, J. L., Daniel, G. R. and Pennebaker, J. W. (2011), 'How Henry Hellyer's Use of Language Foretold His Suicide', *Crisis*, 32(5): 288–92.

Banich, M. T. and Mack, M. (2003), *Mind, Brain and Language: Multidisciplinary Perspectives*. Mahwah, NJ: Lawrence Erlbaum.

Barnden, J. A. (1997): 'Consciousness and common-sense metaphors of mind', in S. Nuallain, P. McKevitt and E. Mac Aogain (eds), *Two Sciences of Mind: Readings in Cognitive Science and Consciousness*. Amsterdam: John Benjamins, pp. 311–40.

Barnden, J. A. (2010), 'Metaphor and Metonymy: Making their Connections More Slippery', *Cognitive Linguistics*, 21(1): 1–34.

Barnden, J. A. (n.d.) ATT-Meta Project Databank online. Available at: http://www.cs.bham.ac.uk/~jab/ATT-Meta/Databank/index.html (accessed: 23 August 2010).

Barnden, J. A. and Lee, M. G. (2001), 'Application of the ATT-Meta Metaphor-Understanding System to an Example of the Metaphorical view of MIND PARTS AS PERSONS', Technical Report CSRP-01-09, School of Computer Science, The University of Birmingham, UK.

Beck, A. T., Ward, C. H., Mendelson, M., Mock, J. and Erbaugh, J. (1961), 'An Inventory for Measuring Depression', *Archives of General Psychiatry*, 4: 561–71.

Biber, D. (1988), *Variation Across Speech and Writing*. Cambridge: Cambridge University Press.

Biber, D., Johansson, S., Leech, G., Conrad, S. and Finegan, E. (1999), *The Longman Grammar of Spoken and Written English*. New York: Longman.

Bloom, L. (1996), 'I Write for Myself and Strangers', in Bunkers and Huff (eds), *Inspiring the Daily: Critical Essays of Women's Diaries.* Amherst: University of Massachusetts Press.

Bloor, T. and Bloor, M. (2004), *The Functional Analysis of English: A Hallidayan Approach* (2nd edn). London: Arnold.

Boase-Beier, J. (2003), 'Mind Style Translated', *Style*, 37(Fall 3): 253–65.

Bockting, I. (1994), 'Mind Style as an Interdisciplinary Approach to Characterisation in Faulkner', *Language and Literature*, 3(3): 157–74.

Bockting, I. (1995), *Character and Personality in the Novels of William Faulkner: A Study in Psychostylistics.* Amsterdam: UP of America.

Brain, T. (2001), *The Other Sylvia Plath.* Harlow: Longman.

Brain, T. (2006), 'Sylvia Plath's Letters and Journals', in J. Gill (ed.), *The Cambridge Companion to Sylvia Plath.* Cambridge: Cambridge University Press.

Bundtzen, L. K. (2006), 'Plath an Psychoanalysis: Uncertain Truths', in J. Gill (ed.), *The Cambridge Companion to Sylvia Plath.* Cambridge: Cambridge University Press.

Butor, M. (1973), *La Modification.* Paris: Bordas.

Calvino, I. (1984), 'Un re in ascolto', *Sotto il sole giaguaro.* Milano: Garzanti, 1986, 59–93.

Cameron, L. (2003), *Metaphor in Educational Discourse.* London: Continuum.

Cameron, L. (2008a), 'Metaphor and Talk', in R. W. Gibbs Jr. (ed.), *The Cambridge Handbook of Metaphor and Thought.* New York: Cambridge University Press.

Cameron, L. (2008b), 'Metaphors Shifting in the Dynamics of Talk', in M. S. Zanotto, L. Cameron and M. Do Couto Cavalcanti (eds), *Confronting Metaphor in Use: An Applied Linguistics Perspective.* Amsterdam: John Benjamins.

Cameron, L. (2013), The Dynamics of Metaphor and Empathy: Plenary Presentation at the RaAM Seminar on Metaphor, Metonymy and Emotions, 2–4 May 2013, Poznan, Poland.

Cameron, L. and Low, G. (2004), 'Figurative Variation in Episodes of Education Talk and Text', *European Journal of English Studies,* 8: 355–73.

Cameron, L. and Stelma, J. H. (2004), 'Metaphor Clusters in Discourse', *Journal of Applied Linguistics*, 1(2): 107–36.

Cameron, L., Low, G. and Maslen, R. (2010), 'Finding Systematicity in Metaphor Use', in L. Cameron and R. Maslen (eds), *Metaphor Analysis: Research Practice in Applied Linguistics, Social Sciences and the Humanities.* London: Equinox, pp. 116–46.

Casasanto, D. (2008a), 'Similarity and Proximity: When Does Close in Space Mean Close in Mind?', *Memory and Cognition*, 36(6): 1047–56.

Casasanto, D. (2008b), 'Who's Afraid of the Big Bad Whorf? Crosslinguistic Differences in Temporal Language and Thought', *Language Learning*, 58(1): 63–79.

Charteris-Black, J. (2012), 'Shattering the Bell Jar: Metaphor, Gender and Depression', *Metaphor and Symbol*, 27(3): 199–216.

Charteris-Black, J. and Musolff, A. (2003), '"Battered Hero" or "Innocent Victim"? A Comparative Study of Metaphors for Euro Trading in British and German Financial Reporting', *English for Specific Purposes*, 22(2): 153–76.

Chung, C. K. and Pennebaker, J. W. (2007), 'The Psychological Function of Function Words', in K. Fiedler (ed.), *Social Communication: Frontiers of Social Psychology*. New York: Psychology Press, pp. 343–59.

Cohn, M. A., Mehl, M. R. and Pennebaker, J. W. (2004), 'Linguistic Markers of Psychological Change Surrounding September 11, 2001', *Psychological Science*, 15(10): 687–93.

Cooper, B. (2003), 'Sylvia Plath and the Depression Continuum', *Journal of the Royal Society of Medicine*, 96(June): 296–301.

Coulthard, M. and Johnson, A. (2007), *An Introduction to Forensic Linguistics: Language in Evidence*. London and New York: Routledge.

Crawford, L. E. (2009), 'Conceptual Metaphors of Affect', *Emotion Review*, 1(2): 129–39.

Deignan, A. (2005), *Metaphor and Corpus Linguistics*. Amsterdam: John Benjamins.

Deignan, A. (2008), "Corpus Linguistic Data and Conceptual Metaphor Theory", in M. S. Zanotto, L. Cameron and M. C. Cavalcanti (eds), *Confronting Metaphor in Use: An Applied Linguistic Approach. John Benjamins*, pp. 149–62.

DelConte, M. (2003), 'Why You Can't Speak: Second-Person Narration, Voice and a New Model for Understanding Narrative', *Style*, 37(2): 204–19.

Demjén, Z. (2007), An investigation of the differences and similarities in Sylvia Plath's representations of herself and her world between two extracts from her journals, MA Dissertation. Lancaster University.

Demjén, Z. (2011a), 'Motion and Conflicted Self Metaphors in the Sylvia Plath's Smith Journal', *Metaphor and the Social World*, 1(1): 7–25.

Demjén, Z. (2011b), 'The Role of Second-Person Narration in Representing Affective States in Sylvia Plath's Smith Journal', *Journal of Literary Semantics*, 40(1): 1–21.

Eggins, S. (2004), *An Introduction Systemic Functional Linguistics*. London: Continuum.

Emmott, C. (2002), '"Split Selves" in Fiction and in Medical "Life Stories": Cognitive Linguistic Theory and Narrative Practice', in E. Semino and J. Culpeper (eds), *Cognitive Stylistics Language and Cognition in Text Analysis*. Amsterdam: John Benjamins.

Faigely, L. and Meyer, P. (1983), 'Rhetorical Theory and Reader's Classifications of Text Types', *Text*, 3(3): 305–25.

Farah, N. (1986), *Maps*. New York: Pantheon.

Fekete, S. (2002), 'The Internet – A New Source of Data on Suicide, Depression and Anxiety: A Preliminary Study', *Archives of Suicide Research*, 6: 351–61.

Fine, J. (2008), *Language in Psychiatry. A Handbook of Clinical Practice*, London: Equinox.

Fludernik, M. (1994a), 'Introduction: Second-person Narrative and Related Issues', *Style*, 28(3): 281–311.

Fludernik, M. (1994b), 'Second-person Narrative as a Test Case for Narratology: The Limits of Realism', *Style*, 28(3): 445–77.

Fludernik, M. (1995), 'Pronouns of Address and "Odd" Third-person Forms: The Mechanics of Involvement in Fiction', in K. Green (ed.), *New Essays in Deixis: Discouse, Narrative, Literature*, Amsterdam: Rodopi.

Fludernik, M. (1996), *Towards a "Natural" Narratology*. London: Routledge.
Fludernik, M. (2000), 'Genres, Text Types, or Discourse Modes? Narrative Modalities and Generic Categoriazation',. *Style*, 34(2): 274–92.
Fowler, R. (1977), *Linguistics and the Novel*. London: Methuen.
Fowler, R. (1986), *Linguistic Criticism*. Oxford: Oxford University Press.
Fowler, R. (1996), *Linguistic Criticism* (2nd edn). Oxford: Oxford University Press.
Fundukian, L. J. and Wilson, J. (eds) (2008), *The Gale Encyclopedia of Mental Health* (2nd edn). Detroit: Gale.
Genette, G. (1980), *Narrative Discourse: An Essay in Method*, trans. J. Lewin. Ithaca: Cornell University Press.
Gibbs, R. W. Jr. and Steen, G. J. (1999), *Metaphor in cognitive linguistics*. Amsterdam: John Benjamins.
Gibbs, R. W. Jr., Leggit, J. S. and Tuner, E. A. (2002), 'What's Special about Figurative Language in Emotional Communication?', in S. Fussell (ed.), *The Verbal Communication of Emotions*. Mahwah: Lawrence Erlbaum.
Gibbs, R. W. Jr., Okonski, L. and Hatfield, M. (2013), 'Crazy Creative Metaphors: Crazy metaphorical minds?', *Metaphor and the Social World*, 3(2): 141–59.
Goatly, A. (1997), *The Language of Metaphors*. London: Routledge.
Goatly, A. (2007), Washing the Brain – Metaphor and Hidden Ideology by Andrew Goatly, Amsterdam/Philadelphia: John Benjamins.
Goatly, A. and LLE Project, Lingnan University (2002–5), Metalude – Metaphor at Lingnan University, http://www.ln.edu.hk/lle/cwd03/lnproject/home.html (accessed: 30 July 2010).
Goossens, L. (1990), 'Metaphtonymy: The Interaction of Metaphor and Metonymy in Expressions for Linguistic action', reprinted in R. Dirven and R. Pörings (eds) (2003), *Metaphor and Metonymy in Comparison and Contrast*. Berlin, New York: Mouton de Gruyter, pp. 349–78.
Grady, J. E. (1997a), *Foundations of Meaning: Primary Metaphors and Primary Scenes*. Unpublished PhD dissertation. University of California, Berkeley.
Grady, J. E. (1997b), 'Theories are Buildings Revisited', *Cognitive Linguistics*, 8(4): 267–90.
Grady, J. E. (1999), 'A Typology of Motivation for Conceptual Metaphor: Correlation vs. Resemblance', in R. W. Gibbs, Jr. and G. J. Steen, *Metaphor in Cognitive Linguistics*. Amsterdam: John Benjamins.
Gray, E K. and Watson, D. (2001), 'Emotion, Mood, and Temperament: Similarities, Differences–and a synthesis', in R. L. Payne and C. L. Cooper (eds), *Emotions at work*. New York: Wiley, pp. 21–43.
Grice, H. P. (1975), 'Logic and Conversation', in P. Cole and J. Morgan, *Syntax and Semantics 3: Speech Acts*. New York: Academic Press, pp. 41–58.
Gross, J. J. (2008), 'Emotion Regulation', in M. Lewis, J. M. Haviland-Jones and L. F. Barrett (eds), *Handbook of Emotions*. New York, London: Guildford Press.
Gumperz, J. (1999), 'On Interactional Sociolinguistic Method', in S. Sarangi and C. Roberts (eds), *Talk, Work and Institutional Order*. Berlin: Mouton de Gruyter.

Haaga, D. A. F., Dyck, M. J. and Ernst, D. (1991), 'Empirical Status of Cognitive Theory of Depression', *Psychological Bulletin,* 110(2): 215–36.

Halliday, M. A. K. (1971), 'Linguistic Function and Literary Style: An Inquiry into the Language of William Golding's *The Inheritors*', in S. Chatman (ed.), *Literary Style: A Symposium*. New York: Oxford University Press, pp. 330–68.

Halliday, M. A. K. (1972), 'Towards a Sociological Semantics. From the Series of Working Papers and Prepublications (14/C, 1972)', edited by Centre Internazionale di Semiotica e Linguistica of the University of Urbino, 1972. Reprinted in J. Webster (eds) (2003), *On Language and Linguistics*. London: Continuum.

Halliday, M. A. K. (1973), '"The Functional Basis of Language" from *Applied Studies towards a Sociology of Language,* Vol. 2, *Class, Codes and Control*', in Basil Bernstein (ed.), published by Routledge and Kegan Paul, 1973, pp. 343–66. Reprinted in Webster, J. (ed.) (2003), *On Language and Linguistics*. London: Continuum.

Halliday, M. A. K. (1994), *An Introduction to Functional Grammar.* London: E. Arnold.

Halliday, M. A. K. (2006), 'Systemic Theory', in K. Brown (ed.), *Encyclopedia of Language and Linguistics*, Vol. 12. London, Amsterdam: Elsevier, p. 443.

Halliday, M. A. K. and Hasan, R. (1976), *Cohesion in English.* Harlow: Longman.

Halliday, M. A. K. and Matthiessen, C. (2004), *An Introduction to Functional Grammar*. Hodder Education.

Hargitai, R., Naszódi, M., Kis, B., Nagy, L., Bóna, A. and László, J. (2007), 'Linguistic Markers of Depressive Dynamics in Self-Narratives: Negation and Self-Reference', *Empirical Text and Culture Research*, 3: 26–38.

Hasson, U. and Glucksberg, S. (2006), 'Does Understanding Negation Entail Affirmation? An Examination of Negated Metaphors', *Journal of Pragmatics,* 38: 1015–32.

Herman, D. (1994), 'Textual *You* and Double Deixis in Edna O'Brien's "A Pagan Place"', *Style*, 28(3): 378–410.

Herman, D. (2004), *Story Logic: Problems and Possibilities of Narrative*. Lincoln: University of Nebraska Press.

Herman, D. (2008), 'Description, Narrative and Explanation: Text-type Categories and the Cognitive Foundations of Discourse Competence', *Poetics Today*, 29(3): 437–72.

Herman, D., Jahn, M. and Ryan, M-L. (2005), *Routledge Encyclopedia of Narrative Theory*. New York: Routledge.

Hidalgo-Downing, L. (2003), 'Negation as a Stylistic Feature in Joseph Heller's Catch-22: A Corpus Study', *Style,* 37(3): 318–41.

Hopper, P. J. and Traugott, E. (2003), *Grammaticalization*. Cambridge: Cambridge University Press.

Hunston, S. (2002), *Corpora in Applied Linguistics*. Cambridge: Cambridge University Press.

Hunt, D. and Carter, R. (2012), 'Seeing through the Bell Jar: Investigating Linguistic Patterns of Psychological Disorder', *Journal of Medical Humanities* 33: 27–39.

Ireland, M. E. and Mehl, M. R. (2014), 'Natural Language Use as a Marker of Personality', in T. M. Holtgraves (ed.), *The Oxford Handbook of Language and Social Psychology*. US: Oxford University Press, pp. 201–18.

Jamison, K. R. (2006), 'Contemporary Psychology and Contemporary Poetry: Perspectives on Mood Disorders', in R. Crawford (ed.), *Contemporary Poetry and Contemporary Science*. Oxford: Oxford University Press.

Jeffries, L. (2009), *Critical Stylistics*. Basingstoke: Palgrave Macmillan.

Kiehl, G. (2005), The Phenomenological Experience of Depression. Available online at: http://www.cgjungpage.org/index.php?option=com_content&task=view&id=638&Itemid=40 (accessed: 13 March 2008).

Kirk, C. A. (2004), *Sylvia Plath: A Biography*. Westport, CT: Greenwood Press.

Koller, V., Hardie, A., Rayson, P. and Semino E. (2008), Using a Semantic Annotation Tool for the Analysis of Metaphor in Discourse. Metaphorik.de 15: 141–60. http://www.metaphorik.de/15/koller.pdf (accessed 12 January 2015).

Kövecses, Z. (2000), *Metaphor and Emotion*. Cambridge: Cambrdige University Press.

Kövecses, Z. (2002a), 'Emotion Concepts: Social Constructivism and Cognitive Linguistics', in S. Fussell (ed.), *The Verbal Communication of Emotions*. Mahwah: Lawrence Erlbaum.

Kövecses, Z. (2002b), *Metaphor: A Practical Introduction*. Oxford: Oxford University Press.

Kövecses, Z. (2010), *Metaphor: A Pratical Introduction* (2nd edn). New York: Oxford University Press.

Kukil, K. (eds) (2000), *The Unabridged Journals of Sylvia Plath*. New York: Anchor Books.

Lakoff, G. (1993), 'The Contemporary Theory of Metaphor', in A. Ortony (ed.), *Metaphor and Thought* (2nd edn). Cambeidge: Cambridge University Press.

Lakoff, G. (1996), 'Sorry, I Am Not Myself Today: The Metaphor System for Conceptualizing the Self', in G. Fauconnier and E. Sweetser (eds), *Spaces, Worlds, and Grammar*. Chicago: University of Chicago Press.

Lakoff, G. and Johnson, M. (1980), *Metaphors We Live By*. Chicago: University of Chicago Press.

Lakoff, G. and Johnson, M. (1999), *Philosophy in the Flesh*. New York: Basic Books.

Lakoff, G. and Turner, M. (1989), *More than Cool Reason: A Field Guide to Poetic Metaphor*. Chicago; London: University of Chicago Press.

László, J., Ehmann, B., Pólya, T. and Péley, B. (2007), 'Narrative Psychology as Science', *Empirical Text and Culture Research*, 3: 1–13.

Leech, G. (1969), *A Linguistic Guide to English Poetry*. Harlow: Longman.

Leech, G. (1993), '100 Million Words of English: A Description of the Background, Nature and Prospects of the British National Corpus project', *English Today* 33, 9(1), Cambridge University Press, pp. 9–15.

Leech, G. (2004), 'Recent Grammatical Change in English: Data, Description, Theory', in Karin Aijmer and Bengt Altenberg (eds), *Advances in Corpus Linguistics: Papers from the 23rd International Conference on English Language Research on Computerized Corpora (ICAME 23) Göteborg 22–26 May 2002*. Amsterdam: Rodopi, pp. 61–81.

Leech, G. and Short, M. (1981), *Style in Fiction*. Harlow: Longman.

Leech, G., Garside, R. and Bryant, M. (1994), 'CLAWS 4: The Tagging of the British National Corpus', in *Proceedings of the 15th International Conference on Computational Linguistics (COLING 94)*. Kyoto, Japan: Kyoto University Press, pp. 622–8.

Marcus, L. (1994), *Auto/Biographical Discourses: Criticism, Theory, Practice*. Manchester: Manchester University Press.

Margolin, U. (1990), 'Narrative you Revisited', *Language and Style*, 23(4): 425–46.

Margolin, U. (1999), 'Of What is Past, Is Passing, or to Come: Temporality, Aspectuality, Modality and the Nature of Literary Narrative', in D. Herman (ed.), *Narratologies: New Perspectives on Narrative Analysis*. Columbus, OH: Ohio State University Press.

McEnery, T. and Hardie, A. (2012), *Corpus Linguistics*. Cambridge, UK: Cambridge University Press.

McGavran, J. H. (1988), 'Dorothy Wordsworth's Journals: Putting Herself Down', in S. Bestock (ed.), *The Private Self: Theory and Practice of Women's Autobiographical Writings*. London: Routledge.

McIntyre, D. (2005), 'Logic, Reality and Mind Style in Alan Bennett's "The Lady in the Van"', *JLS*, 34: 21–40.

McMullen, L. M. and Conway, J. B. (2002), 'Conventional Metaphors for Depression', in S. Fussell (ed.), *The Verbal Communication of Emotions*. Mahwah: Lawrence Erlbaum.

McNeill, L. (2005), Genre Under Construction: The Diary on the Internet. Available online at: http://www.languageatinternet.de/articles/2005/120 (accessed: 14 August 2009).

Meier, B. P. and Robinson, M. D. (2006), 'Does "Feeling Down" Mean Seeing Down? Depressive Symptoms and Vertical Selective Attention', *Journal of Research in Personality*, 40(4): 451–61.

Merlini Barbaresi, L. (2004), 'A Model for Defining Complexity in Descriptive Test Type', *Folia Linguistica*, 38(3–4): 355–81.

Meyer, B. J. F. (1985), 'Prose Analysis: Puposes, Procedures, and Problems', in B. K. Britton and J. B. Black (eds), *Understanding Expository Text*. Hillsdale, NJ: Lawrence Erlbaum Associates.

Morrissette, B. (1965), 'Narrative You in Contemporary Literature', *Comparative Literature Studies*, 2: 1–24.

Morson, G. S. (1981), *The Boundaries of Genre: Dostoevsky's* Diary of a Writer *and the Traditions of Literary Utopia*. Austin: University of Texas Press.

Musolff, A. (2006), 'Metaphor Scenarios in Public Discourse', *Metaphor and Symbol*, 21(1): 23–38.

Myers, D. (2010), *Psychology.* New York: Worth Publishers.

Nettle, D. (2004), 'Evolutionary Origins of Depression: A Review and Reformulation', *Journal of Affective Disorders,* 81(2): 91–102.

Nin, A. (1975), *A Woman Speaks.* London: Butler and Tanner Ltd.

O'Brien, E. (1984), *A Pagan Place.* Port Townsend: Graywolf.

Ortony, A. (1975), 'Why Metaphors are Necessary and Not Just Nice', *Educational Theory,* 25(1): 45–52.

Ortony, A. and Fainsilber, L. (1987), 'The Role of Metaphors in Descriptions of Emotions', in *Proceedings of the 1987 workshop on Theoretical issues in natural language processing* Association for Computational Linguistics, Las Cruces, New Mexico.

Palmer, A. (2004), *Fictional Minds.* Lincoln: University of Nebraska Press.

Partington, Alan (2006), 'Metaphors, Motifs and Similes Across Discourse Types: Corpus-Assisted Discourse Studies (CADS) at Work', in Stefanowitsch and Gries (eds), *Corpus Based Approaches to Metaphor and Metonymy.* Berlin: Mouton de Gruyter.

Pennebaker, J. W. and King, L. A. (1999), 'Linguistic Styles: Language Use as an Individual Difference', *Journal of Personality and Social Psychology*, 77(6): 1296–312.

Pennebaker, J. W. and Lay, T. C. (2002), 'Language Use and Personality During Crises: Analyses of Mayor Rudolph Guiliani's Press Conferences', *Journal of Research in Personality*, 36: 271–82.

Pennebaker, J. W., Mehl, M. R. and Niederhoffer, K. G. (2003), 'Psychological Aspects of Language Use: Our Words, Our Selves', *Annual Review of Psychology*, 54: 547–77.

Pennebaker, J. W. and Stone, L. D. (2003), 'Words of Wisdom: Language Use Over the Life Span', *Journal of Personality & Social Psychology,* 85: 291–301.

Phelan, J. (1994), 'Self-Help for Narratee and Narrative Audience: How I- and You?-Read "How"', *Style*, 28(3): 350–66.

Pólya, T., Kis, B., Naszódi, M., László, J. (2007), 'Narrative Perspective and the Emotion Regulation of the Narrating Person', *Empirical Text and Culture Research*, 3: 50–61.

Pólya, T., László, J. and Forgas, J. P. (2005), 'Making Sense of Life Stories: The Role of Narrative Perspective in Perceiving Hidden Information about Social Identity', *European Journal of Social Psychology,* 35: 785–96.

Power, M. and Dalgleish, T. (1997), *Cognition and Emotion: From Order to Disorder.* Hove: Psychology Press.

Pragglejaz Group (2007), 'MIP: A Method for Identifying Metaphorically used Words in Discourse', *Metaphor and Symbol*, 22(1): 1–99.

Pyszczynski, T. and Greenberg, J. (1987), 'Self-Regulatory Perseveration and the Depressive Self-Focusing Style: A Self-Awareness Theory of Reactive Depression', *Psychological Bulletin*, 102: 122–38.

Quirk, R., Greenbaum, S., Leech, G. and Svartvik, J. (1985), *A Comprehensive Grammar of the English Language*. New York: Longman.

Ramachandran, V. S. (2003), In The Reith Lectures. BBC Radio 4. Available online: http://www.bbc.co.uk/radio4/reith2003/lectures.shtml.

Ramachandran, V. S. and Blakeslee, S. (2005), *Phantoms in the Brain*. London: Harper Perennial.

Ramat, P. (2006), 'Negation', in K. Brown (ed.), *Encyclopedia of Language and Linguistics*, Vol. 8, London, Amsterdam: Elsevier, pp. 559–67.

Rayson, P. (2008), 'From Key Words to Key Semantic Domains', *International Journal of Corpus Linguistics*, 13(4): 519–49.

Rayson, P. (2009), 'Wmatrix: A web-based corpus processing environment, Computing Department, Lancaster University. http://ucrel.lancs.ac.uk/wmatrix/.

Rayson, P. and Garside, R. (2000), *Comparing Corpora using Frequency Profiling*, Proceedings of the Workshop on Comparing Corpora, Thirty-eighth ACL, Hong Kong, 2000, pp. 1–6.

Rayson, P., Archer, D., Piao, S. L. and McEnery, T. (2004a), The UCREL semantic analysis system. In proceedings of the workshop on Beyond Named Entity Recognition Semantic labelling for NLP tasks in association with 4th International Conference on Language Resources and Evaluation (LREC 2004), 25th May 2004, Lisbon, Portugal, pp. 7–12.

Rayson, P., Berridge, D. and Francis, B. (2004b), 'Extending the Cochran Rule for the Comparison of Word Frequencies between Corpora', in *Volume II of Le poids des mots: Proceedings of the 7th Int. Conf. on Statistical analysis of textual data (JADT 2004)*, pp. 926–36.

Reeves, A., Bowl, R., Wheeler, S. and Guthrie, E. (2004), 'The Hardest Words: Exploring the Dialogue of Suicide in the Counselling Process – A Discourse Analysis', *Counselling and Psychotherapy Research*, 4(1): 62–71.

Reitan, R. (2011), 'Theorizing Second-person Narratives: A Backwater Project?', in P. K. Hansen, S. Iversen, H. S. Nielsen and R. Reitan (eds), *Strange Voices in Narrative Fiction*. Berlin: Walter de Gruyter. pp. 147–74.

Richardson, B. (2006), Unnatural Voices: Extreme Narration in Modern Contemporary Fiction. Columbus, OH: Ohio State University

Rodriguez, A. J., Holleran, S. E. and Mehl, M. R. (2010), 'Reading Between the Lines: The Lay Assessment of Subclinical Depression From Written Self-Descriptions', *Journal of Personality*, 78(2): 575–98.

Rude, S. S., Gortner, E. M. and Pennebaker, J. W. (2004), 'Language Use of Depressed and Depression-Vulnerable College Students', *Cognition and Emotion*, 18: 1121–33.

Schiwy, M. A. (1994), 'Taking Things Personally: Women, Journal Writing, and Self-Creation', *NWSA Journal*, 6(2): 234–54.

Schoeneman, T. J., Schoeneman, K. A. and Stallings, S. (2004), '"The Black Struggle": Metaphors of Depression in Styron's Darkness Visible', *Journal of Social and Clinical Psychology*, 23(3): 325–46.

Scott, M. (2004), *WordSmith Tools version 4.* Oxford: Oxford University Press.

Semino, E. (2002), 'A Cognitive Stylistics Approach to Mind Style in Narrative Fiction', in E. Semino and J. Culpeper (ed.), *Cognitive Stylistics: Language and Cognition in Text Analysis.* Amsterdam: John Benjamins.

Semino, E. (2005), 'Mind Style', *Elsevier Encyclopaedia of Language and Linguistics*, 7: 142–8.

Semino, E. (Summer 2007), 'Mind Style 25 Years On', *Style*, 41(2): 153–73.

Semino, E. (2008), *Metaphor in Discourse*, Cambridge: Cambridge University Press.

Semino, E. (2011), 'Metaphor, Creativity, and the Experience of Pain Across Genres', in J. Swann, R. Carter and R. Pope (eds), *Creativity in Language & Literature: The State of the Art.* Basingstoke: Palgrave Macmillan.

Semino, E. and Culpeper, J. (1995), 'Stylistics', in J. Blommaert, J. O. Ostman and J. Verschueren (eds), *Handbook of Pragmatics.* Amsterdam: John Benjamins, pp. 513–20.

Semino, E. and Short, M. (2004), *Corpus Stylistics: Speech, Writing and Thought Presentation in a Corpus of English Writing.* London: Routledge.

Semino, E. and Swindlehurst, K. (1996), 'Metaphor and Mind Style in Ken Kesey's One Flew Over the Cuckoo's Nest', *Style 30,* 143–66.

Schiffrin, D. (1996), 'Narrative as Self-Portrait: Sociolinguistic Constructions of Identity', *Language in Society*, 25: 167–203.

Short, M. (1996), *Exploring the Language of Poems, Plays and Prose.* Harlow: Longman.

Sims, P. A. (2003), 'Working with Metaphor', *American Journal of Psychotherapy*, 57: 528–36.

Smith, C. S. (2003), *Modes of Discourse: The Local Structure of Texts.* Cambridge: Cambridge University Press.

Sontag, S. (1991 [1979, 1989]), *Illness as Metaphor and AIDS and Its Metaphors.* London: Penguin.

Stanley, L. (1992), *The Auto/Biographical I – The Theory and Practice of Feminist Auto/ Biography.* Manchester: Manchester University Press.

Stanzel, F. (1984), *A Theory of Narrative*, trans. C. Goedsche. Cambridge: Cambridge University Press.

Steen, G. J. (1999), 'From Linguistic to Conceptual Metaphor in Five Steps', in Gibbs and Steen (eds), *Metaphor in Cognitive Linguistics.* Amsterdam: John Benjamins.

Steen, G. J. (2007), *Finding Metaphor in Grammar and Usage.* Amsterdam: John Benjamins.

Steen, G. J. (2008), 'The Paradox of Metaphor: Why We Need a Three-Dimensional Model of Metaphor', *Metaphor and Symbol,* 23: 213–41.

Steen, G. J and Gibbs, R. W. Jr. (1999), 'Introduction', in R. W. Gibbs, Jr. and G. J. Steen (eds), *Metaphor in Cognitive Linguistics.* Amsterdam: John Benjamins.

Steen, G. J., Dorst, A. G. Herrmann, J. B., Kaal, A., Krennmayr, T. and Pasma, T. (2010), *A Method for Linguistic Metaphor Identification: From MIP to MIPVU*. Amsterdam: John Benjamins.

Stefanowitsch, A. (2006), 'Corpus-Based Approaches to Metaphor and Metonymy', in A. Stefanowitsch and S. Gries (eds), *Corpus-Based Approaches to Metaphor and Metonymy*. Berlin: Mouton de Gruyter.

Stirman, S. W. and Pennebaker, J. W. (2001), 'Word Use in the Poetry of Suicidal and Nonsuicidal Poets', *Psychosomatic Medicine*, 63: 517–22.

Stout, R. (1947), *How Like a God*. New York: Vanguard Press.

Stubbs, M. (2001), *Words and Phrases: Corpus Studies of Lexical Semantics*. Oxford: Blackwell.

Sweetser, E. (2006), 'Negative Spaces: Levels of Negation and Kinds of Spaces', *Graat*, 35(June): 313–32.

Swoyer, Chris (2008), 'The Linguistic Relativity Hypothesis', The Stanford Encyclopedia of Philosophy (Winter 2008 edn), Edward N. Zalta (ed.), http://plato.stanford.edu/archives/win2008/entries/relativism/supplement2.html (Accessed on 5 September 2010).

Tay, D. (2012), 'Applying the Notion of Metaphor Types to Enhance Counseling Protocols', *Journal of Counseling & Development*, 90: 142–9.

Thayer, R. E. (1996), *The Origin of Everyday Moods: Managing Energy, Tension and Stress*. New York: Oxford University Press.

Thompson, G. (1996), *Introducing Functional Grammar*. London: Arnold.

Thompson, G. (2004), *Introducing Functional Grammar* (2nd edn). London: Arnold.

Thurschwell, P. (2000), *Sigmund Freud*. London: Routledge.

Tolaas, J. (1991), 'Notes on the Origin of Some Spatialization Metaphors', *Metaphor & Symbolic Activity*, 6(3): 203–18.

Toolan, M. (1998), *Language in Literature*. London: Arnold.

Toolan, M. (2001), *Narrative: A Critical Linguistic Introduction* (2nd edn). London: Routledge.

Toolan, M. (2008), Verbal Art: Through Repetition to Immersion. Conference Presentation at Second International Stylistics Conference, China (SISCC), 22–5 October. Available online: http://artsweb.bham.ac.uk/MToolan/ (accessed: 06 January 2011).

van Manen, M. (1997), *Researching Lived Experience: Human Science for an Action Sensitive Pedagogy*. London, Ontario: Althouse.

Vanheule, S., Desmet, M., Groenvynck, H., Rosseel, Y. and Fontaine, J. (2008), 'Belgium the Factor Structure of the Beck Depression Inventory–II: An Evaluation', *Assessment*, 15(2): 177–87.

Wales, K. (1996), *Personal Pronouns in Present-day English*. Cambridge: Cambridge University Press.

Wales, K. (2001), *A Dictionary of Stylistics* (2nd edn). Harlow: Longman.

Werlich, E. (1976), *A Text Grammar of English*. Heidelberg: Quelle and Meyer.

Wilson, A. and Rayson, P. (1993), 'The Automatic Content Analysis of Spoken Discourse', in C. Souter and E. S. Atwell (eds), *Corpus-Based Computational Linguistics*. Amsterdam: Rodopi.

Zimmerman, M. and Coryell, W. (1987), 'The Inventory to Diagnose Depression, Lifetime Version', *Acta Psychiatrical Scandinavia*, 75: 495–9.

Zinken, J. (2003), 'Ideological Imagination: Intertextual and Correlational Metaphors in Political Discourse', *Discourse & Society* 14(4): 507–23.

Index

www.ingramcontent.com/pod-product-compliance
Lightning Source LLC
Chambersburg PA
CBHW050326020526
44117CB00031B/1808
9781350024250